Echoes of Blood: Sri Lanka's Legacy of Violence, Resistance, and Memory

Two Centuries of Killings, Disappearances, and Defiance

(1815-2020)

Sequel to

'CONTOURS OF CONFLICT – THE MAKING & REMAKING OF SRI LANKA'

TUAN B. KAMISS

Dedication

To the fallen and the fearless -
To every soul sacrificed in the name of progress or power, justice or ideology.
To those who fought for freedom, and to those who fought for a cause they held
sacred, no matter the banner they bore.
To the rebels and the loyalists, the visionaries and the defenders, the ones who
stood firm in conviction even when the world trembled around them.
This book is for the lives lost in conflict and in silence, for the voices that rose
and were silenced, for the belief that meaning can be found even in struggle.
May their courage be remembered, and their stories never simplified

Copyrights

Disclaimer

This book is a work of nonfiction based on publicly available sources, historical records, and journalistic accounts. While every effort has been made to ensure accuracy, the author does not claim to provide definitive legal or investigative conclusions. All statements regarding individuals or groups are presented for informational purposes only and should not be construed as accusations or endorsements.

The author and publisher are not liable for any misinterpretation of content and make no representations concerning ongoing legal proceedings or government actions. Readers are encouraged to consult official documents, legal judgments, and primary sources for a more comprehensive understanding of the subject matter.

The views and interpretations expressed in this book are those of the author and do not necessarily reflect those of affiliated organizations, publishers, or contributors. Any resemblance to actual persons or entities outside of cited sources is coincidental and unintended.

Prologue: A Reckoning in Echoes

This book is a sobering chronicle of violence, injustice, and resilience, an unflinching reflection on two centuries of Sri Lanka's turbulent history. From the fall of the Kandyan Kingdom in 1815 and the onset of British Colonial rule to the armed uprisings, communal unrest, and state-sanctioned brutality of the 20th and 21st centuries, the island has been the theatre of repeated conflict. Across generations, blood has been spilled, voices silenced, and truths buried, leaving behind wounds that remain raw and unresolved.

The early chapters delve into the Colonial era, exposing the methods by which resistance was crushed: through mass executions, scorched-earth tactics, and martial law imposed upon indigenous leaders who dared to defy imperial domination. These events planted the seeds of a violent political culture—one that evolved into ethnic tension, civil war, and the systematic disappearance of dissenting voices.

This volume confronts those brutal legacies, from the Insurrections of 1971 and 1989 to the decades-long war in the North and East, and the shadowy political assassinations that continued long after independence. It bears witness to massacres both infamous and forgotten, communal riots that tore neighborhoods apart, and the countless individuals, soldiers, civilians, rebels, and innocents, caught in the crossfire. The narrative does not flinch, nor does it obscure; every account is told with the urgency of remembrance.

But this is not merely a ledger of atrocities. It is, above all, an act of historical reclamation—a call to honor those who have been forgotten and to challenge the selective silences of official memory. By recovering the stories of the disappeared, the murdered, and the maligned, this book seeks accountability in a land where justice has so often been denied. It compels reflection on why violence persists, how power manipulates history, and what it means to endure when others do not.

Scope and Purpose

This book is structured to guide readers through the layered architecture of Sri Lanka's violent past. Each chapter focuses on a distinct era or event, contextualized within broader socio-political currents. The aim is not only to document but to interrogate: to ask how these cycles of violence were allowed to repeat, and what mechanisms, legal, cultural, and psychological, enabled impunity to thrive.

The intended audience is broad:

- Scholars and students seeking a deeper understanding of Sri Lanka's postcolonial trajectory
- Activists and political thinkers confronting the legacy of state violence
- Diaspora communities grappling with inherited trauma
- And any reader who believes that history must be remembered to be transcended

A Personal Reflection

I did not begin this work as a historian. I began as a witness, haunted by stories whispered in homes, etched into gravestones, and carried in the silence of those who survived. Some of these stories are my own. Others were entrusted to me by those who feared they might never be heard. Writing this book has been an act of mourning, of rage, and of hope. It is my attempt to make sense of a nation's fractured soul, and to offer a space where memory might resist erasure.

I do not claim this to be the definitive record of Sri Lanka's troubled past, nor could it be. Many events remain undocumented or inaccessible due to the absence of formal records and the erasure of inconvenient truths. Yet in documenting what I could, this volume aims to serve as a springboard for deeper inquiry. Scholars, students, political leaders, and future generations may find within these pages the starting point for understanding the cultural fault lines and psychological burdens that continue to shape Sri Lankan society.

This book is not simply a chronicle, it is a reckoning. May the stories within stir memory, ignite conscience, and demand accountability. And above all, may they ensure that the voices of the lost are never truly extinguished.

TUAN B. KAMISS
(Author/Compiler)
Calgary
Canada

Table of Contents

Part I: Colonial Crimes & Early Courtrooms

Chapter 1: The Uva–Wellassa Rebellion (1817–1818): A Struggle for Sovereignty

The Uva–Wellassa Rebellion—also known as the Great Rebellion of 1817–1818—was a major uprising against British colonial rule in Sri Lanka (then Ceylon). It was the third and final Kandyan resistance following the signing of the Kandyan Convention in 1815, which ceded the Kingdom of Kandy to the British Crown.

Although the Convention promised to uphold Kandyan customs and protect Buddhist institutions, the British quickly violated these assurances. Their actions alienated both the Kandyan aristocracy and the general populace, setting the stage for revolt.

Several interwoven factors contributed to the outbreak:

• **Violation of the Kandyan Convention:** The British disregarded promises related to local governance and religious protections.

• **Marginalization of Kandyan Chiefs**: Traditional leaders were stripped of authority and treated with disrespect by colonial officials.

• **Economic Exploitation**: Heavy taxation, land confiscation, and disruption of agrarian life fueled resentment.

• **Cultural Insensitivity**: British disregard for Buddhist customs—including interference with sacred relics—deepened tensions.

The rebellion erupted **in October 1817** in the **Uva and Wellassa** regions. Ironically, Keppetipola Disawe—a Kandyan chief originally dispatched by the British to quell the uprising—defected and became its most iconic leader.

Other key figures included:

• **Madugalle Nilame:** A Kandyan noble previously exiled for anti-British activities.

• **Wilbawe (Doraiswamy):** A pretender to the Kandyan throne, proclaimed king by the rebels.

The rebels employed guerrilla tactics, targeting British garrisons and supply lines. They briefly captured strategic towns such as Matale and Kandy, demonstrating widespread support and coordination.

British Counteroffensive

Governor Robert Brownrigg declared martial law and launched a brutal suppression campaign. Reinforcements from British India were brought in, and loyalist Kandyan chiefs like **Molligoda** and **Ratwatte** assisted the British.

Martial Law: Declared across Uva and Kandyan provinces to suppress resistance.

Scorched Earth Policy: British troops destroyed **villages, crops, and irrigation systems** to starve rebels and civilians.

Mass Executions: Over **778 rebels** were executed, imprisoned, or exiled.

Collective Punishment: Families of rebels were stripped of land and rights.

Economic Consequences in Uva–Wellassa

Agricultural Collapse: Thousands of acres of paddy fields and irrigation schemes were destroyed.

Depopulation: Villages were abandoned due to famine and displacement.

Loss of Irrigation Heritage: Ancient systems dating back to King Saddhatissa (137–119 BC) were lost.

Long-Term Poverty: By 2018, Moneragala (in Uva–Wellassa) was identified as **Sri Lanka's poorest district**, a legacy of colonial devastation.

Legacy and Recognition

Though the rebellion was crushed by November 1818, its legacy remains profound:

• Symbol of resistance: Keppetipola is now honored as a **National Hero**.

• Historical reckoning: The rebellion exposed the brutality of colonial rule and the resilience of Kandyan society.

• Cultural memory: Memorials and literature continue to commemorate the fallen, especially in Uva Province.

• Official recognition: In 2011, the Sri Lankan government formally revoked the colonial designation of rebels as traitors, recognizing them as freedom fighters.

Rebel Leaders of Uva–Wellassa
Keppetipola Disawe

Early Life and Background

• Full Name: Rajapaksa Wickramasekera Mudiyanselage Bandaranayake Monarawila Keppetipola

• Born: In Galboda, Matale, Kingdom of Kandy

• Family: Son of Golahela Disawe and Monaravila Kumarihamy; his sister was **Ehelepola Kumarihamy,** mother of the famed child martyr **Madduma Bandara.** *(Please see story below)*

• Position: Held the title of Disawe (provincial governor) under King Sri Wikrama Rajasinghe and later under British rule.

Role in Colonial Transition

• In 1815, Keppetipola was one of the few Kandyan nobles who signed the *Udarata Treaty (Kandyan Convention)*, which ceded the Kandyan Kingdom to the British. He signed in Sinhala, which some historians interpret as a subtle act of resistance.

• Initially served as **Disawe of Uva under British administration**.

The Uva–Wellassa Rebellion (1817–1818)

• In 1817, Governor Brownrigg sent Keppetipola with 500 men to suppress a growing rebellion in Uva.

• Upon meeting the rebels, Keppetipola defected, returned British arms, and declared he would not fight his own people with foreign weapons.

• He was appointed **Maha Adhikaram (Chief Minister) under the rebel king Wilbawe** and led a guerrilla campaign against British forces.

• His leadership helped the rebellion spread rapidly across central Sri Lanka, alarming colonial authorities.

• After months of fighting and British reinforcements from India, the rebellion faltered due to scorched-earth tactics and famine.

• Keppetipola fled to **Nuwara Kalawiya** but was captured on October 28, 1818, along with fellow rebel **Pilimathalawe.**

• On November 25, 1818, he was executed by beheading in Kandy. His skull was sent to Britain for study due to its unusual shape—a grim colonial practice.

• Today, Keppetipola is revered as a **National Hero** of Sri Lanka.

• His courage at the time of execution, calmly reciting Buddhist verses and expressing a wish to be reborn in the Himalayas to attain Nirvana—is legendary.

• In 2011, the Sri Lankan government officially recognized him and other rebels as freedom fighters, revoking their colonial designation as traitors.

Keppetipola Village in Welimada

• Location: Situated in the **Welimada Divisional Secretariat, Badulla District,** Uva Province.

• Elevation: Approximately 1,226 meters above sea level.

• **Historical Significance**: During British rule, the village was known as **Wilson-Tenna**, named after a British general who destroyed the area during the rebellion. It was **renamed Keppetipola in 1968 to honor the Disawe's legacy.**

• Cultural Sites: Includes the Sri Somananda Pirivena and remnants of ancient fortifications.

• Modern Identity: A serene village surrounded by tea plantations and known for its cool climate and historical pride.

Veera Puran Appu

Full Name: **Weerahannadige Francisco Fernando**

Honorific Title: Veera Puran Appu ("Veera" meaning "hero" or "brave" in Sinhala)

Born: November 7, 1812, in Moratuwa, Western Province

Died: August 8, 1848, executed by firing squad at Bogambara Grounds, Kandy

• Puran Appu was born into a modest family and educated at a Wesleyan school in Moratuwa.

• At age 13, he fled his hometown after a violent dispute with a village headman and moved to Ratnapura, where he lived with his uncle—Sri Lanka's first Sinhalese proctor.

• He later settled in Uva Province, where he became increasingly opposed to British colonial rule.

Role in the 1848 Matale Rebellion

Though not directly involved in the Uva–Wellassa Rebellion of 1817–1818, Puran Appu's revolutionary spirit was shaped by its legacy. He emerged as a key leader in the **Matale Rebellion of 1848**, which was sparked by oppressive taxation and economic hardship under British rule.

• On July 28, 1848, he led a successful assault on Matale, capturing the town despite other rebel setbacks.

• He was known for his charisma, military acumen, and unwavering commitment to Sri Lankan sovereignty.

• His final words, as recorded by Governor George Byng, were:

"If there had been half a dozen such men as me to lead, there would not be a white man living in the Kandyan Province."

Legacy and Reverence

• Executed: Captured and executed by the British on **August 8, 1848**, alongside fellow leaders **Gongalegoda Banda** and **Ven. Kudapola Thera**.

• Burial: His body was buried in Matale.

• **National Hero**: Today, Veera Puran Appu is celebrated as a symbol of resistance and patriotism. His name evokes courage and defiance against colonial oppression.

• Cultural Impact: His life has inspired literature, songs, and historical studies across Sri Lanka.

Other Notable Figures

Madugalle Nilame: Early instigator, exiled after sending offerings to deities for British overthrow.

Butawe Rate Rala, **Kivulegedara Mohottala**, and **Millawe Disawa**: Local chiefs who organized protests and joined the rebellion.

Timeline of Battles and Strategic Shifts

Date	Event
Sept 1817	Wilbawe, claiming royal lineage, appears in Wellassa.
Sept 26	British-appointed Muhandiram Haji Marikkar killed by rebels.
Oct 14–16	Major Wilson killed near Bibile; rebellion escalates.
Nov 1817	Keppetipola joins rebels; British declare martial law.
Jan 1, 1818	Rebels formally outlawed; property confiscated.
Feb 21, 1818	Entire Kandyan provinces placed under martial law.
Oct 28, 1818	Keppetipola captured.
Nov 1818	Rebellion collapses after British reinforcements arrive.

Key Sources

1. **Wikipedia – Great Rebellion of 1817–1818**
   Known as the **Uva–Wellassa Uprising**, this was the **third Kandyan War**, sparked by discontent with British rule following the **Kandyan Convention of 1815**.

- Led by **Keppetipola Disawe**, who famously switched sides from the British to the rebels.
  - Rebels proclaimed **Wilbawe** as a pretender to the Kandyan throne.
  - British forces responded with a brutal **scorched-earth policy**, destroying villages, crops, and livestock.
  - Estimated **casualties**: 8,000–10,000 Sri Lankans; 900–2,000 British and collaborators.
2. <u>**AmazingLanka – Uva Wellassa Rebellion and Keppetipola Memorial**</u>
   This source offers a detailed biography of **Monarawila Keppetipola**, the rebellion's iconic leader.
   - He hailed from a noble Kandyan lineage and was revered for his **honor and defiance**.
   - The rebellion was fueled by British disrespect toward Kandyan elites and religious institutions.
   - The British appointed **non-Sinhalese headmen**, further alienating local leaders.
3. <u>**Ozlanka – 1818 Uva-Wellassa Patriots: Never Ever Forgotten**</u>
   This commemorative article reflects on the **205th anniversary** of the uprising.

- It describes the rebellion as **Sri Lanka's first national liberation struggle**.
- British reprisals included **mass executions**, **torture**, and the killing of **all males over 14** in rebel districts.
- The uprising united **Sinhalese, Veddah, Malay, and Muslim communities** in resistance.

The Tragedy of Ehelepola Kumarihamy and <u>Madduma Bandara</u>

A Tale of Loyalty, Brutality, and Heroism in the Kandyan Kingdom

Introduction

*Though my scope of research was from 1815 onward, this story falls just outside that boundary. Yet, it remains one of the most compelling and emotionally charged episodes in Sri Lankan history—a tale of loyalty, betrayal, and extraordinary courage. The tragedy of Ehelepola Kumarihamy and her son Madduma Bandara **unfolded in 1814**, during the final years of the Kandyan Kingdom, and continues to resonate as a symbol of patriotic sacrifice.*

Historical Backdrop

In the early 19th century, the Kingdom of Kandy stood as the last bastion of native rule in Sri Lanka, surrounded by British-controlled coastal territories. **The reigning monarch, King Sri Vikrama Rajasinha**, grew increasingly suspicious of his nobles, fearing betrayal and foreign influence.

One of his most trusted officials, **Ehelepola Maha Adikaram**, the **Disawe of Sabaragamuwa**, was accused of conspiring with the British while he was in Colombo. Unable to capture him, the king turned his fury on Ehelepola's family in Kandy.

The Royal Vengeance In a chilling act of retribution, the king ordered the arrest of Ehelepola Kumarihamy, Ehelepola's wife, along with their four children:

• Loku Bandara (eldest son)
• Madduma Bandara (second son)
• Tikiri Manike and Dingiri Menike (daughters)

On May 17, 1814, the royal executioners carried out a brutal sentence:

• Loku Bandara, overcome with fear, hesitated at the moment of execution.

• Madduma Bandara, just a child of seven or eight, stepped forward and declared:

"Strike me with one blow!"

His composure and bravery stunned the crowd. He was beheaded swiftly.

• The two daughters and Ehelepola Kumarihamy were then **drowned in Bogambara Lake,** their bodies weighted with stones.

This act of cruelty was meant to send a message, but it horrified the Kandyan public and sowed deep resentment against the king.

Legacy and Impact

• The massacre of Ehelepola's family became a turning point in Kandyan history.

• Public outrage helped catalyze the **Kandyan Convention of 1815**, which led to the formal cession of the Kingdom to the British.

• **Madduma Bandara was immortalized as a child hero**, a symbol of unflinching courage in the face of tyranny. Statues and memorials in Kandy and beyond honor his sacrifice, and his story is taught in schools as a lesson in patriotism and moral strength.

Memorials and Commemorations

• **Statue in Kandy**: A statue of Madduma Bandara stands proudly in front of the Sri Dalada Maligawa (Temple of the Tooth) in Kandy, symbolizing his bravery.

• **Annual Commemoration**: Every May 17, a ceremony is held at Ehelepola Raja Maha Viharaya in Matale to honor Madduma Bandara's sacrifice. This date marks the anniversary of his execution in 1814.

• **Literature and Drama**: His story has been retold in songs, poems, books, films, and stage dramas, often portraying him as a child hero who faced death with unmatched courage.

• **Educational Symbol**: Madduma Bandara is frequently cited in Sri Lankan school textbooks as a symbol of patriotism and youthful valor.

The Mortar Legend

Interestingly, one source recounts a more gruesome version of the execution: after the beheadings, the king allegedly ordered Ehelepola Kumarihamy to crush her children's heads in a mortar, threatening her with disgrace if she refused. This version, while not universally accepted, adds a chilling layer to the tragedy and may explain the origin of the "pounded to death" narrative you mentioned earlier.

This story continues to resonate because it's not just about cruelty—it's about resistance, dignity, and the cost of loyalty. If you'd like, I can help you explore how this tale has influenced modern Sri Lankan identity or even help you write a tribute or creative piece inspired by it.

Key Sources

1. Wikipedia – Madduma Bandara Ehelapola

2. Sunday Times – "All in Wax: The Ehelepolas' Tragic Story and the Fall of the Kandyan Kingdom"

3. Daily Mirror – "Ehelepola Kumarihamy: A Heroic Figure"

Chapter 2: The Madulla Massacre (1817) - A Prelude to Rebellion

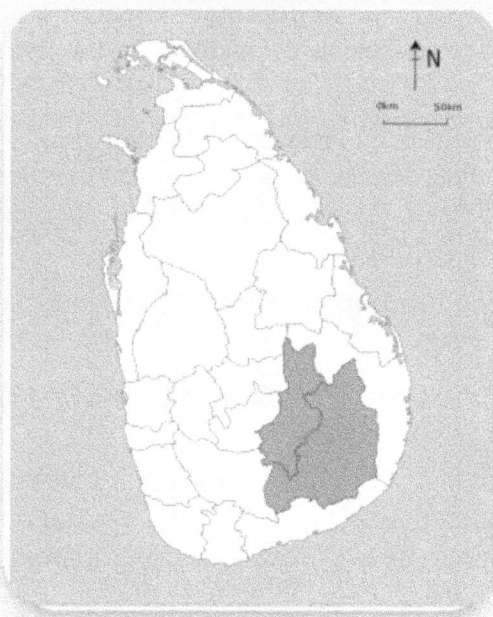

The Madulla Massacre occurred on **December 9, 1817**, in the village of **Madulla**, located in the **Uva Province** of Sri Lanka (then Ceylon). This event unfolded during the early stages of the **Uva–Wellassa Rebellion**, a widespread uprising against British Colonial rule that erupted in response to the erosion of Kandyan sovereignty following the **Kandyan Convention of 1815**.

The Convention had promised to preserve local customs and protect Buddhist institutions, but British administrators quickly reneged on these assurances. Discontent simmered among Kandyan chiefs and villagers, culminating in a series of coordinated revolts across the central highlands.

On **December 9, 1817**, British troops entered Madulla under the pretext of suppressing rebel activity. What followed was a **targeted killing of 22 villagers**, many of whom were suspected of aiding or sympathizing with the nascent rebellion. The massacre was not a result of battlefield confrontation—it was a deliberate act of terror designed to intimidate the local population and deter further resistance.

Eyewitness accounts and later historical analyses suggest that the victims were **unarmed civilians**, and that the killings were carried out without trial or due process. The British forces, operating under martial law, viewed collective punishment as a legitimate tool of colonial governance.

The Madulla Massacre was one of the earliest and most brutal episodes in the Uva–Wellassa Rebellion. It signaled the British intent to crush dissent through **fear and overwhelming force**, rather than negotiation or reform. The massacre also served as a warning to other villages in the region, many of which were later subjected to similar reprisals.

This event helped galvanize support for the rebellion, as news of the killings spread across Uva and Wellassa. Kandyan chiefs such as **Keppetipola Disawe**, who had initially sided with the British, defected and joined the resistance—transforming the uprising into a full-scale war for autonomy.

The Madulla Massacre exemplifies the **systemic violence** employed by the British Empire to maintain control over its colonies. Similar tactics were used in other parts of the world, including India, Africa, and the Caribbean. In Sri Lanka, these acts were rarely investigated, and perpetrators were almost never held accountable.

According to historians and human rights advocates, such massacres constitute **Colonial War Crimes**, though they remain largely unacknowledged in official British narratives.

Today, the Madulla Massacre is remembered as a symbol of **colonial oppression and local resistance**. While overshadowed by larger events like the Uva–Wellassa Rebellion and the 1915 riots, it remains a poignant reminder of the human cost of imperial ambition.

In recent years, scholars and activists have called for greater recognition of such atrocities, urging governments and institutions to **reframe colonial history through the lens of justice and accountability**.

Key Sources

1. **Wikipedia – List of Massacres in Sri Lanka**
   The **Madulla Massacre** occurred on **December 9, 1817**, in the village of **Madulla**, during the early phase of the **Uva–Wellassa Rebellion**.

2. **Sinhalanet – Colonial Crimes in British-Occupied Ceylon**
   This article places the Madulla Massacre within the context of **colonial war crimes**, describing how British forces responded to uprisings with **indiscriminate violence**, including **mass killings**, **torture**, and **scorched-earth tactics**.

   o   The British viewed Kandyan resistance as treason and responded with **collective punishment**, targeting entire villages like Madulla.

3. **Sri Lanka Guardian – British Colonial War Crimes: Unpunished**
   This retrospective explores the **lack of accountability** for colonial atrocities, including the **Madulla Massacre**, and argues that such events were part of a deliberate strategy to **break indigenous resistance**.

4. It highlights the **absence of trials or reparations**, and the enduring silence around massacres like Madulla in mainstream colonial histories.

Chapter 3: Saradiel and Mamala Marikkar - Bandits or Freedom Fighters? (1864)

(Pic: Wikimedia)

Shadows of Utuwankanda — The Legend Begins

The morning mist clings to the jagged ridges of **Utuwankanda** like a secret yet to be spoken. Here, nestled deep in the heart of Sri Lanka's Kegalle District, lies **Saradiel Village** — a place that once throbbed with defiance and danger, and now pulses with memory and mystery. It is the ghost of rebellion, wrapped in jungle green.

This was not just a hideout. It was **Saradiel's Fortress**, his stage, his sanctuary. From these unforgiving heights, he watched the movements of British convoys on the **Colombo-Kandy Road** below, plotting his strikes with mathematical precision. Today, those same roads bring travelers from around the globe — drawn by the legend of a man often called *Ceylon's Robin Hood.*

To reach this fabled Village, one must **veer right at the Utuwankanda Junction**, leaving the bustling highway behind. What follows is not a drive, but an ascent — winding, steep, and laced with the scent of forest. As visitors climb higher, the land sheds its modern veneer and begins to whisper tales of rifles, rebels, and red-coated patrols.

The village itself is rich in reconstructions and relics. **Life-size models**, **exhibits**, and **guided tours** offer glimpses into Saradiel's life, his gang, and the colonial powers that hunted him. Yet the true test of courage lies beyond the village — in the climb to **Utuwankanda's peak**, where Saradiel once vanished into fog and legend.

The final stretch is treacherous. No railings, no mercy — just a craggy path leading up to a **3-square-meter plateau**. Children should not tread here, nor the elderly or infirm. One wrong step near the **precipitous corner** and gravity becomes law. The climb challenges not only strength, but sanity; it is a visceral experience, each footfall echoing the choices Saradiel once made under siege.

Near the summit lies the heart of the tale — a **cave tucked in stone**, surrounded by boulders like silent sentinels. Inside: darkness, chill, and wonder. It's said to hold a **secret tunnel**, perhaps an escape route used by Saradiel and his crew. Few know where it leads. Fewer dares follow.

Visitors who brave the journey are rewarded with more than views. They stand where **freedom took root**, where **loyalty was tested**, and where a rebel chose to fight, not flee. The cave isn't just a passage — it's a portal into the past.

And as the sun casts golden light on the jungle below, it's easy to feel his presence — not as myth, but as man. Watching, waiting, perhaps smiling at the bold few who dared to climb.

The Story of the Legendary Bandits

(Saradiel Village Utumankanda – You Tube pic)

In the mist-draped mountains and jungles of 19th century Ceylon, a tale of daring rebellion unfolded—one that blurred the lines between outlawry and heroism. Led by two figures whose names still echo through history, **Saradiel** and **Mamala Marikkar** carved their legend not from crowns or conquests, but from resistance against colonial domination.

Saradiel, known to some as the "**Robin Hood of Ceylon,**" emerged from the central highlands as a master tactician and a symbol of defiance. Born into humble circumstances, he became a charismatic figure who rallied villagers, freed laborers, and plundered British convoys. Not for personal gain, but to redistribute wealth to those oppressed under colonial rule.

Mamala Marikkar, by contrast, was forged by salt and steel—raised on the coasts and known for his prowess with both blade and ship. He was a rebel of the seas turned ally of the hills, bringing a strategic edge and maritime experience that complemented Saradiel's guerrilla genius.

Together, they formed a rare partnership: one bound not by blood, but by a shared vision of justice and independence.

The alliance launched a series of audacious attacks, beginning with ambushes along trade routes and escalating into assaults on colonial estates. One such estate, ominously called "The Red House," became ground zero for revolution. By torchlight and rifle crack, Saradiel and Marikkar stormed its gates—freeing workers, destroying records, and symbolically defacing its walls with the mark of a lion entwined with a dagger.

Their strategy wasn't one of brute force alone. They manipulated terrain, sabotaged railways, and executed rapid strikes before vanishing into jungle fog. Each raid spread fear and confusion among colonial officials, including seasoned veterans like **Captain Langham**, who quickly learned that these were not ordinary bandits—they were revolutionaries with a plan.

Saradiel and Marikkar's deeds ignited more than flames across plantations; they sparked imaginations. To villagers, they were liberators. To officials, a growing threat. Their ability to unite disparate communities, reclaim resources, and outwit authority became the blueprint for organized resistance. Though their fates eventually met with betrayal and execution, their legend never died.

Saradiel's gang was more than a group of outlaws — it was a resistance cell. His closest ally was **Mamala Marikkar**, a fearless fighter and strategist. Other members included:

Bawa – known for his stealth and tracking skills

Samath – a scout who monitored British movements

Hawadiya – the gang's arms handler

Kirihonda – a lookout stationed in the hills

Sirimale – once loyal, later the traitor who sealed their fate

Together, they orchestrated raids across the Colombo-Kandy corridor, targeting colonial wealth and redistributing it among the poor. Their hideout at **Utuwankanda** gave them a tactical advantage, allowing them to monitor traffic and plan ambushes.

In **March 1864**, Saradiel's luck ran out. **Sirimale**, once a trusted member, turned informant and tipped off the police. On **March 21**, Saradiel and Marikkar were lured to a house in **Mawanella**, where a police unit lay in wait.

Sergeant Ahamath fired the first shot, wounding Saradiel

Mamala Marikkar retaliated, killing **Constable Sabhan**, the first Sri Lankan Policeman to die in the line of duty

Surrounded and outnumbered, the duo surrendered to **Assistant Government Agent F.R. Saunders** and the **Ceylon Rifles**

Fall of the Thunder Riders

Dawn broke with gunfire in Mawanella. Saradiel and Marikkar, cornered in a shadowed house, fought like lions. **Constable Sabhan**—young, valiant—rushed in first and paid with his life, struck down by Marikkar's gun in one furious moment. The silence that followed was thicker than smoke. Bullets ricocheted, blood spilled, and the rebels—bleeding but defiant—were overwhelmed by the weight of betrayal and the might of colonial rifles.

Bound in chains and flanked by soldiers, Saradiel and Marikkar were paraded through the towns they once liberated. Spectators lined the roads, torn between awe and grief, watching their fallen heroes dragged toward **Kandy**, hearts pounding like the distant war drums they would never hear again.

At **Bogambara Prison**, the noose waited. On **May 7, 1864**, as the sun cast its final amber rays over the hills of Utuwankande, the two rebels met their end—not as bandits, but as legends. The rope tightened, but so did the grip of their legacy. And long after their bodies fell still, the story of Saradiel and Marikkar lived on—etched in stone, whispered in winds, and burned into the spirit of a nation that still dares to defy.

(Pic: Daily FT.lk)

Today **Annual Police Heroes' Day** is observed on **March 21st** to honor the memory of **Constable Sabhan**, the first Sri Lankan police officer killed in the line of duty during the attempted arrest of Saradiel in 1864.

Key Sources

1. **Wikipedia** – Utuwankande Sura Saradiel. Saradiel, born Deekirikevage Saradiel in 1832, was dubbed the "Robin Hood of Sri Lanka" for robbing colonial caravans and redistributing wealth to poor villagers.

2. **Roar Media** – "Sri Lanka's Very Own Robin Hood: Saradiel of Utuwankanda" This article paints Saradiel as a folk hero, shaped by childhood bullying and colonial injustice.

3. Namo Magazine – "Saradiel: Robin Hood of Sri Lanka" This narrative explores Saradiel's multiple arrests and daring escapes, including one from Mahara Prison. Marikkar was captured alongside him, and both were tried and hanged in 1864.

Chapter 4: The Attygalle Murder Case (1906) - "The dead don't speak. But their estates do."

Francis Dixon Attygalle – The Victim of Greed

(Pic: elanka.com.au)

A Colonial Tragedy

In the twilight of colonial Ceylon, Colombo was a city of horse-drawn carriages, stately mansions, and families whose names carried weight in both commerce and society. Among them stood the Attygalles—a dynasty built on graphite mines and coconut estates, with wealth stretching across the Kurunegala district.

At the heart of this legacy was **Francis Dixon Attygalle**, the only **son of Mudaliyar Don Charles Gemoris Attygalle**, a prominent philanthropist and landowner. Following the Mudaliyar's death in 1901, the management of the family's vast estate fell to **John Kotelawala Sr.,** a former Police Inspector who had married Francis's elder sister, Alice Elizabeth Attygalle. The marriage, born of an illicit love affair, had been controversial and initially opposed by the Attygalle family, but it ultimately brought Kotelawala into the fold, and into the family's fortune.

Initially entrusted with the estate due to Francis's minority, Kotelawala soon faced accusations of misappropriation from the Attygalle matriarch, Petronella Attygalle. Legal battles ensued, and with the Governor's intervention, Francis was granted Venia Aetatis, legal adulthood, at just 16, allowing him to reclaim control of the family business.

But the transition was anything but smooth. Stripped of power and embittered by the loss of influence, Kotelawala began plotting his revenge. In 1905, he formed the **Ceylon-Japan Trading Company** and traveled to Japan under the guise of business. While abroad, his former police associates, Singhone Perera and Baron Singho, allegedly hired a gunman named **Piloris**, a Boer War veteran, to assassinate Francis Dixon Attygalle.

On the night of **December 5, 1906**, Francis was shot in the abdomen while standing on the verandah of his residence **in Dias Place, Pettah**. He succumbed to his injuries two days later. The investigation revealed a chilling conspiracy: although Kotelawala was not present at the scene, evidence pointed to his orchestration of the murder through his former police subordinates.

Upon his return to Ceylon in January 1907, Kotelawala was arrested at Colombo Harbour and charged with aiding and abetting the murder. The trial, held at Hulftsdorf under **Justice Alexander Wood Renton**, became one of the most sensational legal proceedings in colonial Ceylon. Before the verdict was delivered, Kotelawala committed suicide in Welikada Prison.

He left behind a widow and three children, **including Sir John Kotelawala**, who would later become the third Prime Minister of independent Ceylon, serving from 1953 to 1956.

Key Sources

1. **Wikipedia** – Attygalle Murder. On December 5, 1906, Francis Dixon Attygalle, heir to a wealthy graphite empire, was shot in the abdomen and later died in hospital.
• The prime suspect was his brother-in-law, John Kotelawala Sr., a former police inspector who had married into the Attygalle family.
• After being accused of embezzlement and mismanagement, Kotelawala was ousted from the family business and allegedly orchestrated the murder.
• He committed suicide in prison before the trial concluded, leaving behind a scandal that rocked colonial society.

2. **Sunday Times** – "The 1907 Attygalle Murder Case: The Kotelawala Connection"

• The case became infamous not only for its legal complexity but also because Kotelawala was the father of future Prime Minister Sir John Kotelawala.

3. **Colombo Telegraph** – "When Giants Clash: The Attygalle Murder Case" This article draws from A.C. Alles' Famous Criminal Cases of Sri Lanka, offering a vivid account of the power dynamics and colonial intrigue:

Chapter 5: The 1915 Sinhalese–Muslim Riots: Ethno-Religious Tensions and Colonial Repression

A Distant Memory from the Past

Over four decades ago, my late father often recounted vivid, harrowing scenes he personally witnessed during the Sinhala-Muslim riots of 1915. At just thirteen years old, a schoolboy at the time, he was forced to flee on foot, covering miles in search of safety. Along the way, he saw hundreds of shops and homes reduced to ashes. His own parents had found refuge in a safer part of Kandy, along Peradeniya Road in Katukelle—a Malay Kampong enclave where many residents were either affiliated with, or retired from, the Malay Regiment. This connection offered protection; the rioters did not dare encroach upon that community.

*During the height of the violence, my father's uncle—his sister's husband—was the Chief Inspector. A towering figure well over six feet tall, he was tasked by British authorities with restoring order in **Matale**, where rioters had descended from Polonnaruwa and were looting Muslim-owned shops. Upon arrival, he found chaos in the heart of the town. Drawing his two swords, he charged into the fray, slashing through the mob and leaving many wounded or scattered. His bold intervention was pivotal in halting further destruction.*

Yet, even after his retirement, my father said, the threat of retaliation lingered—so much so that his uncle's family continued to receive police protection for years to come.

The **1915 Sinhalese–Muslim Riots** were a violent and widespread conflict that erupted in **British Ceylon** (now Sri Lanka) between **Sinhalese Buddhists** and **Muslim Moors**, lasting from **May 28 to August 8, 1915**. Though initially sparked by a local dispute, the riots quickly escalated into a national crisis, prompting the British colonial government to impose **Martial Law** and carry out brutal reprisals.

Background and Causes - Religious and Cultural Tensions

The immediate trigger was a dispute over a **Buddhist Vesak Procession** passing a **Muslim mosque** in **Gampola**. Muslims objected to the use of traditional drums and music near their place of worship.

The conflict reflected deeper **ethno-religious tensions**, especially between **Sinhalese Buddhists** and **Indian Moors**, who had recently gained economic dominance in trade and commerce.

Colonial Policies and Legal Disputes

British laws like the **Police Ordinance of 1865** and **Local Boards Ordinance of 1898** restricted religious expression, including noise during worship.

A legal battle over procession rights culminated in a **Supreme Court ruling** favoring the mosque, which many Buddhists saw as a betrayal of their cultural traditions.

Economic Rivalries

The **Indian Moors**, a subgroup of the Muslim community, had displaced **Ceylon Moors** in trade, especially in rice importation and retail.

This economic shift created resentment among Sinhalese traders and consumers, fueling anti-Muslim sentiment.

Key Leaders and Figures

Sir Robert Chalmers – Governor of Ceylon; criticized for his harsh response and later recalled.

Brigadier General H. H. L. Malcolm – Led military suppression under martial law.

Herbert Dowbiggin – Inspector General of Police; oversaw mass arrests and executions.

Sir Ponnambalam Ramanathan – Tamil legislator who **defended Sinhalese leaders** in the Legislative Council, condemning British excesses.

E. W. Perera – Lawyer and patriot who **smuggled documents to England** in his shoe to expose colonial abuses and rally support for the Sinhalese cause.

Many Sinhalese leaders involved in the **temperance movement** (anti-alcohol campaign) were arrested, despite having no role in the violence.

These arrests were seen as an attempt to suppress emerging nationalist voices.

The Riots and British Response

Date	Event
May 28, 1915	Vesak procession attacked near mosque in Gampola.
May 30–31	Riots spread to Kandy and Colombo.
June 2	Martial law declared in Western and Sabaragamuwa Provinces.
June–August	Summary executions, mass arrests, and destruction of property.
August 30	Martial law lifted.

Casualties: Over **116 deaths**, including **63 killed by Police/military**; **189 injured**; **4,075 shops looted**, **250 burned**, and **17 mosques destroyed**.

The riots exposed the fragility of communal harmony under colonial rule and the dangers of the British **divide-and-rule** strategy.

The repression galvanized nationalist movements, laying the groundwork for future independence efforts.

The event remains a cautionary tale about the manipulation of ethnic tensions for political control.

Sources and Further Reading

Wikipedia: 1915 Sinhalese-Muslim Riots
Sunday Times Heritage Feature
LankaWeb Historical Analysis

During the suppression of the **1915 Sinhalese–Muslim riots**, the British colonial administration relied heavily on **auxiliary forces**, including **Gurkha soldiers from the British Indian Army** and **Malay personnel** who had previously served in the disbanded Ceylon Rifle Regiment.

Gurkha Soldiers

Deployment: Gurkhas were brought in from British India as part of the emergency response to the riots, especially after Martial Law was declared on **June 2, 1915**.

Role: They were tasked with quelling unrest, enforcing curfews, and conducting summary executions under martial law.

Impact: Their presence added a layer of fear and intimidation, as Gurkhas were known for their discipline and combat prowess. They operated under direct orders from British officers and were involved in door-to-door raids and mass arrests.

Malay Soldiers and Police

Background: Many Malays had served in the **Ceylon Rifle Regiment**, which was disbanded in 1873. Afterward, they joined the **Ceylon Police Force** as constables.

Role in 1915: Malay personnel were part of the local policing effort, especially in urban areas like Colombo and Kandy. They assisted in crowd control, guarding key installations, and enforcing colonial ordinances.

Their involvement reflects the complex dynamics of colonial policing, where minority groups were often employed to enforce imperial authority over the majority population.

These forces were instrumental in the brutal suppression of the riots, which resulted in **over 100 deaths**, thousands of arrests, and widespread destruction of property. Their deployment underscores the colonial strategy of using Non-local troops to enforce control and minimize sympathy with the local population.

Authoritative Sources

1. **Wikipedia** – 1915 Sinhalese–Muslim Riots.

Offers a comprehensive overview of the riots, including their origins in Kandy, the spread across provinces, and the colonial response. It details the imposition of martial law, summary executions, and the role of key figures like Governor Robert Chalmers and Brigadier General H.H.L. Malcolm.

2. **LankaWeb** – Historical Analysis of the 1915 Riots

Provides context on the socio-political dynamics between Sinhalese Buddhists and Ceylon Moors, the British policy of divide and rule, and the violent suppression of unrest. It also highlights the colonial military presence and the use of European auxiliaries during the crackdown.

3. **Ceylon Today** – "1915: A Time of Riots"

Explores the cultural and religious tensions that triggered the riots, including disputes over Buddhist peraheras passing mosques. It reflects on the long-term legacy of the riots and their role in shaping communal relations and nationalist sentiment in Sri Lanka.

Chapter 6: Duff House – Colombo's Mysterious Killing (1933)

The murder at Duff House took place on **Sunday, October 15, 1933**, in Colombo, Sri Lanka. It involved the death of **Mrs. Lillian Roslin Seneviratne**, wife of **Stephen Seneviratne**, a Cambridge-educated Barrister turned Agriculturalist.

Stephen Seneviratne was the son of **Attapattu Mudaliyar Solomon** Seneviratne and related to the **Maha Mudaliyar.**

Lillian, his wife, was from the influential **D'Alwis family** and had a history of diabetes and emotional instability. She often expressed fears of dying young like her parents and had a documented tendency toward suicidal thoughts.

Their marriage was turbulent, marked by frequent quarrels, suspicions of infidelity (especially involving a servant named Jessie), and disagreements over property sales.

They moved into **Duff House on Bagatalle Road** in **October 1933**, just weeks before the incident.

On the morning of **October 15**, Lillian was found unconscious in her bedroom with a strong smell of chloroform in the air.

Stephen attempted to revive her with brandy and hot water bottles, and artificial respiration.

Initial medical opinion suggested **suicide by Aspirin overdose**, but later investigations pointed to **Chloroform as the cause of death**, raising suspicions of **homicide**.

The case quickly escalated into one of the most medically complex and legally dramatic trials in Sri Lankan history, culminating in a Supreme Court conviction and a successful appeal to the Privy Council in England.

The Trial Begins

On May 14, 1934, the **Colombo Assizes** opened one of the most sensational trials in Ceylon's legal history: the murder of Mrs. Lillian Roslin Seneviratne by her husband, Stephen Seneviratne. Presiding was **Justice M.T. Akbar, the first Malay Judge of the** Colombo Assizes, known for his intellect and religious conviction. The jury was English-speaking, and the courtroom was packed with legal luminaries and curious onlookers.

Prosecution Team:

Deputy Solicitor General M.W.H. de Silva (later Attorney General and Minister of Justice)
Crown Counsel H.L. Wendt
Police Superintendent J.R.G. Bantock
Dr. M.V.P. Pieris, eminent surgeon, assisting with medical evidence

Defence Team:

R.L. Pereira KC, H.A.P. Sandrasagara KC, Stanley Obeysekera KC

Eric Soysa and P.H.P. Jayatilleke

The defence's strategy was not to prove innocence but to sow reasonable doubt—especially given Mrs. Seneviratne's history of suicidal ideation.

Experts were divided between suicide and homicide theories. The cause of death was Chloroform inhalation, but the mechanism—suicide or homicide—divided experts:

Doctor	Opinion
Dr. S.C. Paul	Death due to syncope from aspirin overdose
Prof. Milroy Paul (his son)	Injuries consistent with chloroform application
Dr. J.S. de Silva	Suicide
Dr. R.L. Spittel	Homicide
Dr. Karunaratne	Probable homicide
Dr. T.S. Nair	Conducted post-mortem

The courtroom resembled a medical seminar, with theories ranging from smothering to syncope and asphyxia.

The Duff House Visit

On June 8, after evidence concluded, the court made an unusual visit to Duff House. An experiment was staged: Inspector Van Cuylenberg lay on a bed and mimicked groans to test audibility. Only the judge and jury foreman were present. The Privy Council later deemed this demonstration irregular and prejudicial.

Witnesses included household staff—Alpina, Mabel Joseph, Seelas, Martin, Banda, Simon the cook, and driver Perera—as well as prominent figures like Mrs. Harry Dias Bandaranaike and Mr. Leo D'Alwis. Their testimonies painted a picture of a troubled marriage, frequent quarrels, and a woman haunted by her own mortality.

Despite the defence's efforts, the jury returned a **5–2 guilty verdict**, and Stephen was sentenced to death. R.L. Pereira's cross-examination was legendary—his bulldog tenacity reportedly caused doctors to faint under pressure.

Appeal to the Privy Council

With no Court of Criminal Appeal in Ceylon, Stephen appealed to the **Privy Council in England**. The case was heard by **Lord Maugham, Lord Roche, and Sir George Rankin**. Representing the Crown were D.B. Sommerville KC and L.M.D. de Silva KC; Stephen was defended by H.I.P. Hallet KC and R.L. Pereira KC.

On **July 29, 1936**, the Privy Council **quashed the conviction**, citing procedural irregularities and misdirection in Justice Akbar's charge to the jury. Stephen was released after 30 months in prison and reunited with his son, Terence.

Key Sources

1 - **Sunday Times** – "Murder by Chloroform at Duff House". This detailed account covers the trial of Stephen Seneviratne, accused of murdering his wife at Duff House, Colombo, in 1933.

2 - **Famous Criminal Cases of Sri Lanka** by A.C. Alles – Volume 1

Chapter 7: Redemption Denied—The Kenilworth Estate Tragedy (1938 or 1939)

(Pic shows Kenilworth Factory, the Office was just on the right corner)

Location: Kenilworth Estate, Ginigathena, Central Highlands of Sri Lanka

Access Routes: Nawalapitiya–Hatton Road or Yatiyantota–Hatton Road

Colonial Context: In the 1930s, British superintendents managed vast tea estates in Sri Lanka's central hills, wielding near-absolute power over labor and logistics.

The Superintendent – Mr. Geoffreys: A principled British official who valued justice tempered with mercy.

- **Estate Culture**: Superintendents were often seen as disciplinarians, not empathetic figures—Roberts' gesture was extraordinary for its time.

The Kenilworth Estate sits nestled among the bright green hills between Nawalapitiya and Hatton, its winding roads brushing past the Yatiyantota pass. The first estate before the Carolina Group, it once bore the tranquil routine of plantation life—until kindness cost a man his life.

Mr. Geoffreys, the estate's Superintendent, was a man of quiet integrity and fairness. In the late 1930s, while poring over the estate accounts, he discovered that the **Chief Clerk** had siphoned Rs. 2,000—a significant sum. When confronted, the clerk crumbled and confessed. But instead of dismissing him outright or calling the police, **Mr. Geoffreys** extended something rare in estate life: mercy. He gave the clerk one month to return the stolen funds, promising consequences only if the deadline wasn't met.

On the final day, Mr. Geoffreys entered his office with tempered expectation, believing he would receive the money and the clerk would be redeemed. Instead, a hidden estate gun waited behind the door. As Mr. Geoffrey took his seat, the Clerk sprang into action—firing a fatal shot at the Superintendent, before turning the weapon on himself in a tragic suicide.

Nearby, in the manager's bungalow by the factory, Mrs. Geoffreys heard the gunshots and assumed someone was hunting pigs near the farm. It wasn't until much later that the unbearable truth reached her: her husband's act of compassion had led to his execution.

Amount Misappropriated: Rs. 2,000 — equivalent to several years' wages for estate workers in the 1930s.

Mr. Geoffrey's Decision: Instead of contacting police, he gave the chief clerk one month to return the stolen funds—a move almost unheard of within the rigid hierarchy.

Date of Reckoning: On the final day, expecting restitution, Roberts walked into the office unaware the clerk had hidden a loaded estate gun.

Mr. Geoffreys stepped into his office, expecting resolution, not tragedy. He sat at his desk, unaware of the loaded estate gun hidden just behind the door. Without a word, the chief clerk—once granted a second chance—reached for the weapon, and in a burst of violence, fired point-blank.

Geoffreys collapsed, his life extinguished in the very place where he'd chosen mercy over justice. In the deafening silence that followed, the clerk turned the gun on himself, ending his life as swiftly as he had taken another.

Just yards away in the manager's bungalow, Mrs. Geoffreys heard the gunshots echo across the estate. She assumed pigs were being culled at the nearby farm—a mundane explanation for an extraordinary horror. But the truth crept in with the speed of disbelief: the sound she'd heard was not routine estate business—it was the sound of betrayal, of a man punished for his kindness. The reverberations of that day would echo through the misty hills for years.

Personal Reflection

As I put the final touches on this chapter, I find myself drifting back to my own short-lived tenure as one of the youngest Chief Clerks of Kenilworth in the 1980s. The memory is vivid, almost surreal. There's every chance I occupied the very same chair where this tragic figure once carried out his daily duties. That thought alone sent a shiver down my spine, as if the weight of history still lingered in the seat's faded arms. I could simply imagine it all—the wooden desk, the quiet tension in the room, the sound of footsteps in the corridor, and then that irreversible moment. Writing this wasn't just a reconstruction; it was a resurrection.

Key Sources

1. Kenilworth Group – **History of Ceylon Tea**

2. Kenilworth Tea Estate – The Teamakers UK

Offers background on the estate's founding, geographic features, and workforce culture. Though focused on tea production, it helps contextualize the estate's social environment, which may be relevant to understanding the conditions surrounding any historical incidents.

3. **Watawala Plantations** – Kenilworth Division

Chapter 8: Servant's Confession – The Pope Murder Case (1941)

(Stellenberg Bungalow Did George Pope Live here? – Pic: historyofceylontea.com)

A Colonial Thriller in the Hills of Pupuressa

The tea-covered hills of **Pupuressa**, Sri Lanka, were cloaked in moonlight on **May 9, 1941**. At the **Stellenberg Estate**, nestled deep in the Central Highlands, Superintendent **George Pope** drove back from a quiet dinner with a fellow planter. Respected and feared in equal measure, Pope had built a reputation for fierce resistance to labor rights—and especially to unionization efforts that were gaining traction under a rising force: the **Ceylon Indian Congress Labour Union**, founded just a year earlier in 1940.

As tensions flared across estates, **Ramasamy Weeraswamy**, a fiery and eloquent laborer, emerged as a local leader aligned with the **Ceylon Indian Congress Labour Union**. He was relentless, pushing for workers' dignity, fair treatment, and union recognition. Pope saw him as a dangerous agitator and fired him. But the CIC Labour Union intervened, forcing Pope to reinstate Weeraswamy—a blow to his pride and power.

Pope's estate became a pressure cooker of resentment and resistance. And it was about to erupt.

Driving along the estate's winding road, Pope's headlights illuminated a pile of **tree trunks blocking the path**. He stepped out of the car to investigate.

In the shadows waited **six men**, armed with **pruning knives**—the tools of their trade now twisted into weapons of revenge. They attacked with calculated fury, leaving Pope gasping and bleeding beside his car.

Inside the tea factory, **Mr. Lodewyke**, the Tea Maker, realized something was wrong when Pope failed to return. He sent workers to search. A man named **Cassim** found the bloodied Superintendent and sprinted back with the news. Police were called, and the investigation kicked off before dawn.

Key discoveries:

A **line room key** lay near Pope's body.

Six laborers were missing at the morning muster.

The key matched the room of **Ramasamy Weeraswamy**, the union activist.

Five suspects were arrested swiftly. But Weeraswamy had vanished.

For **five months**, police scoured plantations across the region. Posters bearing Weeraswamy's face appeared everywhere—from railway stations to roadside kiosks. He was finally caught in a remote village near Kandy and brought to justice.

The Trial That Gripped Ceylon

The courtroom buzzed with tension. Justice **Soertsz** presided over the case as the Crown laid out its argument:

> **Motive**: Conflict between Pope and union-backed workers
>
> **Forensics**: Physical evidence tied to all six suspects
>
> **Eyewitnesses:** Workers placing Weeraswamy at the heart of the plot

The defense tried to cast light on inhumane working conditions and systemic injustices. But the sheer violence of the attack buried any hopes of leniency.

Verdict: Guilty

Sentence: **Death by hanging at Welikada Prison**

The murder shook colonial Ceylon. It revealed the **raw desperation** of the plantation labor force and the brewing storm of organized resistance. Stellenberg Estate never returned to quiet normalcy—locals renamed the stretch of road where Pope fell as **"The Road of Midnight Death."**

Primary References

1. **A.C. Alles – *Famous Criminal Cases of Sri Lanka***
   Volume 1 of this seminal work includes a detailed account of the Pope Murder Case. Alles outlines the background of George Pope, the motive behind the murder, and the role of estate labor unrest. The confession of the servant—who implicated fellow workers and the estate's aspiring union leader—was central to the prosecution's case.

2. **History of Ceylon Tea – "Murder at Midnight" by Bernard VanCuylenberg**
   This article provides a vivid narrative of the murder, describing how Pope was killed in his bungalow and how the investigation unfolded. It also explores the social tensions on the estate and the legacy of the crime in local memory.

3. **Dilmah t-Radio Podcast – "The George Pope Murder in 1941"**
   A 7-minute audio segment recounts the murder and trial, highlighting the role of Ramasamy Weeraswamy, the alleged mastermind behind the plot. It also touches on the confession made by one of the estate servants, which led to the arrest and conviction of the perpetrators.

Part II: Post Independent Era

Chapter 9: "Tomatoes in the Boot" – Bruce Whitehouse - The Estate Murder (1949)

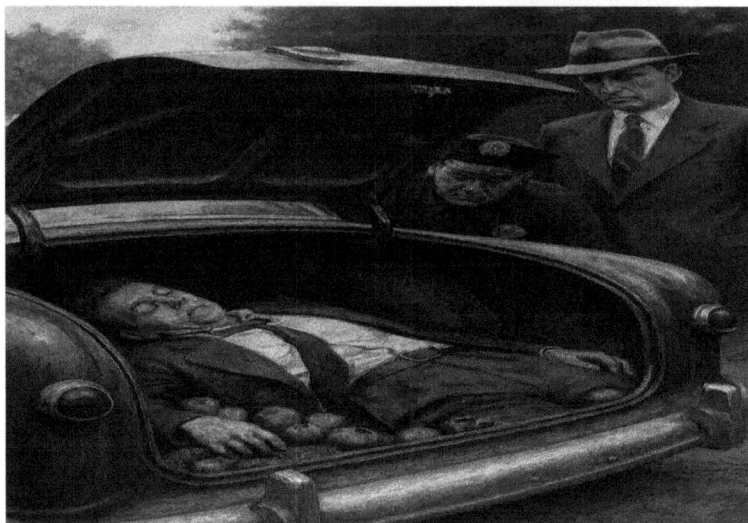

(Recreated Image)

In the lush hill country of **Rakwana, Ratnapura**, amid the whispering tea bushes of the **Madampe Group** Estate, lived **Bruce Whitehouse**, a respected British planter. Known for his routines and gentle disposition, he regularly drove to **Colombo** to collect worker wages and indulge in a quirky passion—**buying tomatoes** from Pettah.

His wife often accompanied him, enjoying the weekend outing. But on one such trip in **1949**, the seemingly tranquil drive became a tragic descent into murder.

Key Characters

Name	Role	Notes
Bruce Whitehouse	Victim	British Estate Superintendent; methodical and kind
Mrs. Whitehouse	Survivor	Wife; bravely tried to save him
Laathara Baas	Antagonist	Colombo underworld boss; mastermind of the robbery
Members of his gang	Perpetrators	Tracked Whitehouse's habits; executed the assault
Rakwana Police	Investigators	Swift in response and arrests
Judges and Prosecutors	Judicial Agents	Oversaw one of the fastest trials of the decade

The Crime at *Thakkali Wanguwa* ("Tomato Bend")

After cashing estate wages and securing his tomato supply, Bruce drove back toward Rakwana. At a **sharp curve along the Colombo–Ratnapura Road**, locally dubbed *Thakkali Wanguwa*, a gang vehicle overtook and blocked them.

Masked assailants rushed out, demanding the cash. Bruce resisted valiantly, but the confrontation turned violent. A gunshot rang through the misty hills—Bruce had been shot point-blank.

In a cruel twist of fate, the gang fled with **two sacks of tomatoes** instead of the full cash haul. Mrs. Whitehouse, visibly shaken, managed to drive to **Palmgarden Estate** seeking help. Her husband died shortly after.

Legal Proceedings and Outcome

Within three weeks, Police tracked down **Laathara Baas** and the gang. The trial was swift but scrupulous:

Three gang members were sentenced to **death by hanging** at **Welikada Prison**.

One received a life sentence and later died in custody.

The court described the crime as **"an act of cold-blooded calculation marred by reckless violence."** The murder caused widespread alarm among colonial estate managers and exposed gaps in rural security.

Bruce Whitehouse's death symbolized more than a crime—it highlighted the vulnerability of planters in remote estates, the unchecked reach of Colombo's criminal underbelly, and the tragic cost of routine.

The curve where he was killed retained the eerie nickname *"Tomato Bend"*, a reminder of how ordinary objects—tomatoes in a boot—can be woven into extraordinary horror.

Historical References

Tales from the Thotum – The Dark Side – *History of Ceylon Tea*
Bernard VanCuylenberg recounts the murder of Bruce Whitehouse, Superintendent of Madampe Group, Rakwana. The article details how Whitehouse's routine trips to Colombo to collect estate wages were tracked by Colombo's underworld, led by the notorious "Laathara Baas." On the day of the murder, sacks of tomatoes placed in the boot alongside cash bags played a bizarre role in the crime's unfolding.

The Bruce Whitehouse Murder in 1949 – Dilmah t-Radio
This 5-minute podcast offers a gripping summary of the murder, adapted from VanCuylenberg's article. It highlights the criminal plot, the fatal ambush, and the symbolic role of the tomatoes in the boot.

Marked for Murder – Bernard VanCuylenberg – *eLanka*
Another retelling of the case, emphasizing Whitehouse's fondness for tomatoes and how their presence in the boot alongside cash bags added a strange twist to the murder narrative.

Chapter 10: Gambling, Greed & Murder – The Turf Club Case (1949)

(Pic: sundaytimes.lk)

The Colombo Turf Club Robbery of 1949

In the waning light of colonial legacy, post-independence Ceylon was a nation caught between tradition and transformation. The British had departed, but their institutions lingered — polished, prestigious, and vulnerable. Among them stood the **Colombo Turf Club**, a glittering relic of empire nestled near **Reid Avenue in Cinnamon Gardens**.

On race days, the **Colombo Racecourse** came alive with spectacle. Ceylonese elites, businessmen, and socialites gathered in tailored suits and silk sarees, placing extravagant bets and parading their status. Beneath the glamour, however, brewed a darker undercurrent — one of financial desperation, unchecked ambition, and criminal ingenuity.

That undercurrent erupted on **January 31, 1949**, in what would become one of the most audacious crimes in the island's history.

The Turf Club's earnings from the previous Saturday's races — a staggering **Rs. 322,000**, equivalent to tens of millions today — were en route to the Chartered Bank in Fort. The cash was transported in locked trunks by a driver from **Armstrong Garage**, a trusted contractor.

But the driver that day wasn't the usual man.

The Mastermind

At the center of the plot was **Nanayakkara Athulugamage Simon de Silva Jayasinghe, alias Aratchirala**. A charismatic and enigmatic figure, Aratchirala was no stranger to Colombo's elite. He moved easily between political circles and business deals, cloaked in charm and whispered rumors of racketeering.

He had connections. He had resources. And he had a plan.

Aratchirala assembled a crew of trusted associates — including a substitute driver, enforcers, and insiders familiar with the Turf Club's operations. His strategy was chillingly precise:

- Eliminate the **regular driver, John Silva**, to avoid suspicion.

- Insert a loyal accomplice in his place.

- Intercept the cash transport en route to the bank.

- Disappear before anyone realized what had happened.

The Murder of John Silva

John Silva was a quiet, dependable man in his early forties. He lived with his family in Wattala and was known for his punctuality and honesty. On the eve of the heist, Silva was lured to **Puttalam** under false pretenses.

There, he was drugged and suffocated — a calculated murder designed to remove the only person who could identify the switch. His body was later discovered tied to a tree, sending shockwaves through the investigation.

On the morning of **January 31**, the substitute driver — posing as Silva — collected the cash trunks from the Turf Club. The route to Fort was familiar, but this time, the vehicle was intercepted. The money vanished. The crew dispersed.

No alarms were raised. No witnesses came forward. For a brief moment, it seemed they had pulled off the perfect crime.

The Trial

The investigation was swift and relentless. Clues emerged — forged identity cards, suspicious telegraphs, and eyewitness accounts from rural petrol stations. The trail led back to Aratchirala and his crew.

The trial was held in the Colombo High Courts, presided over by **Chief Justice Sir Arthur Wijewardene,** a stern and meticulous figure. Over 25 days, more than 100 witnesses testified — including medical experts, bank employees, and forensic analysts.

Journalists from Dinamina and Ceylon Daily News filled the courtroom daily, chronicling every twist. Spectators gasped as forensic evidence linked the murder scene to materials recovered from Aratchirala's property.

The defense was aggressive, accusing police of coercion and fabrication. But Deputy Solicitor General D.C. Rajapakse led a prosecution that was airtight — built on timelines, testimonies, and chilling facts.

The Verdict

On March 27, 1950, the jury returned its verdicts:

- Aratchirala and two others were found guilty of robbery and murder.

- The remaining suspects received varying sentences based on their roles.

- Appeals were filed but swiftly dismissed.

On a humid morning in June 1950, the condemned were led to the gallows of Welikada Prison. Aratchirala, once the embodiment of charm and confidence, reportedly looked up at the hanging rope with cold indifference — his façade finally stripped away.

The Aftermath

The case reverberated across Ceylonese society. It shattered the illusion of safety that surrounded elite institutions and exposed the cracks in a system still clinging to colonial grandeur.

In the years that followed, S.W.R.D. Bandaranaike, a rising political figure, would ban horse racing, citing moral decay and public outrage. The ban symbolized a national desire to break from colonial excess and redefine its values.

Today, remnants of the Turf Club's glory linger in crumbling buildings and faded photographs. But the robbery remains vivid in Sri Lanka's criminal history — not merely for its audacity, but for the symbolic collapse of greed-fueled elitism in a transitioning society.

The murder of John Silva was not simply a casualty of a robbery.

It was the cost of unbridled ambition — played out on the backstretch of colonial Ceylon's final lap.

Primary References

1. **The Sunday Times** – "Turf Club Robbery and Murder in 1949" by Jayantha Gunasekera. This article offers a vivid account of the crime, set against the backdrop of Colombo's elite racing scene. It details the culture of high-stakes gambling at the Havelock Race Course, the social dynamics of the Turf Club, and the events leading up to the robbery and murder. It also explores the fallout among gamblers, racehorse owners, and society figures.

2. **A.C. Alles – Famous Criminal Cases of Sri Lanka, Volume 2**. This volume includes a comprehensive legal and narrative analysis of the Turf Club case. Alles outlines the planning of the robbery, the murder of the club's cashier, and the trial that followed. His work is considered one of the most authoritative sources on Sri Lanka's criminal history.

'3. **Trove – "Big Ceylon Robbery" (Feb 1, 1949)**. This Australian newspaper report confirms the scale of the robbery—£A37,500 stolen from the Ceylon Turf Club—and provides an international perspective on the crime's impact.

Chapter 11: The Cricket Scandal – The Sathasivam Murder Trial (1951–1953)

I still remember how my elder brothers closely followed the sensational story they referred to as The Sathasivam Murder Trial. *Being avid cricket fans, they never missed a single update in* **The Times of Ceylon***, devouring every headline and dissecting each detail in animated discussions that lasted for hours. That memory stayed with me for years, quietly stirring curiosity—until I grew older and set out to understand the case for myself.*

The Trial of Mahadevan Sathasivam

He was the darling of Ceylonese cricket. Mahadevan "Satha" Sathasivam, a flamboyant batsman hailed by legends like Garry Sobers and Frank Worrell as one of the finest stroke-makers they'd ever seen. But on **October 9, 1951**, the man who once danced down the pitch to dispatch bowlers into oblivion was now facing a far more sinister opponent—a murder charge.

His wife, **Paripoornam Anandam Rajendra**, granddaughter of Sir Ponnambalam Ramanathan, was found strangled in the kitchen of their home at No. 7, St. Alban's Place, Bambalapitiya. A mortar had been placed on her neck. The cricketing icon was arrested the next day. The nation gasped. Was this a crime of passion, a scandal of betrayal, or a setup to destroy a sporting hero?

Anandam, mother of four daughters, had filed for divorce weeks earlier, citing infidelity and emotional cruelty. Sathasivam had been romantically linked to Yvonne Stevenson, a foreign national whose presence loomed over the marriage like a storm cloud.

Letters Anandam wrote to Satha while he was in England revealed her anguish:

Enter **Hewa Marambage William**, an 18-year-old cook hired just 11 days before the murder. His testimony became the fulcrum of the trial. William claimed he assisted in the murder, holding Anandam's legs while Sathasivam strangled her. But inconsistencies riddled his account. He had injuries on his face, confessed to stealing jewelry, and was arrested in Tangalle.

He was granted a conditional pardon and turned crown witness, but his credibility quickly unraveled.

Sir **Richard Aluvihare**, then Inspector General of Police, personally took over the investigation despite lacking criminal expertise. Senior officers like **Albert de Silva**, known as "Honest Albert," testified that they were prevented from pursuing the truth. Evidence was allegedly manipulated to frame Sathasivam, while William's confession was reshaped to fit the prosecution's narrative.

The Trial of the Century

Held at the Assizes Court of the Western Province, presided over by **Justice E.F.N. Gratiaen**, the trial lasted 57 days.

Defense Team: Led by Dr. Colvin R. de Silva, a brilliant Trotskyite lawyer and parliamentarian.

Star Witness: Sir Sydney Smith, world-renowned forensic pathologist, flown in from the UK.

Smith challenged the prosecution's timeline and cause of death. His analysis of rigor mortis, body temperature, and digestive contents contradicted William's version of events.

Smith's reconstruction suggested sexual motivation and theft as William's motive. He theorized that Anandam bent down to inspect William's work in the kitchen, triggering a violent assault. The seven-sovereign necklace was missing. The mortar was placed post-mortem to simulate a struggle.

Verdict: Not Guilty

On March 24, 1953, the jury returned a unanimous verdict of "Not Guilty." William was convicted of perjury, but due to his pardon, he walked free. Justice Gratiaen criticized the police for their conduct, and the trial became a textbook example of forensic justice triumphing over prejudice.

Sathasivam spent 625 days in remand prison. He later married Yvonne and moved to Singapore and Malaysia, captaining both national cricket teams.

Final Over

Was it a cricket scandal? Not in the sporting sense. But it was a scandal that rocked the cricketing world, casting a shadow over one of its brightest stars. In the end, truth prevailed, but not without bruises.

The trial was a gripping drama of betrayal, forensic brilliance, and the resilience of a man who refused to be bowled out by fate.

Authoritative References

1. **Mahadevan Sathasivam – Wikipedia.** Offers a comprehensive overview of Sathasivam's cricketing career and personal life, including his arrest and trial for the alleged murder of his wife, Paripoornam Anandam Rajendra. It notes his eventual acquittal after a 20-month remand and a high-profile trial presided over by Justice Noel Gratiaen.

2. **"Murder Isn't Cricket" – The Sunday Times,** Sri Lanka. This feature by Stephen Prins dives deep into the emotional and social fallout of the murder, recounting the events of October 9, 1951, when Anandam was found dead in the garage of their home. It also explores the impact on their children and the public fascination with the case.

3. **The Queen v. Sathasivam – vLex Sri Lanka.** A legal summary of the trial, including rulings on evidence admissibility and judicial reasoning. It highlights the prosecution's attempt to introduce letters from the deceased and the defense led by renowned lawyer Colvin R. de Silva.

Chapter 12: The Knife in the Cane Chair - Galboda's Night of Reckoning (1954)

Back in the early sixties, I was working as a member of the Estate Office staff when a close colleague shared a remarkable and unsettling tale. A fellow employee—someone in a role much like ours—had been convicted of murdering two co-workers at an estate in the Nawalapitiya district. While serving his sentence, the convict transformed his time behind bars into a mission of compassion. He took it upon himself to launch welfare initiatives, offering basic education to unlettered inmates and involving them in productive activities. His efforts earned the respect and praise of the prison authorities, eventually leading to an official pardon. This is the story of a man once branded a murderer—and the redemption he carved for himself.

The train from Colombo Fort wound its way through misty hills and emerald valleys, finally halting at **Galboda station**—a sleepy outpost just past **Mt. Jean**. Among the passengers was a bright-eyed youth named **Somasiri**, freshly graduated from Ananda College, clutching his appointment letter for the Junior Clerk position at Galboda Group.

He was eager, polite, and full of promise. But the estate office, like many colonial remnants, harbored a cruel undercurrent. The Chief Clerk, a man in his forties, took a twisted pleasure in humiliating the newcomer. Practical jokes escalated into public mockery, and the Teamaker often joined in, turning the office into a stage for ridicule. Somasiri endured it all in silence, fearing that retaliation would cost him his job.

One evening, the Teamaker (Factory Officer) hosted a dinner party at his home. The Chief Clerk, several staff members, and Somasiri were invited. The plan was simple: ply the young man with liquor and make him the butt of their jokes once again.

But Somasiri had come prepared.

Days earlier, he had visited the estate blacksmith and requested a custom-made knife, claiming it was for kitchen use. The blacksmith, perhaps too trusting or too indifferent, complied without question.

As the night wore on, laughter turned cruel. Somasiri, humiliated and intoxicated, reached his breaking point. From beneath his jersey, he drew the concealed knife and, in a flash of fury, drove it through the Chief Clerk's chest with such force that it pierced the cane chair behind him. Witnesses later described the scene as surreal—rage incarnate.

The Teamaker tried to intervene. He became the second victim, stabbed in the stomach with the same blade. Panic erupted. Guests fled. Somasiri stood over the bodies, brandishing the blood-soaked knife, daring anyone to come near.

Word reached **Mr. David Murray(?)**, the estate's Superintendent. Calm and composed, he approached the scene. His presence alone seemed to pierce the haze of violence. With gentle words and quiet authority, he convinced Somasiri to surrender the weapon. The police arrived soon after.

At trial, the courtroom heard not just of the murders, but of the torment that preceded them. Witnesses testified to the relentless bullying, the psychological toll, and the toxic culture that allowed it to fester. The judge, moved by the circumstances, sentenced Somasiri to **twenty years** imprisonment—spared from the gallows by the weight of testimony and the strength of his defense.

It was a tragedy born of cruelty, silence, and unchecked power. The plantations buzzed with the tale for years, whispered in estate bungalows and around fires on misty nights. For many, it was a cautionary tale—not just of murder, but of the cost of ignoring suffering.

Prison Life

While details on Somasiri's specific acts of service within prison remain limited in public records, accounts suggest that his conduct and contributions during incarceration were deemed exemplary enough to merit clemency.

His pardon, granted after years of confinement, reflects a broader principle in Sri Lanka's justice system—that rehabilitation and genuine reform can lead to redemption. The Galboda case, once a symbol of tragedy, now carries a quiet reminder that even within the walls of punishment, the possibility of transformation endures.

Verified Historical Sources

1. Tales from the Thotum – The Dark Side – **History of Ceylon Tea**. Bernard VanCuylenberg's article recounts several estate-era murders, including the Galboda case. Though not named explicitly as "The Knife in the Cane Chair," the narrative describes a chilling murder involving a cane chair and a concealed weapon, set in the Galboda estate region. The article explores the psychological tension and betrayal that led to the crime.

2. **Galboda Estate Registry – History of Ceylon Tea**. Provides background on the Galboda estate, its ownership history, and its role in the development of Ceylon's tea industry. While not directly referencing the murder, it situates the estate within the colonial plantation context.

Chapter 13: Secrets in the Tank – The Wirawila Murder (1956)

In the quiet dawn of **January 31st, 1956**, near the edge of the **Wirawila Tank** in Southern Sri Lanka, a fisherman stumbled upon a haunting sight—an elegant woman's body, clothed in a nurse's uniform, floating lifelessly. Beside the tank, a frightened three-year-old girl sat alone, silently watching the water.

The woman was **Lilian**, a mother of two, recently estranged from her husband. She had been working with private medical practitioners in Matara when she entered a relationship with **Sugathadasa**, a wealthy Copra dealer, in 1953. By 1956, their once discreet affair had turned turbulent.

The authorities first suspected **drowning**, noting froth near the nostrils and water-logged lungs. Lilian's identity remained unknown, as the murder had been orchestrated far from her hometown to conceal connections. The killer's hope: that the death would be dismissed as accidental and the body buried nameless.

The mystery unraveled thanks to **Babun Nona**, a woman who had previously rented a room to Lilian and recognized her from a newspaper photo. Her tip prompted investigators to perform a **second autopsy**.

Dr. W.D.L. Fernando, a pioneering forensic pathologist in Sri Lanka, trained under **Sir Sydney Smith** in the UK. His work in this case helped establish forensic pathology as a cornerstone of Sri Lankan criminal justice. He found unsettling signs of **strangulation**—a protruding tongue, signs of struggle, and the lack of water in the stomach. These contradicted the initial conclusion. The presence of fecal matter and defensive bruises pointed clearly to **homicide**.

The breakthrough in the case came from an unexpected witness—the hired driver who ferried Lilian, her daughter, and **Sugathadasa** from Matara to Wirawila that evening. His account filled crucial gaps in the timeline: Sugathadasa's unnervingly cold behavior, his suspicious actions during the journey, and the deliberate choice of a remote location all pointed to something more sinister.

Trial and Verdict

In court, the prosecution pieced together a gripping and disturbing narrative. They exposed Sugathadasa's motive, his calculated attempt to stage the murder as an accident, and the systematic disposal of the body. The evidence presented was damning. The jury unanimously found him guilty of premeditated murder, and the sentence reflected the gravity of his crime.

Beyond delivering justice for Lilian, the trial also underscored the crucial role of forensic science in criminal investigations, marking a significant moment in Sri Lanka's legal history.

This case marked one of the earliest instances in Sri Lankan legal history where **Forensic Pathology** turned the tide of justice.

Authoritative Sources

1. **A.C. Alles – Famous Criminal Cases of Sri Lanka, Volume 1.** This volume includes a detailed account of the Wirawila Tank Murder Case. Alles reconstructs the investigation, trial, and forensic challenges surrounding the discovery of a decomposed body in a rural tank. His legal analysis and narrative style make this one of the most comprehensive sources on the case.

2. **Open Library – Listing for A.C. Alles' Series.** Confirms the inclusion of the Wirawila case in Volume 1 of the series. The listing provides publication details and cataloging information for researchers and readers seeking the original text.

3. **Wikipedia** – A.C. Alles Biography. Offers background on Justice A.C. Alles, his career as a Supreme Court judge, and his role in documenting landmark criminal cases in Sri Lanka, including the Wirawila Tank Murder.

Chapter 14: Bullets in Politics: The Assassination of S.W.R.D. Bandaranaike (1959)

(Pic: dailymirror.lk)

I first documented this story in my book **Contours of Conflict***, and I believe it bears repeating here. Its significance endures—not only due to its chilling details but also because it remains one of the most widely discussed assassinations in the nation's history.*

Solomon West Ridgeway Dias Bandaranaike, the fourth **Prime Minister of Ceylon** (now Sri Lanka), was a charismatic leader who swept to power in 1956 on a wave of Sinhala Buddhist nationalism. His government enacted sweeping reforms, including the controversial "Sinhala Only" language policy, which alienated Tamil minorities and stirred political unrest. But it wasn't ethnic tensions that led to his assassination—it was a tangled web of **political betrayal, personal vendettas, and commercial greed**.

On the morning of **September 25, 1959**, Bandaranaike was meeting constituents at his private residence, **Tintagel**, in Colombo. Among them was **Talduwe Somarama Thero**, a Buddhist monk and lecturer at the College of Indigenous Medicine. Under the guise of presenting a memorandum, Somarama pulled out a **.45 Webley Mark VI revolver** and shot the Prime Minister at point-blank range in the chest and abdomen.

Bandaranaike was rushed to Colombo General Hospital, underwent five hours of surgery, and briefly regained consciousness—reportedly requesting clemency for his attacker. He died the next morning, **September 26**, from internal hemorrhaging.

Magisterial Inquiry

The **Magisterial Inquiry** began **December 14, 1959.**

Venue: Chief Magistrate's Court, Colombo

Charges: Conspiracy to murder and murder

Accused

1. **Talduwe Somarama Thero** – The assassin
2. **Mapitigama Buddharakkitha Thero** – Chief monk of Kelaniya Temple, alleged mastermind
3. **H.P. Jayawardena** – Business associate of Buddharakkitha
4. **Anura de Silva** – Alleged accomplice
5. **Newton Perera** – Police inspector accused of supplying the weapon
6. **Vimala Wijewardene** – Cabinet Minister (later acquitted)
7. **Carolis Amarasinghe** – Ayurvedic physician and SLFP supporter (turned crown witness)

Star Witnesses

Carolis Amarasinghe:

His testimony was pivotal. He revealed meetings at his home where Buddharakkitha, Jayawardena, and Somarama discussed acquiring weapons and practicing shooting. Amarasinghe claimed Somarama told him the target was "Agamathithuma" (the Prime Minister).

Ananda Thero:

A monk who witnessed the shooting and narrowly escaped being shot himself.

Political Conspiracy

The motive wasn't ideological—it was **commercial**. Buddharakkitha had expected lucrative government contracts for shipping and sugar manufacturing. When Bandaranaike refused, citing ethical concerns, Buddharakkitha felt betrayed. Adding fuel to the fire was a personal insult involving **Vimala Wijewardene**, with whom Buddharakkitha was rumored to have a relationship. Bandaranaike allegedly dismissed her complaints about defamatory pamphlets with the remark, "Aren't some of these things true?"

Supreme Court Trial

Date: February 22 – May 10, 1961

Presiding Judge: Justice T.S. Fernando

Outcome:

Somarama, Buddharakkitha, and Jayawardena: Found guilty of conspiracy and murder; sentenced to death

Anura de Silva and Newton Perera: Acquitted

Vimala Wijewardene: Discharged earlier during inquiry

Somarama was hanged in 1962. Buddharakkitha died in prison in 1967.

Bandaranaike's death shocked the nation. His widow, **Sirimavo Bandaranaike**, succeeded him and became the **world's first female Prime Minister**. The assassination exposed the dark underbelly of Sri Lankan politics—where **religious robes masked ruthless ambition**, and **bullets replaced ballots**.

A Turning Point in Sri Lankan Politics

The killing of Prime Minister S.W.R.D. Bandaranaike on September 25, 1959, stands as one of the most pivotal episodes in Sri Lanka's post-independence history. It exposed the deep fault lines within the country's political and religious establishment and triggered a reckoning with the misuse of power, privilege, and ideology.

Bandaranaike, elected in 1956 on a platform of Sinhala nationalism and Buddhist revivalism, faced growing dissent from both minority communities and factions within his own camp. His sweeping reforms—most notably the "Sinhala Only" language policy—alienated Tamil minorities and ignited political turmoil, but the fatal blow came not from ideological opponents. The trigger was pulled from within his own circle: a Buddhist monk, **Talduwe Somarama Thero**, shot the Prime Minister at point-blank range in his Colombo residence.

What appeared to be a lone act of violence quickly unraveled into a web of conspiracy. Investigations revealed that **Mapitigama Buddharakkitha Thero**, a powerful cleric and close associate of the Prime Minister, had orchestrated the assassination out of commercial frustration and personal vengeance. Buddharakkitha had lobbied for lucrative government contracts and, feeling betrayed by Bandaranaike's ethical rebuff, resolved to eliminate him. Alongside Somarama, he enlisted help from business associate **H.P. Jayawardena**, among others.

Court proceedings following the assassination gripped the nation. The trial featured explosive testimony—most notably from **Carolis Amarasinghe**, a former supporter turned Crown Witness—who exposed covert meetings, weapon procurement, and the chilling confession that Bandaranaike was the intended target. The trial culminated in 1961 with guilty verdicts for Somarama, Buddharakkitha, and Jayawardena, all sentenced to death. Somarama was executed in 1962, while Buddharakkitha died in prison years later.

Politically, the assassination triggered seismic shifts. Bandaranaike's widow, **Sirimavo Bandaranaike**, ascended to power in 1960, becoming the **World's First Female Prime Minister** and inheriting a nation rattled by the realization that spiritual robes could conceal political ambition and ruthless intent.

The case left behind a legacy more profound than courtroom verdicts—it shattered idealistic notions of leadership and spotlighted the perils of mixing religion, politics, and commerce. In the backdrop of post-colonial optimism, Bandaranaike's death served as a solemn reminder: in the realm of power, loyalty is rarely unqualified, and betrayal can wear sanctified robes.

Authoritative Sources

1. **Wikipedia** – Assassination of S.W.R.D. Bandaranaike. Provides a detailed timeline of the assassination.

2. **Daily Mirror** – "The Incident That Rocked Ceylon" by D.B.S. Jeyaraj. Offers a rich narrative of the assassination's impact, including the declaration of a state of emergency, the trial proceedings, and the broader political consequences.

3. **Daily FT** – "The Prelate and the Premier"

Focuses on the motives behind the assassination, particularly the role of Mapitigama Buddharakkitha Thera, the chief conspirator. It also details the medical bulletin issued after Bandaranaike's death and the coroner's verdict of homicide due to shock and hemorrhage.

Chapter 15: Kalattawa's Deadly Lies: The Double Murder and Trial of Alfred de Zoysa (1966–1970)

In the mid-1960s, a single case gripped the conscience of Sri Lanka. From tea shops in remote villages to office corridors in Colombo, the Kalattawa Case dominated conversations—an unsettling tale of wealth, deceit, and murder that seeped into the daily rhythms of life.

What made it especially memorable wasn't just the nature of the crime—but the symbol of privilege buried with it. Whispers of a brand-new Austin Cambridge, concealed in haste to erase evidence, became an emblem of the affluence surrounding the scandal. The very act of burying such a prized vehicle sparked fascination and fury alike. It suggested something more than guilt—it revealed arrogance, a belief that money could dig holes deep enough to swallow the truth.

I found myself drawn to the story with unshakable intensity. As each twist surfaced, I devoured every report, every rumor, every courtroom update. It wasn't just news—it was a mirror to the country's shifting social currents, exposing tensions between power and justice.

This wasn't a crime hidden in darkness. It was buried—boldly, literally, and with brazen intent.

The **Kalattawa Double Murder Case**, which unfolded in Sri Lanka between 1966 and 1970, remains one of the most sensational and complex criminal investigations in the country's history.

Centered around the influential businessman and tavern owner **Alfred de Zoysa**, the case involved illicit liquor, vehicle theft, hidden corpses, and a chilling conspiracy that ultimately led to a landmark trial and execution. This Chapter explores the intricate web of deceit, the painstaking investigation, and the dramatic courtroom proceedings that gripped the nation.

Alfred de Zoysa was a well-known figure in **Anuradhapura**, a city steeped in history and sacred significance. He was soft-spoken and charismatic, yet wielded immense influence through his arrack business, irrigation contracts, and land holdings. His taverns were hubs of social activity, and his connections extended to prominent politicians and professionals.

The trouble began in **1966**, when a routine tender for tavern licenses brought **S.R. Kandiah**, a businessman from **Jaffna**, into Zoysa's territory. Kandiah arrived with **Rs. 66,500** to bid for the license, but Zoysa, feeling threatened, attempted to bribe him as a "gift" with **Rs. 65,000** to back off. Kandiah declined and returned to Jaffna—only to be ambushed near **Boo Oya bridge**. His vehicle and cash were stolen in a highway-style robbery orchestrated by Zoysa's men.

Following the robbery, two of Zoysa's employees—**P.K.D. Perera**, a Retired Mechanic, and **Julius Sandrasagara**, a Technical Officer—became liabilities. Both had knowledge of Zoysa's illicit activities, including the stolen **Austin Cambridge** car used in the heist. They were subsequently **murdered**, their bodies burned and buried in Zoysa's **Kalattawa Estate**. Only **Perera's remains** were conclusively identified; **Sandrasagara's body** was never recovered.

The breakthrough came when a young man, **Punchi Bandage Jayasena**, narrowly escaped being burned alive and alerted police. Investigators discovered a **Wadiya** (hut) with a tied-up victim and a can of diesel nearby. This led to Zoysa's arrest and the unraveling of a vast criminal network.

The **Criminal Investigation Department (CID)** launched a meticulous probe, deploying undercover officers disguised as laborers and market vendors.

Key developments included:

Discovery of the **buried Austin Cambridge** car, hidden 15 feet underground in Kalattawa.

Excavation of **charred bones**, a **double belt buckle**, and a **bag frame**, which helped identify Perera.

Testimonies from informants like **Vincent** and **Appuhamy**, who revealed Zoysa's plans to eliminate witnesses.

The CID's efforts were bolstered by officers like **Sergeant M.H.P. Fernando**, **PC U.A. Piyasena**, and **Inspector Upali Seneviratne**, whose undercover work cracked the case wide open.

The Trial: Justice in the Face of Intimidation

The trial began in **1970**, with Zoysa and his accomplices **W. Piyadasa (Kalu Albert)** and **W. Fernando (Willie Mama)** facing charges of **double murder and conspiracy**. Despite attempts to intimidate witnesses and obstruct justice, the prosecution presented compelling evidence:

Forensic analysis of the belt buckle and bones. The **double belt buckle** was the key forensic clue linking Perera to the site.

- Witness accounts of the murders and burial.
- Circumstantial evidence linking Zoysa to the stolen car and illicit distillery.

The jury found all three guilty of **murdering P.K.D. Perera** and **conspiring to murder**. Zoysa and Kalu Albert were sentenced to **death** and hanged in **1972**. Willie Mama died in prison before execution.

The Kalattawa case was groundbreaking for several reasons:

It was one of the **first cases in Sri Lanka** where a conviction was secured **without a complete body**—a legal rarity.

It exposed the **intersection of crime and political influence**, challenging the impunity enjoyed by powerful figures.

It showcased the **tenacity of law enforcement**, especially the CID, in navigating a web of lies and fear.

The case also inspired books, newspaper series, and public discourse on justice, corruption, and the rule of law in Sri Lanka.

"Kalattawa's Deadly Lies" is more than a tale of murder—it is a cautionary saga of unchecked power, betrayal, and the resilience of justice. Alfred de Zoysa's fall from grace serves as a stark reminder that even the most influential cannot escape accountability when truth is unearthed—sometimes, quite literally—from the soil beneath their feet.

The Kalattawa case was a massive undertaking by Sri Lanka's **Criminal Investigation Department (CID)**, involving a coordinated team of officers working across multiple regions. While no single officer was solely in charge from start to finish, several key figures played pivotal roles in leading and cracking the case:

Senior Inspector M.K.J. Perera

Often referred to as the "Captain" of the CID team, he oversaw the broader investigation and coordinated efforts among field officers and forensic experts.

Superintendent of Police (SP) Tyrrell Goonetilleke

He was the CID's top-ranking officer involved in the case and directed major operations, including the excavation of the buried Austin Cambridge car and the search for human remains.

Inspector Upali Seneviratne

Played a hands-on role in evidence gathering and witness tracking. He personally helped identify key forensic clues, such as the double belt buckle that linked the crime to one of the victims.

Undercover & Field Operatives

Sergeant M.H.P. "Batha" Fernando and **Police Constable U.A. Piyasena**

These two CID officers went undercover in Anuradhapura, operated in **Anuradhapura's markets and taverns** posing as laborers and tea shop regulars. Their intelligence work was instrumental in locating informants and uncovering the burial site of the stolen car.

Assistant Superintendent of Police (ASP) A. Mahendran

Coordinated local police efforts in Anuradhapura and worked closely with CID officers during raids and arrests.

SP C. Dhanapala (North Central Division)

Oversaw regional police coordination and supported CID operations during the critical phases of the investigation.

Supporting Officers and Informants

Then Medawachchiya OIC: Nalin Delgoda

Then OIC Crimes: S.S. Navaratnaraja. Pix by M.A. Pushpa Kumara, Ranjith Perera and Amila Gamage

Inspector S.S. Navaratnaraja and **SI Nalin Delgoda**

These officers from the Anuradhapura and Medawachchiya stations were among the first to respond to witness reports and helped apprehend suspects like Alfred de Zoysa.

Informant Hettiarachchige Don Juvan Appuhamy

A tractor driver who revealed the burial site of the stolen car, triggering a cascade of arrests and evidence recovery.

This case was a masterclass in multi-agency coordination, with CID officers working alongside local police, informants, and forensic experts to bring down a powerful criminal network.

Authoritative Sources

1. **The Sunday Times – "Double belt buckle that undid a double murder"**
   This feature by Kumudini Hettiarachchi and team offers a gripping account of the Kalattawa double murder. It details how Alfred de Zoysa, a well-known Anuradhapura businessman, orchestrated the killing of two Jaffna tavern renters over a turf dispute. The discovery of a charred belt buckle in a burned-out vehicle was the key forensic clue that unraveled the conspiracy.

2. **Famous Criminal Cases of Sri Lanka: Alfred de Zoysa and the Kalattawa Murders – A.C. Alles**
   Justice A.C. Alles provides a comprehensive legal and narrative analysis of the case, including the planning, execution, and trial. His book is considered the definitive source on the Kalattawa murders, offering insights into the criminal psychology and procedural intricacies.

3. **Court of Criminal Appeal Judgment – Alfred de Zoysa v. The Queen (1971)**
   This legal document outlines the appeal proceedings, judicial reasoning, and final

verdict. It discusses issues of jury misdirection, character evidence, and the burden of proof—critical elements that shaped the outcome of the trial.

Chapter 16: The Tragedy of Innocence: The Story of Premawathie Manamperi (17 April 1971)

In the annals of Sri Lankan history, few stories evoke as much sorrow, outrage, and reflection as that of **Premawathie Manamperi**. Born on January 18, 1949, in the sacred town of Kataragama, she was a young woman of promise—intelligent, graceful, and deeply rooted in her community. Her life, however, was brutally cut short at the age of 22, leaving behind a legacy of injustice and a haunting reminder of the dangers of unchecked power.

Premawathie was the eldest daughter in a large family, raised by Hendrik Appuhamy and Lilawathi Obeysinghe. She pursued education with passion, passing the **Dharmacharya Examination** and serving as a **Dhamma teacher** at the **Kataragama Dhamma School**. Her commitment to Buddhist teachings and her role as a mentor to young minds reflected a life dedicated to compassion and wisdom.

In 1970, she was crowned **Princess of the Year (AVURUDHU KUMARI)** at a local festival—a title that celebrated not just her beauty, but her poise and popularity. Yet this public recognition would tragically become a catalyst for envy and vengeance.

The 1971 Insurrection and a Fatal Betrayal

During the JVP insurrection in April 1971, Kataragama became a hotspot of unrest. On April 16, Premawathie was falsely accused of being a rebel and arrested by **Sub-Inspector Jayasiri Udawatte**, a Police Officer whose romantic advances she had previously rejected. She was handed over to the army, where **Lieutenant Alfred Wijesuriya** and **Volunteer Officer Amaradasa Ratnayake** subjected her to torture, humiliation, and public degradation.

She was stripped naked, beaten, and forced to walk through town with her hands raised—a grotesque spectacle of cruelty. Near the Kataragama Post Office, she was shot, but remained conscious, reportedly asking for water. She was then buried alive and later shot in the head to ensure her death. A postmortem confirmed she was still alive during burial.

Justice and Its Limits

Her body was exhumed on May 24, 1971, and an inquest led to a trial in the Galle Criminal Court, presided over by Justice D.Q.M. Sirimanne. Wijesuriya and Ratnayake were convicted of attempted murder and sentenced to 16 years of rigorous imprisonment. However, SI Udawatte, the man who orchestrated her arrest, was never charged, and the possibility of sexual assault was never investigated.

The circumstances surrounding her death were riddled with corruption and cruelty. Despite multiple witnesses attesting to her innocence and the personal motives behind her arrest, justice was elusive. While two Army officers were convicted of attempted murder, the Police officer who orchestrated her arrest faced no consequences.

Her story became emblematic of how women's bodies are often weaponized in conflict, and how systemic failures can silence even the most glaring truths.

Cultural Reverberations and Memorials

Premawathie's death sparked national outrage, becoming a rallying cry during the 1977 elections, where J.R. Jayewardene condemned the incident as emblematic of state brutality.

Her story inspired:

• Nahi Werena Verani, a film starring Sangeetha Weeraratne as Premawathie

• A song by Anton Jones, narrating her tragic fate

• A reference in Shehan Karunatilaka's *The Seven Moons of Maali Almeida*, where she symbolizes defiled innocence

In 1979, a memorial was built in Kataragama, featuring a clay pot offering water to pilgrims—a gesture of healing. Sadly, it was later vandalized and obscured with paint and eventually demolished.

Conclusion

Premawathie Manamperi's story is not just a tale of personal tragedy—it is a mirror held up to society. It asks us to confront the consequences of abuse, the fragility of justice, and the enduring strength of memory. Her life, though stolen, continues to speak. It urges us to remember, to question, and to ensure that such horrors are never repeated.

She was a teacher, a daughter, a beauty queen. But above all, she was human. And her humanity deserves to be honored.

Authoritative Sources

1. **Wikipedia – Premawathie Manamperi**
   Offers a detailed account of her arrest, torture, public humiliation, and execution by military personnel during the early days of the 1971 uprising. It also highlights the postmortem findings that revealed she may have been buried alive.

2. **Sunday Times – "Kataragama Beauty Queen Murder Case: The Need to Obey Only Lawful Commands"**
   This article explores the personal and political dimensions of the case, including the alleged motives of police officer Udawatte and the military's role in her death. It also references the film *Nahi Verena Verani*, which dramatized the events.

3. **Reddit – "The 50 Year Anniversary of the Murder of Premawathie Manamperi"**
   A community-sourced summary that includes trial details, the role of Lieutenant Wijesuriya and Amaradasa Ratnayake, and the political fallout. It notes that her murder became a rallying cry for the UNP in the 1977 elections and inspired cultural responses like songs and films.

Chapter 17: The Assassination of Alfred Duraiappah: Politics, Identity, and the Rise of Tamil Militancy (1975)

(Pic: Daily News)

The First Political Martyr of Sri Lanka's Civil Conflict

Alfred Thangarajah Duraiappah was born on June 15, 1926, in Vannarpannai, Jaffna. Educated at St. John's College, he qualified as a Proctor from Ceylon Law College in 1948 and joined the Unofficial Bar of Jaffna. His political career began in 1952 with election to the Jaffna Municipal Council, where he later became Deputy Mayor in 1958.

In 1960, Duraiappah won a seat in Parliament as an Independent candidate, **defeating G.G. Ponnambalam**. He served as Member of Parliament for Jaffna from 1960 to 1965 and later became **Mayor of Jaffna from 1970** until his death in 1975.

Duraiappah aligned himself with the **Sri Lanka Freedom Party (SLFP)**, the ruling party dominated by Sinhalese interests. As SLFP's chief organizer in Jaffna, he secured government funding for infrastructure projects—roads, markets, and public utilities—earning grassroots support.

However, his cooperation with the central government made him a target of Tamil nationalist ire, especially after the 1974 Tamil Research Conference incident, where Sri Lankan police disrupted a public event, resulting in the deaths of 9–11 Tamil civilians. Duraiappah's role as mayor during this tragedy intensified accusations of betrayal.

Assassination and LTTE Involvement

On **July 27, 1975**, Duraiappah was en route to the Varadaraja Perumal Temple in Ponnalai, Jaffna, with his 14-year-old daughter Eesha. As he arrived, masked gunmen ambushed him, shooting him dead. D.K. Rajaratnam, a fellow municipal council member, was also injured.

The assassination was carried out by members of the Liberation Tigers of Tamil Eelam (LTTE). It is widely believed that Velupillai Prabhakaran, then a young militant, personally pulled the trigger, marking the LTTE's first major political killing.

Symbolism and Impact

Duraiappah's killing was politically and symbolically charged:

• **Seen as a traitor**: His SLFP ties and perceived complicity in the 1974 incident made him a target.

• **Militant messaging**: The LTTE aimed to intimidate Tamil politicians who cooperated with the Sinhalese-led government.

• **Strategic escalation:** The murder signaled a new era of targeted political violence in Sri Lanka's north.

In 1978, the LTTE issued a public letter claiming responsibility for Duraiappah's assassination, along with ten others.

Timeline of Key Events

Date	Event
1960	Elected MP for Jaffna
1965	Lost parliamentary seat
1970	Elected Mayor of Jaffna
1974	Tamil Research Conference incident: 11 civilians killed
1975	Assassinated by LTTE at Ponnalai temple. CID assigns **Inspector Bastianpillai** to monitor Tamil political activity.
1977	Tamil United Liberation Front (TULF) becomes the main opposition party, advocating for a separate Tamil state. Ethnic tensions rise further.
Early 1978	Intelligence suggests Uma Maheswaran, a Tamil militant leader, is hiding in Murunkan, Vavuniya District. CID begins planning reconnaissance.
April 7, 1978	Inspector Bastianpillai leads a small team into the Murunkan jungle— Sub Inspector Perampalan, Sergeant Balasingham, and Constable Sriwardene accompany him. They encounter militants disguised as farm workers.
April 7, 1978 (later that day)	LTTE operatives ambush the CID team. Sellakili seizes Bastianpillai's weapon and executes the officers. Their bodies are thrown into a well; the police vehicle is burned.
April 10–13, 1978	CID and military personnel locate the site. Bodies of the officers are recovered. The LTTE claims responsibility via the TULF, asserting symbolic retaliation.

Late 1978	Tamil militants target other Tamil CID officers, including Pathmanathan and Kumar. The pattern of targeted killings intensifies.

Authoritative Sources

1 - **Wikipedia** – Alfred Duraiappah

Provides a comprehensive biography of Duraiappah, including his tenure as Mayor of Jaffna and Member of Parliament. It details his affiliation with the Sri Lanka Freedom Party (SLFP), his development initiatives in Jaffna, and his assassination on 27 July 1975 by members of the emerging Tamil militant movement, widely believed to include Velupillai Prabhakaran.

2 - **Sri Lanka Guardian** – "Traitors and Targets: The Killing of Alfred Duraiappah" This reflective essay explores the ideological framing of Duraiappah as a "traitor" within Tamil nationalist discourse. It traces his political career, the motivations behind his assassination, and how the event catalyzed the normalization of political violence in Tamil militancy.

3 - **The Morning Telegraph** – "Traitors and Targets: The First Bullet in Tamil Politics"
Offers a vivid narrative of the assassination near the Varadaraja Perumal Temple in Ponnalai, Jaffna. It contextualizes the killing as the symbolic "first shot" of Tamil armed struggle, marking the transition from political dissent to insurgency. The article also examines Duraiappah's complex identity as a Tamil Christian aligned with a Sinhalese-majority party.

Chapter 18: The 1976 Anti-Muslim Violence in Puttalam: A Forgotten Chapter of Communal Strife

The 1976 anti-Muslim violence in Puttalam stands as a stark reminder of the deep-rooted ethnic and religious tensions that have periodically erupted in Sri Lanka. Occurring between **31 January and 7 February 1976**, this episode was not merely a spontaneous outburst but a **coordinated campaign of violence** led by Sinhalese mobs, allegedly under the guidance of a Buddhist monk and with the complicity of local authorities. The violence culminated in the **killing of seven Muslims inside the Puttalam Jumma Mosque by police** on 2 February, marking one of the most egregious violations of religious sanctity in the country's post-independence history.

Background and Rising Tensions

The roots of the violence can be traced to the **early 1970s**, when **anti-Muslim sentiment** began to intensify among segments of the Sinhalese population. This hostility was fueled by perceptions of **Muslim economic dominance**, alleged **preferential treatment**, and **land disputes** in regions like Puttalam.

Key contributing factors included:

Economic Rivalry: Muslims were seen as monopolizing trade and commerce in Puttalam, which bred resentment among Sinhalese traders and laborers.

Demographic Shifts: The influx of Sinhalese settlers from the south into the Muslim-majority town created competition over **jobs, land, and public resources**.

State Discrimination: Local Muslims felt marginalized by government policies that favored Sinhalese settlers, particularly in land allocation and employment.

Historical Precedents: The violence echoed the **1915 Sinhalese-Muslim riots**, making it the second major communal clash between the two communities since independence.

The Violence Unfolds

The violence began with **clashes over a bus stand relocation**, which disrupted Muslim businesses and rerouted traffic through Sinhalese areas—an act seen as economically and symbolically exclusionary. Tensions escalated rapidly, culminating in:

11 Muslim deaths, including **7 killed inside a mosque by police gunfire**

Dozens injured, many seriously

271 Muslim homes, 44 shops, and **2 mosques** burned to the ground

Widespread looting and arson, often carried out in broad daylight

The involvement of **Kolitha Thero**, a Buddhist monk, and **Rajapaksha**, the Puttalam Government Agent, was particularly alarming. Both were accused of inciting violence and enabling Sinhalese mobs and police to act with impunity.

This incident reveals the **intersection of ethnic nationalism, economic competition, and state complicity** in communal violence. Scholars like Prof. M.A. Nuhman and Dr. Farzana Haniffa have argued that such violence is often rooted in **commercial rivalry**, not just religious or ethnic hatred.

The 1976 violence in Puttalam:

Exposed the fragility of intercommunal relations in Sri Lanka

Highlighted the role of state actors in perpetuating violence

Set a precedent for future anti-Muslim riots, including those in Galle (1982) and Mawanella (2001)

Despite its severity, the incident remains **underrepresented in mainstream historical narratives**, overshadowed by the larger Tamil-Sinhalese conflict.

The 1976 anti-Muslim violence in Puttalam was not an isolated event but part of a broader pattern of **ethno-religious tensions** in Sri Lanka. Its legacy continues to shape the socio-political landscape, reminding us of the urgent need for **inclusive governance**, **interfaith dialogue**, and **historical reckoning**. Only by confronting these painful chapters can Sri Lanka hope to build a truly pluralistic society.

Authoritative Sources

1. **Wikipedia** – 1976 Anti-Muslim Violence in Puttalam

This entry provides a detailed chronology of the violence, which occurred between 31 January and 7 February 1976. It documents the killing of 11 Muslims, including seven inside the Puttalam Jumma Mosque, and the destruction of 271 homes, 44 shops, and two mosques. The violence was reportedly led by Sinhalese mobs, with complicity from local police and officials, including a Buddhist monk and the Puttalam Government Agent.

2. "Towards Recovering Histories of Anti-Muslim Violence" – **Vijay Nagaraj & Farzana Haniffa.** This research paper examines the Puttalam 1976, Galle 1982, and Mawanella 2001 incidents, arguing that these episodes reflect systemic communal tensions rooted in economic rivalry, land disputes, and political marginalization. It emphasizes how such violence has been overshadowed by Tamil-Sinhala conflict narratives, leaving Muslim experiences underrepresented in mainstream historiography.

3. **Daily News** – "The Muslim–Sinhala Divide: A Dilemma"

This article contextualizes the Puttalam violence within broader economic and political competition between Sinhalese and Muslim mercantile classes. It cites research by Prof. M.A. Nuhman, who argues that commercial rivalry and nationalist rhetoric, dating back to Anagarika Dharmapala's era, played a significant role in fueling communal strife.

Chapter 19: The Killing of CID Inspector Bastianpillai: A Turning Point in Sri Lanka's Ethnic Conflict (1978)

The late 1970s in Sri Lanka were marked by rising ethnic tensions between the Sinhalese-majority government and Tamil minority groups. Among the most prominent Tamil militant organizations was the **Liberation Tigers of Tamil Eelam (LTTE)**, which sought an independent Tamil state in the north and east of the island.

Inspector T.L.B. Bastianpillai, a Tamil officer in the **Criminal Investigation Department (CID)**, was tasked with monitoring Tamil political movements, particularly the **Tamil United Liberation Front (TULF)**, following the assassination of **Alfred Duraiappah**. He was considered one of the CID's top investigators and had even been responsible for security arrangements during the 1976 Non-Aligned Movement Summit in Colombo.

In early 1978, Bastianpillai received intelligence that **Uma Maheswaran**, a leading LTTE figure, was hiding in a farm in the **Murunkan** jungle in the **Vavuniya District**. On **April 7, 1978**, Bastianpillai led a small team of officers—including **Sub Inspector Perampalan, Sergeant Balasingham, and Constable Sriwardene**—into the jungle to investigate.

The Murunkan Massacre – The First Targeted Killing by LTTE

The officers arrived at what appeared to be a farm and approached several men posing as laborers. Unbeknownst to them, LTTE operatives, including **Sellakili**, were hiding nearby. As Bastianpillai lowered his weapon to accept a drink of water, Sellakili struck him and seized his sub-machine gun. In the ensuing chaos:

Bastianpillai and Sergeant Balasingham were shot dead.

Perampalan was wounded and fell into a well, where he was executed.

Constable Sriwardene attempted to flee but was gunned down.

The bodies were mutilated and dumped into the well. The LTTE took the officers' weapons—marking the first time Tamil militants acquired a sub-machine gun—and burned the police vehicle.

Aftermath and Impact

The disappearance of Bastianpillai and his team alarmed police leadership. Days later, their decomposed bodies were discovered in the Murunkan jungle. The LTTE claimed responsibility for the killings via the TULF, sending shockwaves through the government and public.

This incident was pivotal for several reasons:

It marked one of the **first targeted killings of law enforcement** by Tamil militants.

It demonstrated the LTTE's growing operational capability and willingness to confront the state directly.

It led to increased militarization and surveillance in Tamil-majority areas.

The massacre became a **symbolic moment** in the escalation of Sri Lanka's civil conflict.

In the months that followed, the LTTE assassinated other Tamil police officers investigating militancy, including **Inspector Pathmanathan** and **Inspector Kumar**.

Controversies and Legacy

While some accounts portray Bastianpillai as a dedicated officer, others—particularly from Tamil sources—describe him as a **sadistic interrogator** who allegedly tortured young Tamil suspects. This duality reflects the broader complexities of Sri Lanka's ethnic conflict, where victims and perpetrators often shifted depending on perspective.

The Murunkan massacre is now seen as a **precursor to the full-scale civil war** that erupted in the 1980s. It underscored the failure of political reconciliation and the deep mistrust between Tamil communities and the state apparatus.

Authoritative Sources

1. **Murunkan Massacre – Wikipedia**
   This entry provides a detailed account of the **April 7, 1978** ambush in the Murunkan jungles of Vavuniya District, where **CID Inspector T.L.B. Bastianpillai** and three other officers were killed by **LTTE members**, including **Sellakili** and **Uma Maheswaran**. It describes how the police team was lured into a trap and executed, with their weapons seized—marking the LTTE's first acquisition of a sub-machine gun.

2. **Ilankai Tamil Sangam – "T.L.B. Bastianpillai (1941–1978)" by Sachi Sri Kantha**
   Offers a critical perspective on Bastianpillai's role in the CID, portraying him as a feared interrogator among Tamil youth. The article argues that his killing was not only

tactical but symbolic, representing a retaliatory strike against state repression and a psychological turning point in Tamil resistance.

3. **The Ethnic Conflict in Sri Lanka – Academia.edu**
   Provides broader context on the ethnic tensions that led to the rise of Tamil militancy, including the role of state surveillance, political marginalization, and the militarization of Tamil youth. While not focused solely on Bastianpillai, it situates his assassination within the larger trajectory of the conflict.

Chapter 20: The Killing of Iyathurai Indrarajah: A Prelude to Systemic Repression (1979)

The death of **Iyathurai Indrarajah**, a young Ayurvedic college student from Nallur, Jaffna, in **July 1979**, marked a chilling escalation in state-sponsored violence against Tamil civilians. His killing, along with others that night, signaled the beginning of a brutal campaign of repression in the north, laying the groundwork for decades of conflict and mistrust between the Tamil population and the Sri Lankan state.

The Night of Terror: 13 July 1979

On the night of **13 July 1979**, two unmarked vehicles—one a British-built A-40 car and the other a Police Jeep—left the Jaffna Residency, which had been commandeered by Police forces. Their mission: to abduct and eliminate Tamil youths suspected of militant activity.

Among those taken was **Indrarajah**, forcibly removed from his home on Second Lane, Point Pedro Road. He was one of **six young men** abducted that night, including **Inbam (Visvajothi Erattinam) and Selvam (Selvaratnam)**, both previously acquitted of involvement in the assassination of Alfred Duraiappah.

Indrarajah was subjected to **severe physical assault** before being handed over to the Jaffna Hospital. He succumbed to his injuries **two days later**, with multiple fractures and internal trauma. The hospital conducted an inquest despite emergency regulations that had suspended such procedures.

The **Jaffna Magistrate's verdict**, delivered on **8 January 1980**, was unequivocal:

"The death was due to cardio-respiratory failure consequent to renal tubular necrosis consequent to shock and hemorrhage resulting from multiple injuries. There is evidence of assault by Police. I return the verdict of homicide."

Similar verdicts were issued for Inbam and Selvam, whose bodies bore gunshot wounds and signs of torture. The other three youths—**R. Balendra, S. Parameswaran, and S. Rajeswaran—disappeared without a trace**, adding to the growing list of enforced disappearances in the region.

The killing occurred just days before **General T.I. Weeratunga** assumed command of the Northern Province under the **Prevention of Terrorism Act (PTA)**. His appointment coincided with a birthday celebration, underscoring the surreal juxtaposition of festivity and brutality.

This incident:

Exemplified the use of emergency powers to bypass legal safeguards

Deepened Tamil alienation, fueling support for militant movements

Set a precedent for future extrajudicial killings and disappearances

The murder of Iyathurai Indrarajah was not an isolated tragedy—it was a harbinger of the **systemic violence** that would engulf Sri Lanka's north for decades. His death, officially ruled a homicide, remains a powerful symbol of the **impunity and repression** that characterized the early years of the civil conflict.

Authoritative Sources

1. **Pirapaharan: Vol. 1, Chapter 20** – "Jaffna Turned Torture Chamber" by T. Sabaratnam

This chapter provides a harrowing account of the events of 13 July 1979, when multiple Tamil youths—including Ayurvedic College student Iyathurai Indrarajah—were abducted by plainclothes police officers under emergency regulations. Indrarajah was later admitted to Jaffna Hospital with severe injuries and died two days later. The Jaffna Magistrate's inquest ruled his death a homicide, citing cardio-respiratory failure due to shock and hemorrhage from multiple injuries.

2. **Wikipedia** – Tamil Genocide

While focused on broader patterns of violence, this entry contextualizes the 1979 crackdown in Jaffna as part of a longer arc of state-sponsored repression against Tamil civilians. It references targeted killings, disappearances, and torture as tools of control used by the Sri Lankan government during the early stages of the ethnic conflict.

Chapter 21: The 1981 Anti-Tamil Pogrom: Ethnic Violence and Political Complicity

Between **June and August 1981**, Sri Lanka experienced a wave of coordinated anti-Tamil violence across multiple regions, **Jaffna, Ratnapura, Balangoda, Kahawatte, Colombo**, and border villages in **Batticaloa and Amparai**. Far from being spontaneous, the violence was reportedly organized and politically sanctioned, with Sinhalese mobs, Sri Lankan police, and government officials implicated in the attacks.

Targeted Attacks

• Tamil homes, shops, temples, and businesses were systematically looted and burned.

• In the Hill Country, mobs armed with clubs, iron rods, and knives roamed tea estates, committing arson, murder, and rape.

• Tamil civilians were beaten, terrorized, and driven from their homes, often with no protection from law enforcement.

Mass Displacement

• Over 25,000 Tamil plantation workers were rendered homeless in the central highlands.

• An estimated 10,000 villagers were displaced in the Eastern Province.

• Many fled to refugee camps or Tamil- majority areas, deepening ethnic segregation.

Cultural Destruction: The Burning of the Jaffna Public Library

On the night of May 31, 1981, one of the most devastating acts of cultural violence occurred:

The Jaffna Public Library, a repository of over 97,000 rare books, manuscripts, and historical documents, was deliberately set ablaze by state-sponsored mobs and uniformed security forces.

• The library was a symbol of Tamil intellectual heritage, housing palm-leaf manuscripts, ancient texts, and regional newspapers.

• The destruction continued unchecked for two nights, with no intervention from authorities.

• The timing coincided with District Development Council elections, and two senior UNP ministers—Cyril Mathew and Gamini Dissanayake—were present in Jaffna during the violence. This act of was widely seen as an attempt to erase Tamil history and identity and became a rallying cry for Tamil resistance.

Casualties and Trauma

• At least 25 people were killed, though the true number may be higher.

• Scores of Tamil women were reportedly raped.

• Thousands lost homes, livelihoods, and access to education and healthcare.

• The trauma of the pogrom left deep psychological scars and intensified Tamil grievances.

Political Strategy

• The ruling United National Party (UNP) under President J.R. Jayewardene was accused of using the violence to suppress Tamil political activism, particularly the Tamil United Liberation Front (TULF).

• The pogrom coincided with elections and was allegedly designed to intimidate Tamil voters and undermine Tamil autonomy efforts.

Ethnic Tensions

• Decades of discriminatory language policies, land colonization schemes, and economic marginalization had created deep divisions between Sinhalese and Tamil communities.

• The violence was fueled by Sinhalese nationalist rhetoric, which portrayed Tamils as separatists and threats to national unity.

State Complicity

• Eyewitnesses and international observers reported that Police and army units stood by, or actively participated in the violence.

• Government officials failed to intervene, and no one was held accountable for the destruction of the library or the broader attacks.

Legacy and Consequences

• The pogrom radicalized Tamil youth, leading to increased support for militant groups like the Liberation Tigers of Tamil Eelam (LTTE).

• It marked a turning point in Sri Lanka's ethnic conflict, **setting the stage for the Black July** pogrom of 1983 and the civil war that followed.

• The Jaffna Library's destruction remains a symbol of cultural genocide, and its memory continues to shape Tamil identity and calls for justice.

Authoritative Sources

1. **Wikipedia – 1981 Anti-Tamil Pogrom**
   This entry outlines the timeline and scope of the violence, which occurred between **June and August 1981**. It documents the **burning of the Jaffna Public Library**, destruction of Tamil homes and businesses, and the role of **Sinhalese mobs, Sri Lankan police**, and **members of the ruling United National Party (UNP)** in orchestrating the attacks.

2. **[Brian Eads – "The Cover-Up That Failed" (London Observer, 20 September 1981)]**
   Cited in multiple sources, this investigative report describes how the violence in Jaffna was **planned and executed by the predominantly Sinhalese police force**, with **political backing**. It highlights the **systematic nature of the arson and looting**, including the destruction of over **95,000 Tamil manuscripts**.

3. **T. Sabaratnam – *Pirapaharan*, Vol. 1, Chapter 25** Offers a Tamil nationalist perspective on the pogrom, emphasizing the **political complicity** of the UNP government and the **symbolic violence** of burning the Jaffna Library. It argues that the

event marked a turning point in Tamil resistance, pushing many toward armed militancy.

Chapter 22: The Burning of the Jaffna Library (1981)

(Pics from Wikipedia Archives)

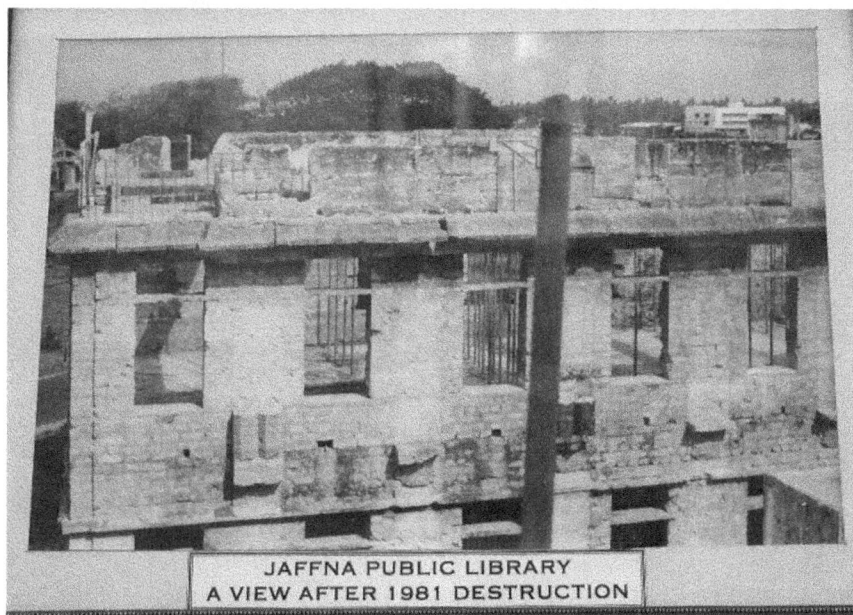

JAFFNA PUBLIC LIBRARY
A VIEW AFTER 1981 DESTRUCTION

Background of the Jaffna Library Burning

Date: Night of **May 31 – June 1, 1981**

Location: Jaffna, Northern Province, Sri Lanka

Library Significance

Contained **over 97,000 books**, including rare Tamil manuscripts, palm-leaf texts, and historical documents

Served as a **symbol of Tamil intellectual and cultural heritage**

One of the **largest libraries in Asia** at the time

Political Context

Occurred during **District Development Council elections**

Tensions were high following the **killing of two Sinhalese policemen** at a Tamil United Liberation Front (TULF) rally

The incident was part of a broader **anti-Tamil pogrom** and repression campaign

Alleged Perpetrators and Execution

1. Sri Lankan Police and Security Forces

• Eyewitness accounts and later investigations suggest that uniformed police officers, plainclothes personnel, and paramilitary units were directly involved in the arson.

• Estimates suggest 100–175 police personnel participated in the destruction.

• The Movement for Inter-Racial Justice and Equality reported that the acts were "well-organized" and carried out by state security forces.

2. **State-Sponsored Sinhalese Mobs**

• The arson was reportedly executed by Sinhalese mobs, many of whom were allegedly supported or protected by state forces.

• The mobs targeted the library as a symbol of Tamil cultural identity, destroying over 97,000 volumes, including ancient palm-leaf manuscripts, historical texts, and rare publications.

3. **Political Oversight**

• Two senior cabinet ministers from the ruling United National Party (UNP)—**Gamini Dissanayake and Cyril Mathew,** were present in Jaffna at the time of the incident.

• Both ministers were known for their hardline Sinhala nationalist views, and multiple sources allege they oversaw or condoned the operation.

• No official inquiry has ever held them accountable, and the incident was not reported in national newspapers at the time.

Civilian Casualties and Impact

Casualties:

- At least **four civilians were killed** during the broader pogrom
- **Reverend Father David**, a scholar and community leader, reportedly **died from shock** days after the burning
- Many **homes and businesses were looted and torched**

Cultural Loss:

- Destruction of **irreplaceable manuscripts**, including works by **Ananda Coomaraswamy** and **Isaac Thambiah**
- Loss of **centuries-old Tamil medical texts**, literature, and historical records

Symbolism:

- The burning became a **rallying cry for Tamil resistance**
- Marked the beginning of **Sri Lanka's descent into civil war**

The burning of the library is widely regarded as a cultural genocide, aimed at erasing Tamil intellectual heritage. Despite widespread condemnation, no one has been held legally accountable for the destruction. The event is often cited as a precursor to the Sri Lankan Civil War, deepening ethnic divisions and mistrust.

Timeline: Burning of the Jaffna Public Library

Date	Event
May 31, 1981 (Evening)	Tensions rise during District Development Council elections in Jaffna.
June 1, 1981 (Early Hours)	*Library Set Ablaze*: Over 97,000 Tamil books and manuscripts destroyed.
June 1–2, 1981	*Other Attacks*: TULF office, Hindu temples, and newspaper offices also targeted.
June 1981	*Civilian Casualties*: At least 4 killed; widespread looting and trauma reported.
Post-June 1981	*Global Outcry*: International condemnation; Tamil diaspora begins commemorations.
1998–2003	*Reconstruction*: Library rebuilt, but many rare texts lost forever.
Present Day	Annual memorials held; event remembered as cultural genocide.

References:

Ruins of the Jaffna Library in 1991 (Getty Images)

Historical Reflection from Tamil Guardian

Wikipedia archives on the Burning

Chapter 23: Shooting of Two Cyclists – June 1981 & Murder at Madhu – Mid-1981

Repression and Radicalization in Jaffna: The Aftermath of Thiagarajah's Assassination

In the lead-up to the District Development Council elections in June 1981, tensions in northern Sri Lanka reached a boiling point. On **24 May 1981**, **A. Thiagarajah**, a Tamil politician aligned with the ruling United National Party (UNP), was assassinated by members of the People's Liberation Organisation of Tamil Eelam (PLOTE) while addressing a rally in **Moolai, Jaffna**. He succumbed to his injuries the following day.

The assassination triggered a heavy-handed response from the Sri Lankan government, which deployed additional police and military units to the North. The move was framed as a security measure ahead of the elections, but it quickly evolved into a campaign of intimidation against Tamil civilians.

Alleged Shooting Incident

During this period of heightened militarization, multiple reports emerged of arbitrary violence against Tamil youth. One such incident involved two Tamil youths cycling near Jaffna town, who were allegedly stopped and shot at close range by armed personnel, reportedly Sinhalese policemen.

• Though not formally investigated, the incident was buried under broader reports of violence and unrest.

• The motive appeared to be intimidation and collective punishment, aimed at suppressing Tamil dissent.

This climate of fear contributed to:

• Widespread resentment among Tamil civilians

• Radicalization of Tamil youth, many of whom joined militant groups like LTTE and PLOTE

• Loss of trust in law enforcement and state institutions

Religious Sanctity and Later Violence: The Case of Madhu Church

While Madhu Church, a revered Catholic shrine in Mannar District, remained a neutral zone during much of the early conflict, it later became a flashpoint for violence.

- The most documented massacre at Madhu Church occurred on 20 November 1999, during clashes between the Sri Lankan Army and LTTE.

- Shelling near the Church killed at least **40 civilians**, including children and pilgrims seeking refuge.

- The incident was condemned internationally and cited in UNHCR and human rights reports as a violation of religious sanctity and humanitarian law.

Symbolism and Implication

- The violation of sacred spaces like Madhu Church shocked the local Catholic community and underscored the disregard for religious sanctity by warring parties.

- Though **not tied to 1981**, the Madhu massacre became emblematic of the civilian cost of the war and the erosion of safe zones.

The assassination of Thiagarajah and the subsequent repression in Jaffna marked a turning point in Tamil political consciousness. While the Madhu Church incident belongs to a later chapter of the conflict, both events reflect the systemic violence and erosion of trust that fueled Sri Lanka's descent into civil war.

Timeline of Events – 1981

Date	Event	Location	Description
June 1981	Shooting of Two Cyclists	Near Jaffna	Two Tamil youths riding bicycles were reportedly shot by Sri Lankan security forces. The incident occurred during heightened military presence following the assassination of UNP candidate Thiagarajah.
Mid-1981	Murder at Madhu	Madhu, Mannar District	A Tamil civilian was allegedly abducted and murdered by state forces near the sacred Madhu Church area, a site revered by both Tamil Catholics and Sinhalese Buddhists.

References

Shooting of Two Cyclists – June 1981

1. **Colombo Telegraph** – "May 31–June 4, 1981: Five Days of State Terror in Jaffna" by Santasilan Kadirgamar

This article documents the early days of June 1981 in Jaffna, when Tamil civilians were targeted by state forces. It references sporadic acts of violence, including attacks on individuals such as Tamil policemen and civilians. While the shooting of two cyclists is not named explicitly, the piece situates such incidents within a broader pattern of intimidation and brutality during the District Development Council elections.

2. **Wikipedia** – 1981 Anti-Tamil Pogrom

Provides context for the violence that swept across Tamil regions in June 1981. It notes that police and armed mobs engaged in looting, arson, and killings, with over 25 confirmed deaths. Though the cyclists' shooting is not individually listed, it aligns with the documented pattern of targeted killings and harassment of Tamil civilians.

Murder at Madhu – Mid-1981

1. List of Massacres in Sri Lanka – Wikipedia

While this list does not explicitly mention a murder at Madhu in mid-1981, it catalogs numerous attacks on Tamil civilians during the early 1980s, including massacres in Mannar and Vavuniya. Given Madhu's location in the Mannar District and its symbolic religious significance, the incident may be part of broader patterns of violence not individually documented.

2. Colombo Telegraph – "Five Days of State Terror in Jaffna"

Again, while not naming Madhu directly, this source discusses the climate of fear - and repression in Tamil areas during mid-1981. It references reports by MIRJE (Movement for Inter-Racial Justice and Equality), which documented abuses in Jaffna, Vavuniya, and surrounding regions—including religious sites and civilian shelters.

Chapter 24: Kandarmadam Incident & Navaratnarajah Killing: Leadup to Black July Progrom (1983)

1983 Navaratnarajah Killing and the **Kandarmadam Incident**, both of which occurred in the lead-up to and during the Black July pogrom, reflecting the intensifying violence against Tamil civilians.

1983 Killing of Navaratnarajah

Navaratnarajah was a respected Tamil lawyer and **former Member of Parliament from Jaffna**. Known for his moderate political stance and advocacy for Tamil rights through legal and parliamentary channels, he was a prominent figure in Sri Lanka's Tamil community.

Circumstances of the Killing

- **Date: July 1983** (exact date not widely documented)
- **Location**: Colombo
- **Incident**: During the height of the Black July riots, Navaratnarajah was reportedly **dragged out of his home by Sinhalese mobs**, beaten, and **killed in cold blood**.
- His murder was part of a broader pattern of **targeted killings of Tamil intellectuals and professionals**, aimed at crippling Tamil civil society.

His death sent shockwaves through the Tamil community, symbolizing the **collapse of legal and political protection** for Tamil citizens.

- It marked a shift from **random mob violence** to **deliberate assassinations** of Tamil leaders.

Note: Due to press censorship and lack of formal investigation, the exact date and circumstances remain poorly documented, but his death is acknowledged in Tamil diaspora narratives and oral histories.

1983 Kandarmadam Killings

Kandarmadam, a suburb of Jaffna, was a bustling Tamil residential and commercial area. In the months leading up to Black July, tensions were already high due to military presence and political unrest.

Incident Details

- **Date**: May–June 1983
- **Perpetrators**: Sri Lankan military and police units

Events:

- Security forces **burned down Tamil-owned shops** in Kandarmadam.
- **Private homes were raided**, and **valuables looted**.

- Civilians were **beaten and harassed**, with reports of **murders and disappearances**.

The violence was part of a **broader campaign of intimidation** following the District Development Council elections, which had been boycotted by Tamil nationalist groups.

Significance

- The Kandarmadam attacks were **precursors to Black July**, demonstrating the **militarization of Tamil areas** and the **erosion of civilian safety**.
- It highlighted the **collusion between state forces and nationalist thugs**, setting the stage for the Island-wide pogrom that followed.

Both incidents—Navaratnarajah's murder and the Kandarmadam attacks—underscore the **systematic targeting of Tamil civilians and leaders** in 1983. These events weren't isolated; they were part of a **coordinated strategy of repression** that culminated in Black July and ignited the civil war.

Timeline: Prelude to Black July — 1983 Tamil Civilian Killings

Date	Event
May–June 1983	*Kandarmadam Attacks*: Security forces burn shops, raid homes, loot property, and harass Tamil civilians in Jaffna suburb.
June 1983	*District Development Council Elections*: Tamil parties boycott elections; government repression intensifies.
July 1983	*Killing of Navaratnarajah*: Former MP and respected Tamil lawyer dragged from home and murdered by mobs in Colombo.
July 24, 1983	*Ambush in Jaffna*: LTTE kills 13 Sri Lankan soldiers, triggering massive backlash.
July 25–30, 1983	*Black July Pogrom*: Sinhalese mobs, with reported police complicity, kill up to 3,000 Tamils, destroy property, and displace tens of thousands.
August 1983	*Aftermath*: Global condemnation grows; thousands of Tamils flee the country; the seeds of civil war are firmly planted.

This timeline reveals how the events weren't isolated flashes of violence — they were linked steps in a tragic unraveling. The **Kandarmadam attacks** and **Navaratnarajah's assassination** didn't just precede Black July — they **foreshadowed** it, showing a deliberate and escalating campaign against Tamil lives and voices.

Authoritative Sources

1. **Black July – Wikipedia**

Offers a comprehensive overview of the Black July pogrom, including its immediate trigger—the ambush and killing of 13 Sri Lankan soldiers by the LTTE on 23 July 1983. While the

Kandarmadam and Navaratnarajah incidents are not named explicitly, the article situates the pogrom within a broader pattern of ethnic tension, state complicity, and escalating violence.

2. **Colombo Telegraph** – "40th Anniversary of Black July" by Karikalan S. Navaratnam This reflective piece discusses the political climate leading up to July 1983, including President J.R. Jayewardene's inflammatory remarks and the use of the Prevention of Terrorism Act to suppress Tamil dissent. It describes how state repression and nationalist rhetoric laid the groundwork for the pogrom and implies that earlier killings—such as those of Tamil civilians and activists—contributed to the rising tensions.

3. **Sri Lanka Campaign** – "Black July 1983, 40 Years On" This report places Black July within a longer trajectory of ethnic violence, noting that the seeds of the pogrom were sown in the years prior, including unresolved communal riots and targeted killings. It references the Presidential Truth Commission (2001), which investigated violence between 1981 and 1984, potentially encompassing the Kandarmadam and Navaratnarajah incidents.

Notes on Documentation Gaps

The Kandarmadam Incident and the killing of Navaratnarajah are referenced in Tamil nationalist literature and oral histories but remain underrepresented in mainstream archival sources. These events are often cited as provocations or retaliatory acts that intensified Tamil-Sinhalese tensions in Jaffna prior to the July 1983 pogrom.

Chapter 25: The Spark That Lit the Fire: 1983 Ambush and Black July

Black July – The Week That Shattered a Nation

In July 1983, Sri Lanka descended into one of the darkest chapters of its history. What began as a retaliatory ambush by Tamil militants quickly spiraled into a **state-condoned pogrom** against Tamil civilians. The violence, concentrated between **July 24 and July 30**, left thousands dead, tens of thousands displaced, and marked the **beginning of a brutal civil war** that would last nearly three decades.

The **Liberation Tigers of Tamil Eelam (LTTE)** ambushed a Sri Lankan Army patrol in **Thirunelveli**, killing 13 soldiers. The attack was a response to earlier military operations and marked a strategic escalation by Tamil militants. The government's reaction was swift—but not against the perpetrators. Instead, **Tamil civilians became the target**.

Organized Violence

Mobs armed with **axes, knives, and petrol bombs** roamed the streets of **Colombo**, attacking Tamil homes and businesses.

Electoral lists were reportedly used to identify Tamil households.

Police and military units were accused of standing by—or even participating.

- Over **18,000 homes** and **5,000 shops** were destroyed.

- The **Indian Overseas Bank** and **Tamil-owned establishments** were looted and burned.

- The **economic base of the Tamil community** was systematically dismantled.

Prison Massacres

On **July 26 and 28, Sinhalese inmates** murdered **53 Tamil prisoners** inside **Welikada Prison,** with alleged complicity from prison guards.

Timeline of Events: July 23–30, 1983

Date	Event	Description
July 23	LTTE Ambush	LTTE militants ambushed an army patrol in Thirunelveli, Jaffna, killing 13 soldiers.
July 24	Riots Begin	News of the ambush reaches Colombo. Anti-Tamil mobs begin attacking Tamil homes and businesses.
July 25	Escalation	Violence spreads to other cities including Kandy, Galle, and Matara. Tamil shops are looted and burned.
July 26	Prison Massacre	35 Tamil prisoners are killed by Sinhalese inmates at Welikada Prison, Colombo.
July 27	Continued Pogrom	Mobs, often aided by security forces, continue attacks. Indian High Commission and Tamil-owned banks are targeted.
July 28	Second Prison Massacre	18 more Tamil prisoners are murdered at Welikada. Total prison deaths reach 53.
July 29–30	Aftermath	Violence begins to subside. Over 150,000 Tamils are displaced. International condemnation grows.

Global Reaction and Diaspora Exodus

India, **Canada**, and **European nations** condemned the violence.

Tens of thousands of Tamils fled to **India**, **Europe**, and **North America**, forming the **Tamil diaspora**.

The events of Black July became a **rallying cry for Tamil nationalism** and led to a surge in LTTE recruitment.

Long-Term Impact

Civil War Ignited: Black July is widely recognized as the **start of the Sri Lankan Civil War,** which lasted until **2009**.

Radicalization: Tamil youth, disillusioned by the state's failure to protect civilians, joined militant groups in droves.

Impunity: No one has been held accountable for the atrocities committed during this week.

Human and Property Casualties during the week of Black July (July 24–30, 1983)

Human Casualties

Category	Estimated Figures
Deaths	Between **400 and 3,000** (some sources report up to **5,638** killed)
Disappeared	At least **466** individuals
Injured	Over **2,000** people
Raped	Approximately **670** Tamil women
Displaced	Around **150,000** Tamil civilians became homeless

Property Damage

Type	Estimated Loss
Homes Destroyed	Over **18,000** Tamil-owned homes
Shops Burned	More than **5,000** Tamil businesses and shops
Economic Cost	Estimated at **$300 million USD**

These figures reflect the **scale and brutality** of the pogrom, which was not only a humanitarian catastrophe but also a **deliberate attempt to dismantle the Tamil community's economic and cultural foundations**.

Black July was not a spontaneous riot—it was a **premeditated pogrom** that exposed deep-rooted ethnic divisions and institutional failures. The scars remain etched in the collective memory of Sri Lanka and its diaspora. Understanding this week is essential to grasping the origins of the conflict and the urgent need for **truth, reconciliation, and justice**.

Authoritative Sources

1.   **Wikipedia – Black July**. Offers a comprehensive overview of the anti-Tamil pogrom that erupted following the LTTE ambush of a Sri Lankan Army patrol in Tinneveli, Jaffna, which killed 13 soldiers on 23 July 1983. The violence began in Colombo the next day and spread nationwide, resulting in the deaths of hundreds to thousands of Tamil civilians, destruction of shops, homes, and temples, and the displacement of over 150,000 people.

2.   **Groundviews** – "Anti-Tamil Pogrom of July 83: Root Causes Unaddressed Even After 40 Years" This article reflects on the political complicity behind the violence, noting that the UNP-led government under President J.R. Jayewardene failed to prevent or condemn the attacks. It situates Black July within a longer history of ethnic discrimination, including earlier pogroms in 1956, 1958, 1977, and 1981, and highlights how the 1983 events catalyzed the Tamil diaspora and militant recruitment.

3.   **HuffPost** – "Black July: Remembering the 1983 Riots in Sri Lanka". Provides a vivid narrative of the LTTE ambush, describing how mines and gunfire decimated the army patrol known as Four Four Bravo. The article recounts how the delayed funeral of the soldiers in

Colombo turned into a flashpoint for mob violence, leading to mass killings, arson, and looting. It also explores the emotional impact on Tamil militants, including Prabhakaran, and how the event marked a decisive shift toward armed struggle.

Chapter 26: The Kent and Dollar Farm Massacres — Seeds of Ethnic Violence (1984)

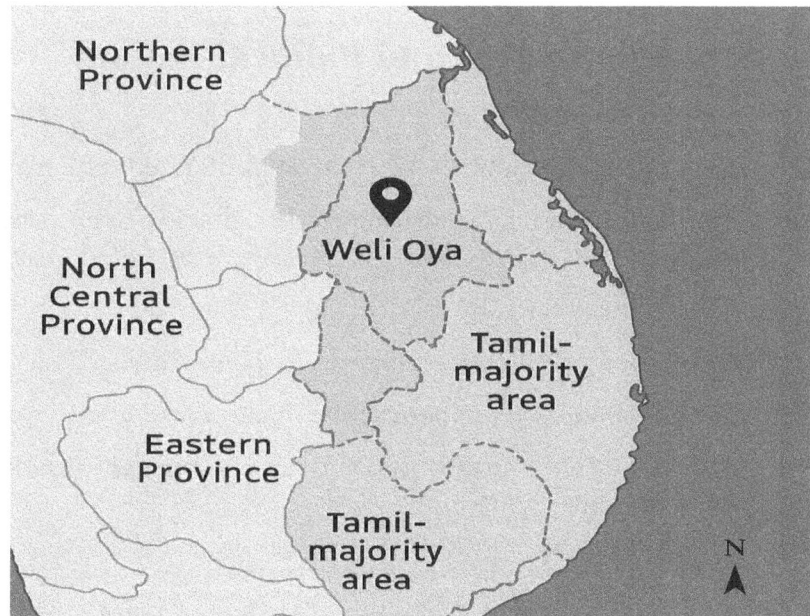

Weli Oya and the Politics of Colonization

In the early 1980s, the Sri Lankan government initiated a controversial colonization program in the **Weli Oya** region, a strategically located area bordering the Tamil-majority Northern and Eastern provinces. The aim was to settle Sinhalese families, including released prisoners and ex-combatants, in what had previously been Tamil-owned farmland, notably the **Kent** and **Dollar Farms** near **Manal Aru in the Mullaitivu district.**

Originally leased in 1965 and later donated by a Tamil landowner to house Indian Tamil refugees, the farms were forcibly taken over by the state in 1984. The Tamil families were evicted under the pretext of national security, and the land was converted into open prisons for Sinhalese settlers. This move was widely seen as an attempt to alter the demographic balance and suppress Tamil separatist sentiment.

The Massacre: November 30, 1984

On the night of November 30, 1984, approximately 50 armed LTTE cadres launched a coordinated attack on both Kent and Dollar Farms. Traveling in two buses, they were armed with submachine guns, automatic rifles, and grenades.

• At Kent Farm, the attackers stormed the settlement, killing Sinhalese prisoners, their families, and home guards.

- Simultaneously, Dollar Farm was attacked with similar brutality.

In total, **82 people were killed,** including civilians, military personnel, and prison guards. The LTTE claimed the farms were militarized settlements, but the killings shocked the nation and marked the first large-scale massacre of Sinhalese civilians during the civil war.

Strategic Impact and Political Fallout

The massacre had far-reaching consequences:

- It derailed the government's plan to establish Israeli-style militarized settlements in the region.

- Sinhalese settlers began fleeing en masse, fearing further attacks. Even appeals from senior officials like Ravi Jayewardene, son of President J.R. Jayewardene, failed to stem the exodus.

The National Security Council responded by reinforcing the colonization effort:

- Establishing the **Weli Oya Brigade Headquarters near Kent Farm**.

- Arming and training Sinhalese villagers in paramilitary tactics.

- Building new towns like **Janakapura**, named after **General Janaka Perera**, and **Kalyanipura**, named **after his wife**.

Controversies and Human Rights Concerns

The Kent and Dollar Farm settlements were not merely agricultural projects—they were symbols of ethnic engineering. Reports emerged of abductions and sexual violence against Tamil women by security forces and prisoners, further inflaming tensions.

The LTTE's attack, while condemned for its brutality, was also interpreted by some Tamil nationalists as a retaliatory strike against forced displacement and state-sponsored colonization. However, the massacre deepened ethnic divisions and legitimized militarized responses from the state.

Reflection

The Kent and Dollar Farm massacres were a turning point in Sri Lanka's civil war. They exposed the volatile intersection of ethnic politics, militarization, and land colonization. The events also underscored the dangers of using settlement schemes as tools of demographic manipulation, especially in conflict zones.

For many Sinhalese families, the massacre remains a traumatic memory of vulnerability and loss. For Tamils, it is a reminder of displacement and marginalization. And for Sri Lanka as a whole, it stands as a cautionary tale of how state policy can inflame communal tensions when justice and equity are sacrificed for strategic gain.

Timeline: Kent & Dollar Farm Massacres (1984)

Date	Event

1965	Kent and Dollar Farms leased by Tamil entrepreneurs from the Sri Lankan state.
1978	Farms donated by a Tamil landowner to house Indian Tamil refugees displaced by the 1977 anti-Tamil pogrom.
Oct 1983	Superintendent of Police Arthur Herath labels Tamil farmers as "terrorists," initiating pressure to evict them.
June 1984	Vavuniya police raid the farms; Tamil families assaulted and forcibly relocated to the hill country.
Mid 1984	Government converts farms into **open prisons**, settling **450 Sinhalese prisoners and families** under a colonization scheme.
Nov 30, 1984	**LTTE attacks Kent and Dollar Farms**: • ~50 cadres arrive in buses • Armed with rifles, machine guns, grenades • 82 people killed, including civilians, guards, and military personnel.
Dec 1984	National Security Council responds by reinforcing colonization efforts and militarizing Weli Oya region.
1988–1989	Sinhala colonization of Weli Oya escalates: • **Over 3,364 families, including ex-convicts, settled** • **Towns like Janakapura and Kalyanipura established.**

Authoritative Sources

1. **Kent and Dollar Farm Massacres – Wikipedia**
   This entry provides a detailed account of the **30 November 1984 attacks** by the **Liberation Tigers of Tamil Eelam (LTTE)** on two farming settlements in **Mullaitivu District**. It documents the killing of **82 people**, including **Sinhalese prisoners, their families, and security personnel**, using **submachine guns, rifles, and grenades**. The article also explores the **political backdrop**, including the state's colonization program that resettled Sinhalese prisoners in Tamil-majority areas.

2. **Special Report No. 5 – University Teachers for Human Rights (Jaffna)**
   This report critically examines the **Manal Aru (later renamed Weli Oya) colonization scheme**, under which the Kent and Dollar Farms were converted into **open prisons** and used to settle Sinhalese convicts. It highlights how this policy—driven by **National Security Minister Lalith Athulathmudali**—was perceived as an aggressive demographic intervention, fueling Tamil resentment and triggering militant retaliation.

3. **Colombo Telegraph – "Border Aggression and Civilian Massacres in Sri Lanka" by Dr. Rajan Hoole**
   This article situates the massacres within a broader pattern of **state-sponsored colonization and ethnic engineering**. It discusses how **Sinhalese settlers were used**

as human shields, and how the **military-civilian nexus** in border regions contributed to escalating violence and displacement.

Chapter 27: The Jaya Sri Maha Bodhi Massacre (1985)

(Pic: lakpura.com)

On a quiet Sunday morning, **May 14, 1985**, the sacred city of **Anuradhapura**—a spiritual heartland for Sri Lankan Buddhists—was shattered by one of the most brutal attacks in the island's history. The Liberation Tigers of Tamil Eelam (LTTE) launched a coordinated assault targeting civilians and religious worshippers, marking the first major LTTE operation outside Tamil-majority areas.

LTTE cadres hijacked a bus and stormed the Anuradhapura Central Bus Station, opening fire indiscriminately on civilians waiting for transport.

They then proceeded to the **Jaya Sri Maha Bodhi shrine**, one of the most sacred Buddhist sites, and gunned down monks, nuns, and pilgrims in cold blood.

The attackers used automatic weapons, killing **146** Sinhalese men, women, and children, and injuring over 85 others.

Before retreating, they entered **Wilpattu National Park**, where they **massacred 24** wildlife department employees, leaving only one survivor.

The operation was reportedly ordered by LTTE leader Velupillai Prabhakaran, executed by Mannar commander **Victor** and **his subordinate Radha**.

The LTTE claimed the massacre was retaliation for the Valvettiturai killings, where the Sri Lankan Army had killed 70 Tamil civilians earlier that year.

In later years, the LTTE controversially alleged that the attack was planned with support from **Indian intelligence (RAW)**.

The massacre triggered anti-Tamil riots in Anuradhapura:

- Tamil-owned shops and homes were looted and burned
- 15–20 Tamil civilians were killed, including some burned alive
- A Sri Lankan Army Corporal, enraged by the killings, shot dead 9 Tamil civilians who had sought refuge in an Army Camp before being killed himself by his commanding officer.
- Over the next two days, 75 Tamil civilians were killed in retaliatory violence.

This massacre marked a turning point in Sri Lanka's civil conflict:

- It shattered the illusion that violence was confined to Tamil-majority regions.
- It deepened ethnic polarization, fueling cycles of revenge and mistrust.
- It exposed the vulnerability of sacred spaces and civilian life in the face of escalating militancy.

Timeline: Jaya Sri Maha Bodhi Massacre (1985)

Date	Event
May 14, 1985	LTTE hijacks a bus and enters **Anuradhapura**. - Opens fire at **central bus station**, killing civilians indiscriminately. - Proceeds to **Jaya Sri Maha Bodhi shrine**, massacring monks, nuns, and pilgrims. - **146 Sinhalese civilians killed, 85 injured**. - Attackers retreat through **Wilpattu National Park**, killing **24 wildlife staff**.
May 15–16, 1985	**Retaliatory anti-Tamil riots** erupt in Anuradhapura: - Tamil shops and homes looted and burned. - **15–20 Tamil civilians killed**, some burned alive. - A Sri Lankan army corporal kills **9 Tamil civilians** before being shot by his commander. - Total of **75 Tamil civilians** killed in two days of reprisals.
Later in 1985	LTTE claims attack was **retaliation for Valvettiturai massacre**. Allegations surface of **Indian intelligence (RAW)** involvement.

Authoritative Sources

1. <u>**Wikipedia – Anuradhapura Massacre**</u>
   This entry provides a detailed account of the **May 14, 1985,** attack, in which **LTTE cadres hijacked a bus**, entered **Anuradhapura**, and opened fire at the **main bus station** before proceeding to the **Jaya Sri Maha Bodhi shrine**. There, they **massacred 146 Sinhalese men, women, and children**, including **monks and nuns** engaged in worship. It was the LTTE's **first major operation outside Tamil-majority areas** and marked a turning point in the ethnic conflict.
2. <u>**Borealis Threat & Risk – "146 Buddhist Pilgrims Killed in the Anuradhapura Massacre"**</u> This article by Phil Gurski reflects on the **religious and symbolic nature** of the attack, emphasizing the LTTE's targeting of **devout Buddhist pilgrims** at one of the most sacred sites in Sri Lanka. It underscores the **shock and horror** that followed, and how the massacre deepened ethnic divisions and fueled retaliatory violence.

3. **Hiru News – "LTTE Attack on Jaya Sri Maha Bodhi Marks 28 Years"**
A commemorative report noting the **anniversary of the massacre**, highlighting its **brutality and impact** on national consciousness. It reinforces the sacredness of the site and the trauma inflicted on the Buddhist community.

Chapter 28: The Kumudini Boat Massacre: Terror on the Waters of Delft (1985)

On **May 15, 1985**, a government-operated ferry named **Kumudini** (also known as *Kumuthini*) became the site of a brutal massacre when **Sri Lankan Navy personnel** boarded the vessel and **murdered at least 23 Tamil civilians**, including women and children. The ferry was traveling between the **islands of Delft and Nainativu** in the **Jaffna District**, a region heavily affected by the ethnic conflict. This massacre was part of a **cycle of retaliatory violence** that followed a series of deadly attacks between the Sri Lankan military and the LTTE.

The massacre occurred during a period of escalating violence:

May 10, 1985: The Sri Lankan Army carried out the **Valvettithurai massacre**, killing **70 Tamil civilians** in retaliation for LTTE landmine attacks.

May 14, 1985: The LTTE responded with the **Anuradhapura massacre**, killing **120 Sinhalese civilians**.

May 15, 1985: The Kumudini massacre unfolded as part of a **series of reprisal attacks** targeting Tamil civilians.

The **Northern Province**, especially the Jaffna islets, had become a militarized zone, with **Navy camps stationed on nearby islands**. Civilians traveling by boat were increasingly vulnerable to harassment, interrogation, and violence.

According to eyewitness accounts documented by **Amnesty International** and Tamil media sources:

The **Kumudini ferry**, carrying **72 passengers**, was intercepted mid-sea by a **fiberglass boat** carrying **eight armed men**, believed to be **Sri Lankan Navy personnel**.

Six men boarded the ferry, dressed in **T-shirts and blue trousers or shorts**, typical of Navy uniforms.

Passengers were ordered to the **forepart of the boat**, then forced **below deck**.

One by one, passengers were called to the upper deck, told to **shout their name, age, address, and destination**—loudly enough to **drown out the cries of victims** being murdered.

Victims were **hacked to death** with **knives, axes, and rifles**. Blood and severed body parts were strewn across the deck.

- Survivors described being **stabbed and thrown onto piles of corpses**, including a mother whose **baby was killed** and a woman who survived with **deep wounds to her neck and head**.

At least 23 people were killed, though some sources cite **up to 36 fatalities**.

Survivors included **Saro Rasaratnam** and **Annaladchmi Sivalingam**, whose testimonies reveal the **terror and brutality** of the attack.

Injured passengers were taken to **Jaffna Hospital**, while families on Delft Island learned of the massacre only through **news reports**.

The **Kumudini ferry**, once a lifeline for islanders, became a **symbol of fear and loss**.

The massacre highlighted the **insecurity of Tamil civilians** under Navy occupation and the **impunity of state forces**.

A **memorial jetty** was renamed **Kumuthini Jetty** in honor of the victims.

Annual commemorations are held on **Delft Island**, including **religious observances** and **literary tributes**, such as the poetry collection *Blood's Rumble*.

The **Kumudini Boat Massacre** was not an isolated incident—it was part of a **systematic campaign of terror** against Tamil civilians during Sri Lanka's civil war. The calculated nature of the killings, the targeting of unarmed passengers, and the lack of accountability reflect the **depth of ethnic violence** and the **failure of justice mechanisms**. Remembering this tragedy is essential to understanding the **human cost of conflict** and the **urgent need for reconciliation and truth-telling**

Authoritative Sources

1 - **Wikipedia** – Kumudini Boat Massacre. This entry documents the events of 15 May 1985, when Sri Lankan Navy personnel boarded the ferry Kumudini en route from Delft Island to Nainativu and killed at least 23 Tamil civilians, including women and children.

2 - **Tamil Guardian** – "Victims of Kumuthini Boat Massacre Remembered 38 Years On"

3 - **Tamil Heritage** – "Kumuthini Boat Massacre 15.05.1985" Offers first-person survivor accounts, including harrowing descriptions of how passengers were stabbed, thrown overboard, and left for dead.

Chapter 29: The Trinco–Habarana Road Massacre - Terror on Good Friday (1987)

In **April 1987**, the Sri Lankan government had declared a unilateral ceasefire in hopes of drawing the LTTE into negotiations backed by India. It was a time of religious observance, **Good Friday for Christians**, and **Sinhala and Tamil New Year** preparations for others. But peace was short-lived. On **April 17,** the Liberation Tigers of Tamil Eelam (LTTE) launched one of the most brutal attacks on civilians in the history of the conflict.

The Massacre also known as the Aluth Oya Massacre or Good Friday Massacre

The attack occurred between the 123rd and 129th mileposts on the **Trincomalee–Habarana Road, near Kitulotuwa**, a remote jungle stretch.

LTTE cadres, dressed in uniform, ambushed five vehicles: three buses, two lorries, and a private car.

The vehicles were forced off the road, and passengers—mostly Sinhalese civilians returning home for the holidays—were ordered out.

Victims were robbed, beaten with clubs, and then shot with automatic weapons.

Those who tried to hide inside the buses were also hunted down and killed.

Among the dead were 12 off-duty security personnel, many chil ildren, and entire families.

Casualties:

127 civilians killed
64 seriously injured
Survivors escaped by playing dead among the bodies.

Timeline Summary

Date	Event
April 11, 1987	Government declares **unilateral ceasefire**
April 17, 1987	**LTTE ambushes vehicles** on Trinco–Habarana Road; 127 killed
April 21, 1987	LTTE attacks **Jayanthipura village**, killing 15 civilians
April 25, 1987	LTTE detonates **car bomb in Pettah**, killing 113 civilians

The massacre was a direct challenge to the ceasefire, undermining peace efforts and escalating ethnic tensions.

It demonstrated the LTTE's ability to strike deep into Sinhalese-majority territory, far from their northern strongholds.

The brutality of the attack shocked the nation and led to heightened military operations in the region.

The Joint Operations Command deployed over 150 armed police and soldiers to secure the area.

Victims were transported to hospitals in Polonnaruwa.

The massacre was widely condemned, including by international observers, and marked a turning point in public perception of the LTTE's tactics.

The Trinco–Habarana Road massacre remains one of the most notorious atrocities of the Sri Lankan civil war. It exposed the vulnerability of civilians during ceasefires and highlighted the fragility of peace in a deeply divided nation. For many Sinhalese families, it was a day of irreversible loss. For the country, it was a grim reminder that terrorism does not pause for diplomacy.

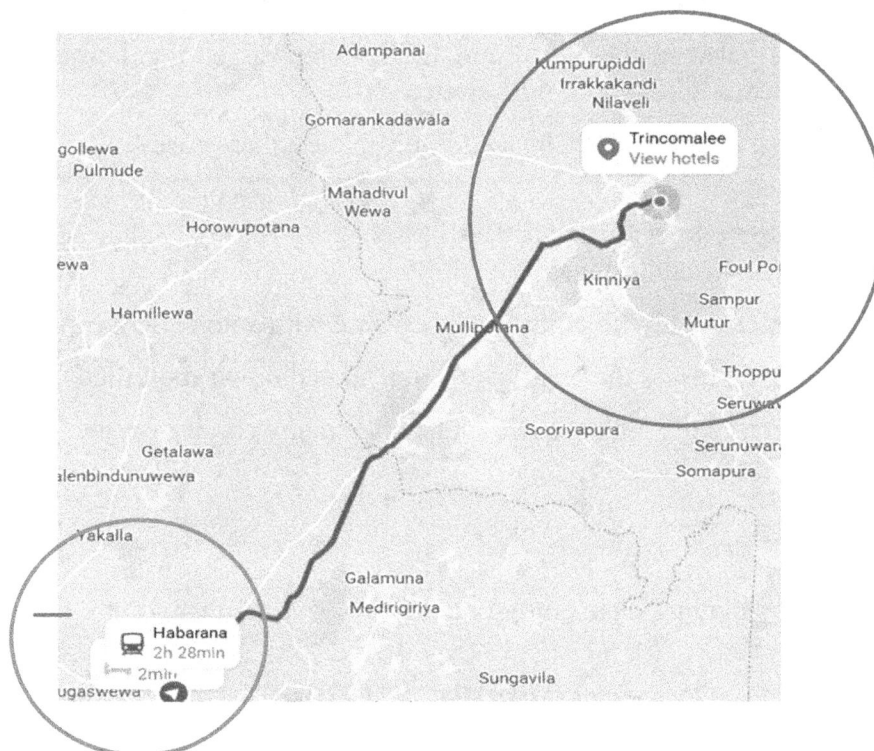

Authoritative Sources

1. **Wikipedia – Aluth Oya Massacre**
   This entry documents the **April 17, 1987,** massacre, also known as the **Habarana Massacre** or **Good Friday Massacre**, in which **LTTE cadres ambushed a convoy of vehicles** on the **Trincomalee–Habarana Road** near **Kitulotuwa**.

2. **UPI Archives – "Separatist Rebels Ambushed Five Vehicles"** This contemporary report describes how **LTTE rebels stopped three buses and two trucks**, separated **Sinhalese from Tamil passengers**, and **executed the Sinhalese**.

3. **Sunday Observer – "When Tiger Terrorists Massacred 127 Civilians in Habarana".** Offers a retrospective account of the massacre, emphasizing the **brutality of the killings**, the **timing during Sinhala and Tamil New Year**, and the **impact on**

national psyche. It also notes that **more than 70 people were seriously injured**, many of whom were airlifted for treatment.

Chapter 30: Inferno in Pettah – The 987 Bombing That Shook Colombo

It was **April 21, 1987**. Colombo, the Capital of Sri Lanka, was slowly stirring back to life after the **Sinhala and Hindu New Year holidays**. Pettah, the city's commercial heart, was bustling with commuters, vendors, and families. The central bus station was packed with people waiting to board overcrowded buses home. At 5:20 PM, that ordinary day turned into a nightmare.

A car bomb, weighing approximately 80 pounds (36 kg), detonated in the middle of the bus terminal. The explosion tore through the station, creating a 10-foot crater and igniting six buses. The blast was heard ten miles away. Within seconds, the air was filled with screams, smoke, and the smell of burning flesh and metal.

Dr. B.J. Masakorala, at the Colombo General Hospital, was summoned urgently. He described the scene as "Dantean"—a flood of dead, dying, and maimed civilians arriving in ambulances, vans, and even tuk-tuks driven by anonymous Samaritans.

"The wards of the Accident Service had to bear the intrusion and thrust of 63 bodies, 25 dying patients and 249 injured within a space of 30 to 45 minutes," Dr. Masakorala recalled. "There were no registration formalities. Bureaucratic rules were abandoned. We just treated whoever came in."

The hospital staff worked tirelessly, improvising triage systems and converting wards to accommodate the wounded. Sheets were later prepared to document the victims—many of whom remained unidentified.

Survivor Testimonies: Lives Shattered

A Father's Blindness

One man, blinded in the blast, lamented that he would never see the face of his newborn child. His wife was pregnant at the time. "His biggest sorrow," said sociologist Indika Bulankulame, "was not the pain or the disability—but the fact that he would never see his baby's face".

A Young Woman's Lost Dream

A young woman in her early twenties, who had aspired to become an air stewardess, suffered severe facial injuries. Her dream ended in that moment. "She spoke of a sense of 'completeness' she had before the blast," Bulankulame noted. "Now, she was always striving to reclaim that lost wholeness.

A Taxi Driver's Voice

Bulankulame's research was inspired by a chance encounter with a taxi driver whose voice was hoarse and raspy. When asked, he revealed it was due to injuries sustained in the Pettah bombing. His story was one of many—ordinary people whose lives were irrevocably altered.

As news of the bombing spread, Sinhalese mobs took to the streets in fury. Tamil-owned shops were stoned, and cars were stopped to identify Tamil passengers. The Sri Lankan police imposed a curfew and intervened to suppress the riots.

The attack was attributed to Tamil militant groups—EROS and the LTTE. It was a calculated strike, timed to inflict maximum civilian casualties and sow terror in the heart of Colombo.

The Pettah Bomb Blast remains one of the deadliest terrorist attacks in Sri Lanka's history. It exposed the vulnerability of civilian infrastructure and the brutal tactics of insurgent warfare. Yet, beyond the statistics, it is the stories of survivors—the father who cannot see, the woman who lost her dream, the taxi driver with a scarred voice—that remind us of the human cost of conflict.

Authoritative Sources

1. **Wikipedia – Colombo Central Bus Station Bombing**
   This entry details the **April 21, 1987, car bombing** at the **Pettah central bus terminal**, carried out by the **Eelam Revolutionary Organisation of Students (EROS)** and attributed to the **LTTE**. The explosion killed between **113 and 150 people**, injured over **200**, and left a **10-foot crater** in the ground. Six buses were destroyed, and the **Bank of Ceylon Pettah branch** was heavily damaged.

2. **BBC On This Day – 1987: Tamil Tigers Blamed for Bus Garage Blast**
   This report confirms that the bomb exploded during **rush hour**, targeting civilians, mostly **Sinhalese Buddhists**—and triggering **retaliatory riots** across Colombo. It situates the attack within the broader ethnic conflict and notes that **Colombo was placed under curfew** following the violence.

3. **Sri Lanka Guardian – "Pettah Bomb '87: A Doctor's Story" by Dr. B.J. Masakorala.**
   A firsthand account from the **Accident Service triage officer**, describing the **chaotic aftermath** at Colombo General Hospital.

Chapter 31: Arantalawa Massacre – The Day Innocence Was Slain (1987)

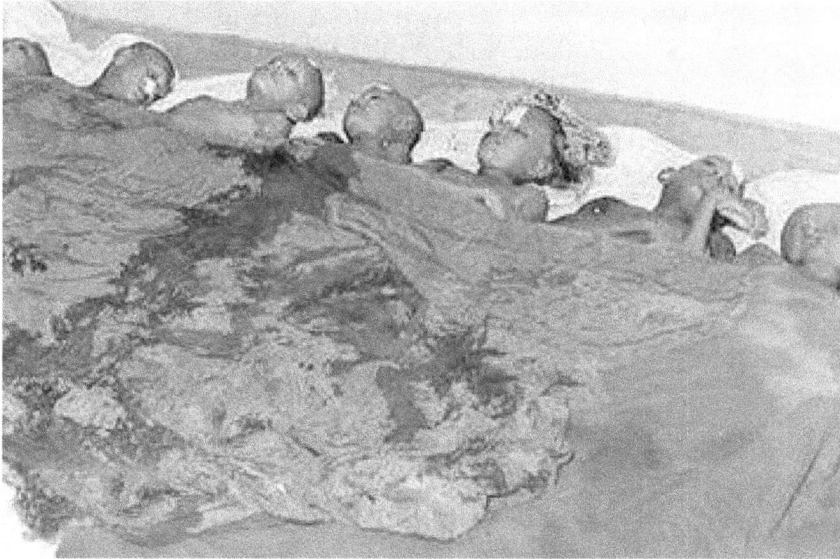

(Pic: Wikipedia)

A Pilgrimage Interrupted

Date: June 2, 1987, Location: Arantalawa, Ampara District, Eastern Sri Lanka

On a quiet morning in June, a group of **33 Buddhist monks**—most of them young novices aged between 7 and 18—boarded a bus from **Mahavapi Vihara**, heading toward the sacred **Kelaniya Raja Maha Vihara**. Accompanied by their mentor, **Ven. Hegoda Indrasara Thera,** and a few laypersons, they were on a peaceful pilgrimage, embodying the spiritual heart of Sri Lanka's Theravada tradition.

As the bus passed through the remote village of **Nuwaragalatenna**, it was halted by approximately 20 armed cadres of the Liberation Tigers of Tamil Eelam (LTTE), who were disguised as Sri Lankan security personnel. Mistakenly believing them to be government forces, the driver allowed them aboard. Under gunpoint, the monks and laypersons were forced into the nearby Arantalawa jungle.

Once deep in the forest, the LTTE militants demanded money and valuables. The monks complied. Then, without warning, the attackers shot the driver dead and turned on the monks.

The militants opened fire on the unarmed monks. Those who tried to flee were chased down and hacked with swords and knives. The Vinaya—the Buddhist monastic code—prohibited the monks from defending themselves. In minutes, 31 novice monks and 4 civilians lay dead. The jungle echoed with the cries of children in saffron robes.

One monk survived but was permanently disabled. He lives today with physical scars and emotional trauma that never healed.

A van driver who had been shot at near the site alerted the Special Task Force (STF). Home guards, hearing gunfire, rushed to the scene. They found the bus abandoned in the jungle, surrounded by bodies. Survivors were rushed to hospital, critically wounded.

The Arantalawa Massacre was not just a physical attack, it was a spiritual assault. The monks represented purity, peace, and the cultural soul of the Sinhalese Buddhist majority. Their murder shocked the nation and the world.

The Divaina newspaper interpreted the massacre as a strategic move by the LTTE to provoke ethnic backlash and deepen divisions between Sinhalese and Tamil communities.

In 2003, a monument was built at the massacre site. In 2013, a memorial museum was opened, featuring the very bus in which the monks were traveling. Inside, the final moments of the massacre are recreated—a haunting tribute to lives lost.

The Arantalawa Massacre remains one of the darkest chapters in Sri Lanka's civil war. It is remembered not only for its brutality but for the innocence of its victims. The image of child monks, slaughtered in their robes, continues to haunt the national conscience.

Authoritative Sources

1. **Wikipedia – Aranthalawa Massacre**
   This entry provides a comprehensive account of the **June 2, 1987 massacre**, in which **33 Buddhist monks—mostly novices aged 7 to 18—and 4 civilians** were brutally killed by **LTTE cadres** near the village of Aranthalawa in the Ampara District.

2. **AmazingLanka – Monument of Aranthalawa Massacre**
   Offers a vivid narrative of the attack and its aftermath, including the creation of a **memorial museum** using the original bus. The article emphasizes the **spiritual and emotional impact** of the massacre, describing how the monks were unable to defend themselves due to the Vinaya code, and how the chief priest, **Ven. Hegoda Indrasara Thera**, was killed while pleading for the novices' lives.

3. **SinhalaNet – Aranthalawa Bhikkhu Massacre 27th Anniversary**
   Reflects on the massacre's legacy, noting that it remains one of the **most brutal attacks on religious clerics** in modern history. The article discusses the **LTTE's strategic intent** to provoke ethnic backlash and deepen communal divisions, and how the massacre is commemorated annually across Sri Lanka.

Chapter 32: Gonawala Sunil: The Rise and Fall of Sri Lanka's Most Infamous Political Enforcer (1987)

(Sunil & his wife – Pic: Lankaweb)

In the turbulent political landscape of Sri Lanka during the late 20th century, few figures embodied the nexus of crime and power as chillingly as **Sunil Perera**—better known as **Gonawala Sunil**. His life was a grim testament to how political patronage can elevate a convicted criminal into a feared enforcer, and how that same power can ultimately lead to a violent end.

Born in **1944 in Kelaniya**, Sunil Perera was one of eight brothers in the Gonawala Perera family, which maintained deep ties to the **United National Party** (UNP). By the late 1970s, Sunil had emerged as a dominant underworld figure, wielding influence through extortion, intimidation, and political muscle. His rise coincided with a period of intense political polarization, where loyalty to the ruling party often translated into unchecked authority.

Sunil's notoriety peaked in 1981 when he was convicted for the rape of a 17-year-old girl—a crime that shocked the nation. Rather than serving his full sentence, Sunil was granted a **Presidential Pardon by President J.R. Jayewardene on July 7, 1981**, coinciding with Sri Lanka's 50th anniversary of universal franchise. The pardon was so conspicuously tailored to his case that it became known as "Sunil Samawa"—Sunil's Amnesty.

Political Patronage and Expanding Influence

Following his release, Sunil's influence only grew. He was appointed an **All-Island Justice of the Peace**, a move that stunned legal circles and underscored the depth of his political connections. He became a bodyguard to **Ranil Wickremesinghe, then Minister of Education,** and was frequently seen welcoming UNP leaders at the airport. His presence at high-level political events signaled a disturbing fusion of state power and criminal enterprise.

The Batalanda Controversy

Sunil's residence in the **Batalanda Housing Complex** later became a focal point of controversy. The **Batalanda Commission Report**, which investigated human rights abuses during the 1988–

89 JVP insurgency, alleged that the complex was used as a torture chamber. Sunil was reportedly linked to the site and frequently seen visiting Wickremesinghe's bungalow nearby. While no formal charges were brought against Wickremesinghe, the report cast a long shadow over both men's reputations. Members of Sunil's family were also implicated in violent attacks, including the assault on the Sapugaskanda Police Station in 1989.

Alleged Role in the Welikada Prison Massacre

The Welikada Prison Massacre during Black July 1983 remains one of the most horrifying episodes in Sri Lanka's post-independence history. When racial violence spilled into Welikada Prison, 53 Tamil prisoners were murdered in two waves—on July 25 and July 27.

Though Gonawala Sunil was **never formally charged**, his name has long hovered over the events like a specter. Investigative reporting and eyewitness accounts suggest that Sunil was present in the prison during the attacks and may have been involved in discussions surrounding them. His connections to **Rogers Jayasekere**, a key prison figure, and his ability to manipulate prison dynamics made him a likely facilitator. While no direct evidence places him wielding weapons, his patronage and presence were seen as instrumental in creating the conditions for the massacre. The International Commission of Jurists later stated that the killings could not have occurred without connivance from prison officials.

The Fall: Death by Assassination

Despite his unchecked power, Sunil's reign ended violently. **On June 25, 1987**, he was gunned down at his home in Kelaniya by unknown assailants. His death marked the collapse of a criminal empire built on fear, political protection, and impunity.

Gonawala Sunil's life is a cautionary tale of how state power can be weaponized through criminal proxies. His rise was enabled by a political system that blurred the lines between governance and gangsterism. His fall, though inevitable, did little to dismantle the structures that allowed such figures to thrive.

Even today, his story serves as a stark reminder of the dangers of unchecked political patronage and the urgent need for institutional accountability in safeguarding democracy.

Timeline of Power, Crime, and Collapse

Year	Event	Details
1944	**Birth of Sunil Perera**	Born in Kelaniya, Sri Lanka, into the politically connected Gonawala Perera family.
Late 1970s	**Rise in the Underworld**	Emerges as a dominant criminal figure with strong ties to the ruling United National Party (UNP).
1981 (Early)	**Conviction for Rape**	Found guilty of raping a 17-year-old girl. Sentenced to 10 years in prison.
July 7, 1981	**Presidential Pardon**	Released by President J.R. Jayewardene during the 50th anniversary of universal

		franchise. The pardon becomes known as "Sunil Samawa."
1981–1983	**Political Empowerment**	Appointed All-Island Justice of the Peace. Becomes bodyguard to Ranil Wickremesinghe and gains visibility in UNP circles.
July 25 & 27, 1983	**Welikada Prison Massacre**	53 Tamil prisoners killed during Black July riots. Sunil allegedly present and linked to planning circles, though never formally charged.
1988–1989	**Batalanda Allegations**	Batalanda Housing Complex reportedly used as a torture site during JVP insurgency. Sunil frequently seen at the location.
1989	**Sapugaskanda Police Station Attack**	Family members of Sunil implicated in violent attacks during political unrest.
June 25, 1987	**Assassination**	Gunned down at his home in Kelaniya by unknown assailants. Marks the end of his criminal-political reign.
Post-1987	**Legacy and Controversy**	His story remains a symbol of political impunity and the dangers of criminal patronage in democratic systems.

Authoritative Sources

1. **Wikipedia – List of Sri Lankan Mobsters**
   This entry profiles **Sunil Perera alias Gonawala Sunil**, highlighting his criminal career from **1977 to 1987**. He was convicted of **raping a 17-year-old girl in 1981** yet received a **presidential pardon** from **President J.R. Jayewardene** on **7 July 1981**, coinciding with Sri Lanka's 50th anniversary of universal franchise. Shockingly, he was later appointed an **all-island Justice of the Peace (JP)** and served as a **bodyguard to Ranil Wickremesinghe**, then Minister of Education.

2. **Colombo Telegraph – "Black July: Justice Of Peace Gonawela Sunil And The Killings In Prison" by Rajan Hoole** This investigative piece explores Gonawala Sunil's alleged role in the **Welikada Prison Massacre of 1983**, where **53 Tamil prisoners were killed**. It describes how Sunil, with **UNP patronage**, wielded influence over prison staff and was reportedly involved in orchestrating violence. The article also critiques the **tailor-made amnesty** that freed him, dubbed "**Sunil Samawa**" by critics.

3. **LankaWeb – "How the UNP Gave Birth to the Underworld – Rapist Gonawala Sunil Dies Under a Hail of Bullets"** This article recounts Sunil's **death by assassination on 25 June 1987** at his home in Kelaniya. It also links him to the **Batalanda torture chamber**, suggesting he illegally occupied a house near the site and was closely tied to powerful political figures in the Gampaha District.

Chapter 33: The Assassination and Aftermath of Vijaya Kumaratunga: A Political Tragedy in Sri Lanka (1988)

Vijaya Kumaratunga was more than a beloved film star—he was a rising political figure whose assassination on **February 16, 1988,** sent shockwaves through Sri Lanka. His death, during a time of intense political unrest, remains one of the most controversial and emotionally charged events in the country's modern history.

Born in **1945**, Kumaratunga captivated audiences with his performances in over **120 films**, earning the title of **Most Popular Actor** multiple times. But his transition into politics was equally impactful. He founded the **Sri Lanka Mahajana Pakshaya (SLMP)** and advocated for peace and reconciliation during the height of the **JVP insurgency**.

On that fateful day in **Polhengoda, Colombo**, Kumaratunga was shot at close range by an assassin linked to the **Deshapremi Janatha Viyaparaya (DJV)**—a militant offshoot of the **Janatha Vimukthi Peramuna (JVP)**. His vocal support for the **Indo-Sri Lanka Accord** and criticism of the JVP's violent tactics made him a target. The killing was widely seen as politically motivated, and the DJV even distributed leaflets justifying the act.

Investigation and Commission Findings

• **Initial Investigation**: Marred by delays, political interference, and suspicious disappearances.

• **Lionel Ranasinghe** was arrested in March 1989, confessed, and later disappeared under mysterious circumstances.

• **Tarzan Weerasinghe** was reportedly detained in 1990–1991, but his presence was denied by officials. He also vanished, allegedly after interrogation.

Presidential Commission (1995–1996)

Appointed by President Chandrika Kumaratunga, Vijaya's widow.

- Led by Justices Sarath N. Silva, P. Ramanathan, and D. Jayawickrema.

- Concluded that a prima facie case existed against:

  - **President Ranasinghe Premadasa** – for motive and suppression of investigation

  - **Minister Ranjan Wijeratne** – for illegal interference in the investigation

No formal charges were brought, as both were deceased by the time of the findings.

The case remains unresolved, symbolizing the deep entanglement of politics and violence in Sri Lanka's history. Kumaratunga's death robbed the nation of a charismatic leader who might have bridged ethnic and political divides. His legacy lives on through his films, his political ideals, and the continued efforts of those who seek justice and reconciliation.

Authoritative Sources

1. **Wikipedia** – Assassination of Vijaya Kumaratunga

This entry provides a detailed account of the February 16, 1988, assassination of Vijaya Kumaratunga, a popular actor and founder of the Sri Lanka Mahajana Pakshaya (SLMP). He was shot outside his home in Polhengoda, Colombo, by members of the Deshapremi Janatha Viyaparaya (DJV), the armed wing of the JVP. The article outlines his political rise, his advocacy for peace and devolution, and the national mourning that followed his death.

2. **Colombo Telegraph** – "The Vijaya Kumaratunge Assassination" by Rajan Hoole

This investigative piece delves into the Presidential Commission's findings, which implicated President Premadasa and Minister Ranjan Wijeratne in obstructing the investigation. It details how the suspected assassin, Lionel Ranasinghe, confessed but was later shielded from further inquiry. The article also explores the political rivalry between Kumaratunga and Premadasa, suggesting that Kumaratunga's growing popularity and pro-devolution stance made him a threat to hardline factions.

3. **Sri Lanka Guardian** – "The Second JVP Insurgency (Part 2)" by Tisaranee Gunasekara

This source situates Kumaratunga's assassination within the broader context of the 1987–1989 JVP insurgency. It highlights his initial sympathy toward the JVP, his later criticism of its violence and racism, and his efforts to build a United Socialist Alliance (USA) as a progressive alternative. His murder is portrayed as a strategic elimination of a charismatic leftist leader who opposed both Sinhala nationalism and authoritarianism.

Chapter 34: The 1987–1989 JVP Insurrection: A Marxist Uprising and Its Tragic Legacy

(Pic: The Island)

The 1987–1989 Janatha Vimukthi Peramuna (JVP) insurrection in Sri Lanka marked one of the most violent and politically complex chapters in the island nation's post-independence history. Led by the Marxist-Leninist JVP, this uprising was not merely a rebellion against the Government—it was a manifestation of deep-rooted socio-political grievances, ideological fervor, and nationalist sentiment. The insurrection resulted in tens of thousands of deaths, widespread disappearances, and a legacy of trauma that continues to shape Sri Lanka's political landscape.

The JVP was **founded in 1965 by Rohana Wijeweera,** a radical Marxist who envisioned a socialist revolution in Sri Lanka. After a **failed uprising in 1971**, the group was banned but later re-emerged with renewed vigor in the 1980s. The second insurrection was fueled by opposition to the Indo-Sri Lanka Accord and the presence of Indian Peace Keeping Forces (IPKF), which the JVP viewed as a threat to national sovereignty and Sinhalese identity.

The movement evolved from its Marxist roots into a more nationalist and militarized force, targeting not only government institutions but also civilians perceived as collaborators. The JVP's military wing, the **Deshapremi Janatha Viyaparaya (DJV),** orchestrated assassinations, bombings, and strikes that paralyzed the country.

Between **1987 and 1989**, Sri Lanka descended into chaos. The JVP's campaign of terror included:

- Targeted killings of politicians, academics, and journalists
- Sabotage of infrastructure and public services
- Intimidation of civilians through curfews and propaganda

In response, the Sri Lankan government launched brutal counter-insurgency operations. Paramilitary groups such as the **Black Cats** and **Eagles of the Central Hills** were deployed, often operating with impunity. The state's reaction was swift and merciless, leading to mass arrests, torture, and extrajudicial executions.

The human cost of the insurrection was staggering. Estimates suggest:

- **60,000–80,000 people were killed**, including insurgents, civilians, and security personnel
- **20,000+ individuals disappeared**, many presumed dead

These figures reflect not only the scale of violence but also the breakdown of legal and moral norms during the conflict. Families were left without answers, and entire communities were traumatized by the pervasive fear and repression.

By late 1989, the insurrection had been crushed. Rohana Wijeweera was captured and killed, and the JVP's leadership was dismantled. Emergency conditions were lifted, but the scars remained.

The insurrection left behind:

- A legacy of unresolved disappearances and human rights violations
- A cautionary tale about the dangers of political extremism and state overreach
- A transformed JVP, which later re-entered mainstream politics as a democratic socialist party

The 1987–1989 JVP insurrection was a tragic convergence of ideology, nationalism, and violence. It exposed the fragility of democratic institutions and the devastating consequences of political polarization. While Sri Lanka has moved forward, the echoes of this dark period continue to resonate in its collective memory and political discourse.

Timeline of Key Events During the 1987–1989 JVP Insurrection

Here's a chronological overview of major incidents and killings that shaped the JVP uprising in Sri Lanka:

1987

April: The insurrection begins as the JVP mobilizes against the Indo-Sri Lanka Accord and the presence of Indian Peace Keeping Forces (IPKF).

Mid-1987: Emergence of the Deshapremi Janatha Viyaparaya (DJV), the JVP's militant wing, which begins targeted assassinations and sabotage operations.

1988

Throughout the Year:

- Widespread strikes and curfews enforced by the JVP.
- Assassinations of political figures, including members of the ruling United National Party (UNP).
- Attacks on police stations and military installations by DJV operatives.

Late 1988:

Pro-government paramilitary groups such as the Black Cats and Eagles of the Central Hills begin retaliatory operations, leading to mass killings and disappearances.

1989

July 28: Security forces allegedly open fire on a JVP rally, killing **129 people** in one of the deadliest single-day incidents.

Throughout 1989:

- Necklacing (a brutal form of execution) becomes widespread.
- Thousands of suspected JVP members and sympathizers are abducted or executed without trial.

November:

- **Rohana Wijeweera**, the JVP founder, is captured and killed.
- Other senior leaders, including **Upatissa Gamanayake** and **Keerthi Vijayabahu**, are also eliminated.

December 29: The insurrection officially ends with the dismantling of the JVP's militant infrastructure.

Aftermath

- Estimated **60,000–80,000 deaths** and **20,000+ disappearances** during the insurrection.
- Operation Combine launched by Sri Lankan Armed Forces to suppress remaining insurgents.

Timeline of Key Events and Assassinations

1986

Dec 15: **Daya Pathirana**, student leader of the **Independent Students Union**, was abducted and murdered near Bolgoda Lake. His death is considered the first politically motivated killing of the insurrection.

1987

Jul 31: **Jinadasa Weerasinghe,** UNP MP for Tangalle, was shot dead in Angunakolapelessa.

Aug 18: **Keerthisena Abeywickrama**, UNP MP for Deniyaya, was killed in a bombing at Parliament.

Dec 12: **DIG Terrence Perera**, Director of the Counter Subversive Division, was assassinated in Battaramulla.

Dec 23: **Harsha Abeywardena,** Chairman of the UNP, was shot in Wellawatte.

1988

Daya Sepali Senadheera, UNP MP for Karandeniya, was killed.

- Feb 16: **Vijaya Kumaranatunga,** actor and founder of the SLMP, was assassinated in Colombo. **(Subsequently contested)**

May 1: **G. V. S. de Silva**, District Minister and UNP MP, was killed in Galle.

May 20: **Nandalal Fernando**, UNP General Secretary, was shot in Wellawatte.

Sep: **Merrill Kariyawasam**, UNP MP for Agalawatte, was assassinated.

1989

Mar 8: **Prof. Stanley Wijesundera**, Vice Chancellor of University of Colombo, was shot in his office.

May 1: **DIG Bennet Perera,** Director of CID, was killed in Mount Lavinia.

Jul 31: **Premakeerthi de Alwis**, beloved broadcaster and lyricist, was murdered in Colombo.

Aug 13: **K. Amaratunge**, Chief News Editor of Rupavahini, was assassinated.

Sep 12: **Dr. Gladys Jayawardene**, Chairperson of the State Pharmaceutical Corporation, was shot in Slave Island.

Sep 13: **Sagarika Gomes**, artist and newscaster, was killed.

Oct 3: **Neville Nissanka**, lawyer, was shot in Miriswatta.

Nov 17: **D. C. Athukorala**, Chief Engineer at Colombo Port Authority, was assassinated.

Nov 13: **Rohana Wijeweera and Upatissa Gamanayake, top JVP leaders**, were captured and executed by government forces.

Dec 29: **Saman Piyasiri Fernando**, DJV military wing leader, was killed, marking the collapse of the insurrection.

Intellectuals and Professionals Targeted

The JVP's strategy included eliminating influential voices in academia, media, and civil service:

- **Chandratne Patuwathavithane,** Vice Chancellor of University of Moratuwa
- **Lesley Ranagala**, UNP MP for Borella
- **Lionel Jayatilake**, former minister
- **Thevis Guruge**, pioneering broadcaster
- **Rev. Fr. Michael Paul Rodrigo**, Catholic priest and social activist
- Ven. Kotikawatte Saddhatissa Thera and Ven. Pohaddaramulle Premaloka Thero, Buddhist monks were assassinated.

Alleged Government Involvement

While the JVP was responsible for a large number of killings, some high-profile deaths were attributed to pro-government paramilitary squads or state actors, especially toward the latter part of the insurrection:

Premakeerthi de Alwis, a beloved broadcaster, was reportedly killed by pro-government paramilitary squads, not the JVP.

Richard de Zoysa, a journalist and human rights activist, was abducted and murdered in 1990. His death was widely believed to be the work of state-linked death squads, and it sparked international outrage.

Wijedasa Liyanarachchi, a lawyer, died from torture injuries while in police custody, pointing to direct involvement by Sri Lanka Police.

Padmasiri Thrimavitharana, a medical student and activist, was reportedly tortured and killed by pro-government paramilitary groups.

Nandathilaka Galappaththi, a JVP political secretary, was also allegedly tortured and killed by paramilitary squads.

These incidents suggest that counterinsurgency efforts may have included **extrajudicial** killings, especially targeting suspected JVP members or sympathizers. The **Operation Combine**, led **by Minister Ranjan Wijeratne**, was a major military campaign that aimed to crush the JVP, and it has been linked to mass disappearances and executions.

Shadows in Uniform — The Black Cats, Eagles of the Central Hills, and the Blurred Lines of State Power

The 1987–89 JVP Insurrection was not only a battle between rebels and the state—it was a war fought in the shadows. As the government struggled to contain the Marxist uprising, paramilitary groups emerged, operating with unclear mandates, covert support, and deadly efficiency. Among these, the Black Cats and Eagles of the Central Hills became infamous for their brutal tactics and ambiguous ties to the state.

The Black Cats: Enforcers in the Dark

Formed around **1989**, the Black Cats were **aligned with the United National Party (UNP)** and operated as an **anti-communist paramilitary force**.

Though **not officially recognized**, they were one of **13 death squads** reportedly **sponsored by the government** to suppress the JVP.

Their operations included:

Targeted assassinations of leftist politicians and activists.

Suppression of press freedom, including the killing of over **800 individuals** linked to anti-UNP publications.

The **Eppawala massacre**, where civilians suspected of JVP ties were executed.

The Eagles of the Central Hills: Vigilantes with a Badge

This far-right paramilitary group was composed of **off-duty police and military personnel**, often acting with **tacit approval from local authorities**.

Their ideology fused **Sinhalese nationalism** with **anti-communist fervor**, making them natural enemies of the JVP.

Notable atrocities:

Kandy Massacre (Sept 1989): In retaliation for JVP killings, the Eagles murdered over **250 civilians**, many of whom had no proven links to the insurgency.

Peradeniya University Massacre: Fourteen custodial staff were executed, allegedly for supporting JVP activities.

The existence of these groups raises troubling questions:

Were they rogue militias or unofficial arms of the state?
Did the government outsource its dirty work to avoid accountability?
How much did political leaders know—or approve—of their actions?

Evidence suggests:

Informal links to the UNP and **cooperation with police units**, despite official denials.
Political protection and **lack of prosecution**, even after massacres.
Overlap in personnel between state forces and paramilitary squads.
This ambiguity allowed the state to **wage a war without fingerprints**, blurring the line between **legitimate counterinsurgency** and **state-sponsored terror**.

The legacy of these groups is a cautionary tale:

They **eroded public trust** in law enforcement and governance.

They **complicated post-conflict reconciliation**, as victims were denied justice.

They **set a precedent** for future conflicts, where **violence could be outsourced** and **accountability evaded**.

The insurrection left an indelible scar on Sri Lanka's political and social landscape. Over 60,000 people were killed or disappeared. The assassinations were not random acts of violence—they were calculated moves to dismantle the state's intellectual, political, and moral backbone. The trauma of this era continues to reverberate through Sri Lankan society, shaping its political discourse and collective memory.

Personal Reflection:

While I have been able to document most of the atrocities committed by both the JVP and Police/Security personnel during the insurrection, I encountered troubling gaps in the historical record.

Notably absent are the accounts of several known victims from that period:

__Policeman Adjumain__, whose entire family was reportedly massacred in a retaliatory JVP attack; __Mr. Hettiarachi, Superintendent of Aislaby Estate in Bandarawela__; and the __Superintendent of Ampitikande Estate in Bandarawela__, whose name I have regrettably been unable to trace. Their stories deserve rightful recognition in this book. Yet, despite extensive searching, I could not locate any formal records of these individuals on public websites.

Authoritative Sources

1. **Wikipedia – 1987–1989 JVP Insurrection**
   Offers a comprehensive overview of the **armed revolt led by the Janatha Vimukthi Peramuna (JVP)**, a Marxist–Leninist party, against the Sri Lankan government. It details the **timeline (April 1987 to December 1989)**, the role of the **Deshapremi Janatha Viyaparaya (DJV)** as the JVP's military wing, and the **death toll**, which is estimated between **60,000 and 80,000**, including thousands of **disappearances and extrajudicial killings**.

2. **Facts.net – "35 Facts About JVP Insurrection"** Provides digestible insights into both the **1971 and 1987–1989 uprisings**, highlighting the JVP's ideological evolution, its **targeting of civilians and officials**, and its transformation into a **legitimate political party** in the 1990s. It also explores the **social and economic conditions** that fueled the rebellion.

3. **Outlook India – "Colombo Diaries: The Bloody JVP Uprisings in Sri Lanka"** A gripping journalistic account from the summer of **1988**, offering **on-the-ground observations** of the violence in the Sinhala heartland. It describes **bodies dumped in rivers, anti-India sentiment**, and the **climate of fear** that engulfed the country. This piece adds a **human dimension** to the insurrection's brutality and the psychological toll on civilians.

Chapter 35: Dr. Rajani Thiranagama - A Voice Amid the Silenced Palmyras (1989)

(Pic: dbsjeyarfaj.com)

Born on February 23, 1954, in Jaffna, Sri Lanka, **Rajani Rajasingham Thiranagama** was raised in a Tamil Christian family. As the second of four daughters, she pursued medicine at the University of Colombo, where she became active in student politics. Her marriage to **Dayapala Thiranagama**, a Sinhala Buddhist student leader, defied ethnic and religious divisions—a reflection of her deep commitment to unity and justice. After completing her medical internship in Jaffna and Haldumulla, Rajani joined the University of Jaffna as a lecturer in anatomy in 1980. By the mid-1980s, she was appointed head of the department.

Activism and Human Rights Work

Her academic career soon became intertwined with activism. Rajani co-founded the **University Teachers for Human Rights (UTHR-J)** in Jaffna and co-authored the landmark book *The Broken Palmyra*, a daring exposé of atrocities committed during Sri Lanka's civil war. In a time of suppression, her voice carried sharp clarity. She documented human rights abuses by all sides—including the LTTE, Indian Peace Keeping Force, and the Sri Lankan government. Her work broke the mold of partisan narratives, earning both admiration and hostility.

The Broken Palmyra challenged the silence, and its publication marked her as a threat.

The Assassination

On **September 21, 1989**, while cycling home from a lecture in Thirunelvely, Rajani was shot and killed. Witnesses reported that she turned when someone called her name—then came the bullets. Though speculation surrounded the perpetrators, many believe the LTTE, which she had once supported, was responsible. Her criticism of their authoritarian tactics had made her a target.

To her loved ones, the motive was painfully clear: she spoke truth, and in war, truth is dangerous.

Legacy and Impact

Rajani's death was not just the loss of a life—it was a moral reckoning. Her daughter, Sharika Thiranagama, has carried forward her legacy as a Professor of Anthropology at Stanford University, exploring themes of identity, displacement, and resistance.

Her story reached global audiences through the documentary *No More Tears Sister (2005),* and in 2007, *UTHR-J* received the **Martin Ennals Award for Human Rights Defenders**, honoring the group's—and Rajani's—unflinching commitment to justice.

Her writings continue to resonate in academic and activist circles, reminding us that dissent is not betrayal—and that humanity must always surpass ideology.

Key Sources

1. **Wikipedia – Rajani Thiranagama**
   Offers a comprehensive biography of **Dr. Rajani Thiranagama**, including her early life, medical career, political activism, and assassination on **21 September 1989** in **Jaffna**. It details her transformation from LTTE sympathizer to outspoken critic, and her role as **co-founder of University Teachers for Human Rights (Jaffna)**. She was killed by **LTTE gunmen**, allegedly in retaliation for her public criticism of their authoritarianism and abuses.

2. **UTHR – Remembering Rajani**
   This tribute from the **University Teachers for Human Rights (Jaffna)** reflects on Rajani's legacy as a **feminist, academic, and moral voice** during a time of terror. It highlights her co-authorship of *The Broken Palmyrah*, a landmark book that exposed **atrocities committed by all parties**—including the **Sri Lankan state**, **Indian Peace Keeping Force**, and **Tamil militant groups**. Her death is described as a **moral crisis** for the Tamil community and a symbol of the silencing of dissent.

3. **Colombo Telegraph – "Remembering Rajani"** This article commemorates Rajani's life and work, emphasizing her **cross-ethnic marriage**, her refusal to flee Jaffna despite threats, and her efforts to establish **Poorani**, a shelter for war-affected women. It also discusses how her assassination forced UTHR-J members underground yet inspired them to continue documenting human rights violations with unwavering integrity.

Chapter 36: The Schoolboys of Embilipitiya – State Terror (1989–1990)

(Embilipitiya Central College)

Between 1989 and 1990, the quiet town of **Embilipitiya** in southern Sri Lanka became the epicenter of one of the most harrowing episodes of **State-sponsored terror** in the country's post-independence history. Known as the ***Embilipitiya Schoolboys Affair***, this tragedy involved the **abduction, torture, and disappearance of at least 32 teenage boys**, (*Number of Victims: Some sources cite 32, others mention 48 schoolboys. The Embilipitiya Disappeared Schoolchildren's Parents' Organisation (EDSCPO) investigated 48 cases*) most of them students at **Embilipitiya Central College**. The perpetrators were **Sri Lankan Army personnel**, allegedly acting on the orders of a **vindictive school principal**, with the tacit approval—or deliberate blindness—of higher authorities. This essay explores the roots of the atrocity, the mechanisms of terror, the long struggle for justice, and its enduring legacy.

The late 1980s were marked by the **Second JVP insurrection**, a violent Marxist uprising led by the **Janatha Vimukthi Peramuna (JVP)**. In response, the Sri Lankan government launched a brutal counterinsurgency campaign. The **Southern Province**, including Embilipitiya, was under heavy military control, and **mass disappearances, extrajudicial killings, and torture** became routine. It is estimated that **over 30,000 people** were killed or disappeared during this period.

Most of the victims were **aged 14 to 19**, attending Embilipitiya Central College. They were not insurgents, nor politically active. Their only crime, it seems, was **mocking the school principal's son**, **Captain Chaminda Galappathy**, over a love letter he had written to a girl. The principal, **Loku Dayananda Galappathy**, allegedly compiled a list of students to be "dealt with" and used his connections with the **Sevana Army Camp** to orchestrate their abduction.

The Mechanism of Terror

Abductions

- Students were taken from classrooms, homes, and even cricket matches.
- Army vehicles and personnel from the **Sevana Camp** were identified by witnesses.
- Some parents were tricked into handing over their children, believing they would be released after questioning.

Torture and Disappearance

- Victims were detained at Sevana Camp, tortured, and never seen again.
- One boy was forced to swallow **glass shards and keys**.
- Mass graves were later discovered at **Sooriyakanda**, containing bones, school uniforms, and personal items. *(Mass Grave Details: The Sooriyakanda mass grave was discovered in 1994, not immediately after the events. Forensic analysis was limited and criticized.)*

The Struggle for Justice

Human Rights Task Force

Led by **Justice J.F.A. Soza**, the HRTF documented the disappearances and pushed for accountability.

Soza's reports implicated **Principal Galappathy**, **Colonel R.P. Liyanage**, and other army officers.

Legal Proceedings

In 1994, the **Attorney General's Department** finally filed charges against Galappathy and several soldiers.

- The **Ratnapura High Court** trial concluded in **1999**:
- **Galappathy and six soldiers** were sentenced to **10 years of rigorous imprisonment**.
- **Captain Chaminda** and **Brigadier Liyanage** were **acquitted**, sparking outrage.

The Embilipitiya case was not an isolated incident. It reflected a **systemic breakdown of rule of law**, where:

- **Military Officers acted with impunity**, often for personal vendettas.
- **Judicial institutions were powerless** or complicit.
- **Political leaders denied responsibility**, with some even promoting the accused.

The **Attorney General's delays**, **intimidation of witnesses**, and **media silence** further entrenched this culture.

Legacy and Lessons

The Embilipitiya tragedy remains a **symbol of state terror**, where **innocent children were sacrificed** to protect egos and power. It teaches us:

The **importance of independent institutions** and **civil oversight**.

The **need for historical reckoning**, not just legal closure.

That **justice delayed is justice denied**, especially for the voiceless.

Despite the convictions, **many perpetrators escaped punishment**, and the **families of the victims continue to grieve**, some still searching for remains and answers.

The Schoolboys of Embilipitiya were not rebels, criminals, or threats—they were children caught in the crossfire of a brutal regime and a vengeful educator. Their story is a chilling reminder of how **personal vendettas can be weaponized by state machinery**, and how **silence and complicity** can bury truth. But through the courage of grieving parents, human rights defenders, and journalists, their voices echo still.

Survivor and Family Voices from Embilipitiya – With References

Sisira Kuma Gunaratne – Father of Nalin Gunaratne

"Four years I had waited, and I immediately felt it was my child. I wasn't able to reconstruct my thoughts. My mind was scattered to pieces."

— Quoted in The Independent, January 1994

Sisira Gunaratne, a bulldozer mechanic, spent years searching for his son Nalin, who was abducted in January 1990. When mass graves were discovered at Sooriyakanda, he recognized a piece of striped cloth matching Nalin's sarong among the remains. His grief and disbelief became emblematic of the parents' anguish.

Wimal Piyasaman – Former Student Witness

"He threatened us. He said the same thing that happened to the others would happen to us if we didn't stop bothering his son."

— Reported in The Independent

Piyasaman recalled how Principal Galappathy stormed into a classroom and issued threats after students mocked his son's love letter. Several boys who had laughed at the letter were abducted shortly after.

Unnamed Mother – On Seeking Help from the Principal

"We soon realised our mistake."

— Quoted in The Independent

Some parents initially turned to Principal Galappathy, believing his army connections could help free their children. They later understood he was the orchestrator of the disappearances.

Justice J.F.A. Soza – Human Rights Task Force

"These cases cannot absolve the State from responsibility."

— From HRTF Annual Report, August 1993, cited in Colombo Telegraph

Justice Soza's investigations and reports were instrumental in documenting the disappearances and pushing for legal action. He emphasized that the state bore ultimate responsibility for the crimes.

Justice P.H.K. Kulatilaka – Court of Appeal

"What pricked my judicial mind was what persuaded these men in uniform to help this layman accused principal to get rid of these innocent young ones."

— *From Sunday Observer, July 2014*

Justice Kulatilaka presided over the appeal and expressed deep concern over the motives and complicity of military personnel in executing the principal's vendetta.

Key Sources

1. **American Institute for Sri Lankan Studies – EDSCPO Fonds**
   This archive documents the work of the **Embilipitiya Disappeared Schoolchildren's Parents' Organisation (EDSCPO)**, founded in 1991 to investigate the **abduction, torture, and disappearance of 48 teenage boys** from **Embilipitiya Central College**. The records include **court documents, newspaper clippings, and investigative reports**, many of which implicate **military personnel at the Sevana Army Camp** and **school principal Loku Galappathy**.

2. **The Independent – "Report from the School of Death" by Tim McGirk (1994)**
   A deeply moving investigative piece recounting the discovery of **mass graves on Mount Sooriya**, where the remains of the missing boys—including **school uniforms and personal items**—were unearthed. It follows the journey of grieving parents like **Sisira Gunaratne**, who searched for years and ultimately identified his son's sarong among the bones.

3. **Colombo Telegraph – "Embilipitiya Schoolboys' Affair: The Thin End of the Wedge" by Rajan Hoole**
   This article situates the tragedy within the broader context of **state terror during the JVP uprising**, highlighting how **Principal Galappathy colluded with military officers** to eliminate suspected student activists. It references the **Human Rights Task Force's 1992 report**, which confirmed the role of the **Sevana Army Camp** in the disappearances and details the **1999 trial verdict** that sentenced Galappathy to **10 years of rigorous imprisonment**.

Chapter 37: Richard de Zoysa: A Voice Silenced, A Legacy That Speaks (1990)

(Pic: litspring.com)

In the turbulent landscape of Sri Lanka's political history, few names evoke as much reverence and sorrow as **Richard Manik de Zoysa**. A journalist, poet, actor, and human rights activist, de Zoysa was a man of many talents and convictions. His abduction and murder on **February 18, 1990**, during a time of intense political unrest, marked a turning point in the country's reckoning with state-sanctioned violence. More than three decades later, his life and death remain a haunting reminder of the dangers faced by those who dare to speak truth to power.

Born on **March 18, 1958**, in Colombo, Richard was the son of **Lucien de Zoysa**, a Sinhalese intellectual, and **Dr. Manorani Saravanamuttu**, a Tamil physician. His mixed heritage gave him a unique perspective on Sri Lanka's ethnic complexities. Educated at **S. Thomas' College, Mount Lavinia**, he quickly distinguished himself as a gifted student, winning accolades in drama and debate. His portrayal of Shakespearean characters earned him national recognition as **Best Actor in the English medium** in 1972.

Richard's artistic journey flourished in the 1980s. He starred in **Yuganthaya** (1983), a film directed by **Lester James Peries**, where he played **Malin Kabalana**, a sensitive and socially conscious character. His performance was lauded for its emotional depth and nuance. He also appeared in *The Way of the Lotus* (1987), a psychological drama exploring Buddhist philosophy.

Beyond the stage and screen, Richard was a fearless journalist and poet. He headed the **Colombo Office of Inter Press Service**, an international news agency, and was known for his incisive reporting on human rights abuses and political corruption. His poetry, including works like *Animal Crackers* and *Lepidoptera*, reflected the anguish and unrest of Sri Lanka's civil strife. Writing under the pseudonym **Angela de Silva***, he used allegory and symbolism to critique authoritarianism and violence.

Richard was also a vocal critic of the **Premadasa Regime**, which was accused of deploying death squads to suppress dissent. His activism placed him in the crosshairs of powerful forces, but he remained undeterred, believing in the transformative power of truth and art.

In the early hours of **February 18, 1990**, armed men stormed Richard's home in **Welikadawatte**, Colombo. In front of his mother and associate, he was forcibly taken without explanation. The next day, his body was found on a beach in **Moratuwa**, 12 miles south of Colombo. He had been **shot in the head and throat**, and his **jaw was broken**—a brutal execution meant to silence a voice that had grown too powerful**.

His mother, **Dr. Manorani Saravanamuttu**, identified two of the abductors and later saw one— a high-ranking Police Officer—on television. Despite her testimony and legal efforts, no arrests were made. Both she and her lawyer, **Batty Weerakoon**, received death threats, and the investigation stalled amid political pressure.

Richard's murder sent shockwaves through Sri Lanka and the international community. It became a defining tragedy of the decade, symbolizing the **State's impunity** and the peril faced by journalists and activists. His death galvanized human rights movements and led to increased scrutiny of government practices.

His mother became a tireless advocate for missing persons until her death in 2001. Richard's friend and fellow journalist **Taraki Sivaram**, who identified his body, would later suffer a similar fate in 2005.

Richard's life continues to inspire. His poetry is studied for its literary brilliance and political insight. His story has been referenced in books, documentaries, and memorials. He remains a symbol of resistance, a martyr for free expression, and a reminder that even in death, truth endures.

Richard de Zoysa was more than a victim—he was a visionary. His intellect, artistry, and courage challenged the status quo and gave voice to the voiceless. Though his life was stolen, his legacy lives on in every journalist who dares to report the truth, every poet who writes against injustice, and every citizen who demands accountability.

In 2005, three police officers were indicted but acquitted due to lack of credible evidence.

Pseudonym "Angela de Silva": This claim appears in some accounts but lacks widespread verification in major biographies or academic sources.

** *Details of Torture*: While his injuries are confirmed, specific methods (e.g., broken jaw) are cited in multiple reports but not officially detailed in court records.

Key Sources

1. **Wikipedia – Richard de Zoysa**
   Offers a comprehensive biography of de Zoysa, a journalist, actor, and human rights activist. He was abducted from his home on **18 February 1990** and found dead the next day on a beach in Moratuwa. His murder is widely believed to have been carried out by a **state-linked death squad**, and his mother, **Dr. Manorani Saravanamuttu**, later identified one of the abductors as a senior police officer.

2. **Daily Mirror – "The Heritage of Richard de Zoysa as a Victim of State-Terror"**
   This article reflects on de Zoysa's legacy as a writer, poet, and activist

3. **International Commission of Jurists – Magisterial Inquiry into the Homicide of Richard de Zoysa**. Documents the legal proceedings following his murder, including the **inquest**, **identification of suspects**, and **death threats** received by his mother and legal counsel. The ICJ sent an observer to monitor the inquiry, underscoring the **international concern** surrounding the case.

Chapter 38: Echoes of Prayer and Gunfire – The Kattankudy and Eravur Mosque Massacres (1990)

(Remembrance after 33 years Pic: slguardian.org)

Timeline of Events

Date	Event
July 1983	Black July riots mark the beginning of Sri Lanka's civil war
1987–1990	Rising tensions between Tamil and Muslim communities in Eastern Province
August 3, 1990	Kattankudy Mosque Massacre: Over 147 Muslims killed during prayer
August 11–12, 1990	Eravur Mosque Massacre: Between 116 and 173 Muslims killed in coordinated attacks*
October 1990	LTTE forcibly expels over 75,000 Muslims from Northern Province
May 2009	Civil war ends with the defeat of the LTTE

* Death tolls: Vary across sources due to lack of formal investigations and mass burials

Kattankudy Mosque Massacre – August 3, 1990

In the heart of Eastern Sri Lanka, the town of Kattankudy—home to a dense Muslim population—became the site of one of the most horrific massacres in the country's history. During Isha prayers, when hundreds of worshippers were prostrating in devotion, approximately 30 armed Tamil militants, allegedly affiliated with the LTTE, infiltrated four mosques disguised as Muslims.

They opened fire indiscriminately with automatic rifles and hurled grenades into the prayer halls. Worshippers were shot in the back and side, many killed instantly. Survivors described scenes of unimaginable horror: blood-soaked prayer mats, bodies piled across the mosque floors, and the cries of the wounded echoing through the night.

- Death toll: **Initially estimated at 100, later confirmed to exceed 147**
- Targeted mosques: Meer Jumma Mosque, Hussainiya Mosque, and two others
- Method: Disguise, infiltration, mass shooting
- Impact: Deep trauma, mass displacement, annual day of mourning

Eravur Mosque Massacre – August 11–12, 1990

Just days after the Kattankudy Massacre, the nearby town of Eravur was attacked in a coordinated assault. Around 30–40 militants, allegedly LTTE, split into groups and stormed five Muslim villages: **Surattayankuda, Michnagar, Meerakerni, Punnakuda, and Saddam Hussein village**.

The attackers dragged Muslims from their homes and executed them in the streets. In one particularly gruesome incident, a pregnant woman** was disemboweled and her unborn child stabbed. Homes were looted and burned, and entire communities were left shattered.

Death toll: **Between 116 and 173 Muslims** killed
Method: House-to-house executions, mutilation, arson
Memorial: Noorussalam Mosque memorial arch built in 2003
Aftermath: Mass displacement, heightened ethnic polarization

** Pregnant woman incident: Reported in survivor accounts, but not officially documented in all sources

Ethnic Tensions and Motives

The massacres were part of a broader campaign of ethnic cleansing by the LTTE, aimed at removing Muslims from Tamil-claimed territories. Muslims were increasingly targeted due to their perceived collaboration with government forces. In retaliation, Tamil civilians also suffered attacks, creating a vicious cycle of violence.

- **Expulsion**: In late 1990, over 75,000 Muslims were forcibly expelled from the Northern Province

- **LTTE Denials**: Despite eyewitness accounts, the LTTE denied responsibility for both massacres

- **State Response**: Criticized for failing to protect Muslim communities and for delayed intervention

- **Legacy**: Deepened mistrust between ethnic groups, complicated post-war reconciliation

The Kattankudy and Eravur massacres remain among the darkest chapters in Sri Lanka's civil war. They are stark reminders of the devastating consequences of ethnic hatred and political extremism. Sacred spaces—mosques meant for peace and prayer—were transformed into sites of carnage.

These events underscore the urgent need for:

- Interfaith dialogue to rebuild trust between communities
- Historical accountability through transparent investigations
- Education and remembrance to prevent future atrocities
- Justice and reparations for survivors and displaced families

The massacres at Kattankudy and Eravur were not random acts of violence—they were calculated assaults on identity, faith, and community. They remind us that peace is not merely the absence of war, but the presence of justice, truth, and compassion. As Sri Lanka moves forward, it must confront these painful truths to ensure that no prayer is ever again interrupted by gunfire.

Image credit: Asanka Brendon Ratnayake – For The Washington Post

Key Sources:

Kattankudy Mosque Massacre – 3 August 1990

1.   **Wikipedia** – Kattankudy Mosque Massacre. This entry details how around 30 armed LTTE militants, disguised as Muslims, entered two mosques—Meera Jummah and Hussainiyya—during Isha prayers and opened fire on over 300 worshippers, killing 147 men and boys. Victims were shot in the back or side while prostrating, and grenades were hurled into the prayer halls. The massacre occurred amid rising tensions following the breakdown of peace talks and retaliatory violence between Tamil and Muslim groups.

2.   **Colombo Telegraph** – "Reliving Bloodshed & Trauma 27 Years On" by Seyed Alavi Sheriffdeen A deeply personal account from a survivor whose father and 10-year-old brother were among the victims. The article describes the emotional scars left on the community and how the mosques remain sacred memorials to the lives lost. It also contextualizes the massacre within the broader pattern of LTTE violence against Muslims in the Eastern Province.

Eravur Mosque Massacre – Late July 1990.

3.   **Groundviews** – "Statement on 25th Anniversary of Mass Killings in Batticaloa" This statement commemorates the mass killings and disappearances in Eravur, Sathurukondan, and Kattankudy, noting that armed Tamil groups attacked Muslim worshippers and villages in July and August 1990, including a mosque shooting in Eravur that killed several civilians. It emphasizes the long-term trauma and fractured relationships between Tamil and Muslim communities in the Eastern Province.

Chapter 39: Ranjan Wijeratne—A Life of Power, A Death of Shock (1991)

In the turbulent political landscape of Sri Lanka, few figures embodied both authority and controversy like **General Ranjan Wijeratne**. Born on **April 4, 1931**, into a prominent family with ties to Sri Lanka's first Prime Minister, D. S. Senanayake, Wijeratne's life was shaped by privilege, ambition, and an unrelenting drive to impose order on chaos.

From Tea Fields to Power Corridors

Ranjan Wijeratne's early career was rooted in the plantation economy. Apprenticing under Carlyle De Kretser, he rose to become **General Manager of the Demodara Group**—the largest tea estate in Ceylon. His leadership extended to the **Planters' Association of Ceylon**, the **Colombo Tea Traders' Association**, and the **Tea Research Institute**, earning him a reputation as a titan of the industry.

But his ambitions stretched beyond agriculture. In 1977, President Jayewardene recognized his administrative acumen and brought him into the public sector. Wijeratne quickly assumed influential roles, including **Permanent Secretary to the Ministry of Agricultural Development** and **Chairman of the Land Reform Commission**.

By the mid-1980s, Wijeratne had transformed into a military and political force. Commissioned into the **Sri Lanka Army Volunteer Force**, he founded the **2nd Battalion of the Sri Lanka Rifle Corps.** His entry into politics in 1988 marked a new chapter—one defined by confrontation and control.

As **Minister of Foreign Affairs and State Minister for Defence under President Premadasa**, Wijeratne became the face of the government's counterinsurgency efforts. He led Operation Combine, which dismantled the JVP's violent uprising. His approach to the LTTE was equally uncompromising. "I am going all out for the LTTE. I never do anything in half measures," he declared in Parliament, signaling his intent to crush Tamil separatism with military might.

Timeline of Key Events

Year	Event
1931	Born on April 4 in British Ceylon to a prominent family with ties to Prime Minister D. S. Senanayake.
1950s–1970s	Rose through the ranks of the tea industry, becoming General Manager of Demodara Group and chairing major trade associations.
1977	Invited by President J. R. Jayewardene to join the government sector.
1984	Commissioned as Lieutenant Colonel in the Sri Lanka Army Volunteer Force; founded the 2nd Battalion, Sri Lanka Rifle Corps.
1988	Became Chairman and later General Secretary of the United National Party (UNP).
1989	Appointed to Parliament via National List; became Minister of Foreign Affairs, Minister of Plantation Industries, and State Minister for Defence.
1989–1990	Led Operation Combine to crush the JVP rebellion; took a hardline stance against the LTTE.
1991	Assassinated on March 2 in Colombo by a remote-controlled car bomb, widely believed to be the work of the LTTE.
Posthumous	Promoted to General; awarded honorary Doctor of Laws by Kotelawala Defence Academy.

Assassination and Aftermath

On **March 2, 1991,** Wijeratne's life was cut short in a devastating car bomb attack on Havelock Road, Colombo. The explosion killed him, five Special Task Force officers, and thirteen civilians. Though no group claimed responsibility, the LTTE was widely suspected.

His death was a seismic blow to the Premadasa administration. It exposed vulnerabilities in the government's security apparatus and intensified the civil conflict. In recognition of his service, Wijeratne was posthumously promoted to General and honored with an honorary doctorate.

Patriot or Authoritarian?

Ranjan Wijeratne remains one of Sri Lanka's most polarizing figures. To some, he was a patriot who stood firm against terror and chaos. To others, he was a symbol of authoritarianism, wielding power with little regard for nuance or dissent.

His legacy is etched into the nation's history—a reminder of the cost of power in a country at war with itself. Whether admired or criticized, Wijeratne's life and death continue to provoke reflection on leadership, sacrifice, and the fragile balance between order and justice.

Key Sources

1. **BBC On This Day – 2 March 1991: Sri Lankan Hardliner Among 19 Killed in Blast**
This report details the **car bomb explosion in Colombo** that killed **Deputy Defence Minister Ranjan Wijeratne**, along with **five bodyguards and 13 civilians**. The bomb was remotely detonated during morning rush hour, and although no group claimed responsibility, suspicion fell on the **LTTE**, given Wijeratne's aggressive military campaign against them.

2. **Colombo Telegraph – "The Assassination of Ranjan Wijeratne" by Rajan Hoole**
This investigative piece explores the **political implications** of Wijeratne's death, noting that he was a **key strategist** in suppressing both the **JVP insurgency** and the **LTTE rebellion**. It raises questions about whether the LTTE acted alone, citing **logistical anomalies and prior warnings**. The article also examines his complex relationship with **President Premadasa**, suggesting internal tensions within the ruling UNP.

3. **Wikipedia – Ranjan Wijeratne**
Provides a full biography, tracing his career from **tea planter and corporate executive** to **Foreign Minister and State Minister for Defence**. It notes his **posthumous promotion to General**, his role in **military modernization**, and his reputation as a **blunt, uncompromising figure** in Sri Lankan politics.

Chapter 40: The Palliyagodella Massacre: A Village Silenced by War (1992)

In the early hours of **October 15, 1992**, the quiet village of **Palliyagodella**—also known as **Palliyathidal**—in **Sri Lanka's North Central Province** became the site of one of the most brutal and underreported atrocities of the country's civil war. Home to a predominantly Muslim population, the village had long lived in fear of the Liberation Tigers of Tamil Eelam (LTTE), whose campaign for a separate Tamil state increasingly targeted Muslim communities.

What unfolded that morning was not just a massacre—it was a calculated act of terror designed to erase a community and send a message. The story of Palliyagodella is a haunting reminder of how civilians, especially religious minorities, became pawns in a violent struggle for territory, identity, and control.

Anatomy of the Massacre

The LTTE assault was swift and merciless. Survivors described militants shouting, "We will kill everyone and then celebrate in your mosque," as they moved from house to house. Grenades were hurled into the mosque where villagers had gathered for safety. Those who fled were hunted down and killed with machetes and gunfire. Among the dead were at least 45 children and several pregnant women.

The villagers, armed only with shotguns provided by the military, were no match for the LTTE's automatic rifles and explosives. The attack lasted nearly four hours before army helicopters arrived—too late to prevent the carnage.

The exact number of victims remains disputed, but all accounts agree: the massacre was one of the deadliest single-day attacks on civilians during Sri Lanka's civil war.

Timeline of Key Events

Time & Date	Event
Pre-October 1992	Villagers report extortion and threats from LTTE; request protection from government forces.
October 14, 1992	Military issues shotguns to villagers—insufficient against LTTE's automatic weapons and explosives.
October 15, 1992 – 4:00 AM	LTTE militants (estimated 500–1,000) surround Palliyagodella and launch coordinated attack.
4:15 AM	Grenades thrown into mosque; ~40 killed instantly.
4:30–8:00 AM	Civilians massacred with machetes and gunfire; pregnant women, children, and entire families targeted.
8:00 AM	Army helicopters arrive; LTTE withdraws.
Following Days	Victims buried in mass graves near the mosque; village abandoned for three years.
Post-1992	No road access for over a decade; survivors displaced and traumatized.

Death Toll and Discrepancies

Source	Estimated Deaths
Sri Lankan Government	166-171
Eyewitnesses & BBC	Up to 285
Children	At least 45
Pregnant Women	Several, including unborn babies

Ethnic Tensions and LTTE Strategy

The massacre was not random. It was part of a broader LTTE strategy **to ethnically cleanse** Muslims from areas they sought to control. Despite decades of coexistence, the LTTE began viewing Muslims as collaborators with the Sinhalese-dominated government. Palliyagodella, situated between Tamil and Sinhalese regions, was seen as a buffer community—one the LTTE wanted removed.

The state's response was tragically inadequate. Despite warnings and requests for protection, the military failed to prevent the attack or intervene in time. The massacre exposed deep flaws in the government's ability to safeguard vulnerable communities.

"I was lying among six bodies. Lying in their blood."

— *Pitchathambi Ishabdeen*, shopkeeper and survivor

The survivors of Palliyagodella carry scars that go beyond physical loss. The village was abandoned for years, its roads left inaccessible, its story largely forgotten in national discourse. No major memorials honor the victims. Media coverage was limited, and the massacre remains absent from many official narratives of the war.

Yet Palliyagodella is more than a footnote—it is a symbol of forgotten suffering. It urges Sri Lanka to confront the full scope of its wartime atrocities, not just those that fit dominant narratives. Justice, remembrance, and reconciliation must include all communities, especially those whose voices have been silenced.

Key Sources

1. **Wikipedia – Palliyagodella Massacre**
   This entry documents the **15 October 1992 massacre** in the village of **Palliyagodella**, located in Sri Lanka's North Central Province. A force of **approximately 1,000 LTTE cadres**, including **female fighters and child soldiers**, attacked the village, killing between **166 and 285 civilians**, most of them **Muslim men, women, and children**. The LTTE reportedly threw **grenades into mosques**, used **machetes and guns**, and targeted **pregnant women and children**, with **45 children among the dead**.

2. **BBC – "Sri Lanka's Forgotten Massacre" by Andrew Hosken**
   This investigative feature recounts the massacre through **eyewitness testimony**, including that of **Pitchathambi Ishabdeen**, a local shopkeeper who survived by hiding among corpses. The article emphasizes how the village was **abandoned for years**, and how the massacre was part of the LTTE's campaign to **ethnically cleanse Muslim communities** from areas they sought to control.

3. **University Teachers for Human Rights (Jaffna) – Report 11, Chapter 7**
   This human rights report provides **contextual analysis**, noting that the massacre followed **tensions between the LTTE and Muslim villagers**, who had requested protection from the Sri Lankan military. It critiques the **state's inadequate response**, including the issuance of **shotguns to villagers**, which proved useless against the LTTE's assault. The report also highlights the **psychological trauma and displacement** that followed.

Chapter 41: The 1993 Jaffna Lagoon Massacre: A Tragic Passage Through War

On **January 2, 1993**, the serene waters of the **Jaffna Lagoon**—also known as the **Kilaly Lagoon**—became the site of a brutal massacre. **Sri Lankan Navy personnel** attacked a convoy of boats carrying **Tamil civilians**, killing between **35 and 100 people***. This massacre, one of the most harrowing episodes of Sri Lanka's civil war, exposed the vulnerability of civilians caught between warring factions and the devastating consequences of militarized zones.

Some sources cite 14 to 35 depending on the report and date.

Historical Background

The **Sri Lankan Civil War** began in **1983**, following the **Black July pogrom**, and lasted until 2009.

The **Jaffna Peninsula**, a stronghold of the **Liberation Tigers of Tamil Eelam (LTTE)**, was largely cut off from the rest of the country.

The **Elephant Pass military base** blocked land access, forcing civilians to use boats to cross the lagoon for medical care, family visits, or escape.

The LTTE also restricted land travel, making the lagoon the only viable route for many civilians.

Events Leading to the Massacre

Prior to January 2, **15 civilians** had already been killed while attempting to cross the lagoon, causing boat operators to halt services.

This left **800 people stranded** on both sides of the lagoon without food or shelter.

On January 2, boat operators resumed travel, and civilians began crossing in **small batches of 15–20 per boat**.

The Attack: January 2, 1993

A **Sri Lankan Navy gunboat**, equipped with a cannon, was patrolling the lagoon.

A **speedboat**, commonly used by the LTTE but unarmed, attempted to flee upon spotting the Navy vessel.

The Navy opened fire on **passenger boats**, mistaking them for rebel transports, and continued firing for **up to 30 minutes**.

Note: Speedboat Incident: A speedboat commonly used by LTTE was seen fleeing, which may have triggered the Navy's attack. However, no return fire was reported, and the speedboat was unarmed.

Survivors reported:

Gunfire and stabbing of passengers, including women and children.
Looting of valuables from the dead.
Bodies dumped into boats and set on fire.

Casualties and Recovery

35 bodies were recovered, many **mutilated or burned beyond recognition**.

Only **18 victims were identified**; the rest were buried without names.

Five injured survivors were treated at **Kilinochchi District Hospital**, with one later dying from injuries.

Hospital Treatment: Five injured survivors were treated at Kilinochchi Hospital, with one later dying—this is confirmed in Red Cross documentation.

Eyewitnesses described Navy personnel towing boats with corpses and setting them ablaze.

Political and Military Context

The government claimed the boats were transporting **LTTE cadres**, though no weapons were found.

The massacre occurred in a **Militarized "No-Go" zone**, where civilians were often treated as combatants.

The incident deepened **Tamil distrust** of the state and intensified calls for **international accountability**.

The **Jaffna Lagoon Massacre** was a chilling reminder of the human cost of civil war. Civilians, caught between military suspicion and rebel control, paid the ultimate price for simply trying to survive. The massacre not only highlighted the brutality of the conflict but also underscored the need for **humanitarian protections** in war zones. Decades later, the tragedy remains etched in the memory of Sri Lanka's Tamil community and continues to fuel demands for **justice and reconciliation**.

Key Sources

1. **Wikipedia** – Jaffna Lagoon Massacre

This entry details the January 2, 1993, massacre, when Sri Lankan Navy patrol boats attacked a flotilla of civilian boats crossing the Kilaly (Jaffna) Lagoon. The boats were transporting Tamil civilians between the north and south shores due to land routes being blocked by both the Elephant Pass military base and LTTE restrictions. Estimates of the death toll range from 35 to 100, though only 14 bodies were recovered, with reports suggesting others were burned along with their boats.

2. **UTHR (J) – Report 10, Chapter 0:** "Massacre in the Jaffna Lagoon"

This human rights report offers a detailed reconstruction of the events, including press coverage, eyewitness accounts, and government responses. It notes that 16 boats, each carrying about 20 passengers, were attacked, and that only six boats reached the mainland. Survivors described tracer rounds flying past, panic, and screams as the Navy opened fire. The report critiques the military's blanket assumption that all lagoon traffic was LTTE-related, leading to indiscriminate violence.

3. **DayHist – "The Jaffna Lagoon Tragedy**: A Dark Chapter in Sri Lankan Civil War History"
This article situates the massacre within the broader ethnic and military tensions of the civil war. It recounts how fishermen and families were caught in the crossfire of a naval operation targeting suspected LTTE movements, and how the lack of accountability and conflicting narratives deepened the trauma. Eyewitnesses described sudden gunfire and chaos, with civilians unaware they were entering a militarized no-go zone.

Chapter 42: The Assassination of Lalith Athulathmudali: A Political Tragedy in Sri Lanka (1993)

*It was more than just the loss of a respected statesman—it felt personal. The assassination of **Lalith Athulathmudali** sent shockwaves through the nation, but for me, it struck terrifyingly close to home. He was gunned down at a rally just steps from my residence in Colombo, on grounds that have since become a living monument: **Lalith Athulathmudali Playground**. To many, he was a brilliant orator, a reformist, and a contender for the highest office. To me, he was a rare example of political integrity. As **Minister of Education**, his insistence on transparent, area-based school admissions not only cleaned up a notoriously corrupt system— it quietly ensured that my daughter could walk through the gates of a leading Colombo school without bribes or backdoor influence. His vision touched lives in ways grand and intimate. That's why the news of his murder didn't just sadden me—it shook something deep within.*

Lalith Athulathmudali was one of Sri Lanka's most distinguished politicians, known for his intellect, eloquence, and reformist vision. Educated at **Oxford and Harvard**, he served as a Cabinet Minister in multiple portfolios including **Trade, National Security, and Education**. He was instrumental in launching the **Mahapola Scholarship Fund**, which benefited thousands of University students across the country.

His political career, however, was marred by increasing tensions within the ruling **United National Party (UNP)**. After being sidelined by President **Ranasinghe Premadasa**, Athulathmudali attempted to impeach him in 1991, citing abuses of power. The motion failed, and Athulathmudali was expelled from the UNP. He then formed the **Democratic United National Front (DUNF)** and emerged as a formidable opposition figure.

(Place of the assassination – Pic: sundaytimes.lk)

On the night of **April 23, 1993**, while addressing a political rally in **Kirulapana**, Colombo, Athulathmudali was fatally shot. His bodyguard was also injured in the attack. The assassination occurred just weeks before the **Western Provincial Council elections**, where Athulathmudali was contesting for Chief Minister.

The murder sent shockwaves through the nation, not only because of the loss of a prominent leader but also due to the murky circumstances surrounding the killing.

Initial investigations by the **Sri Lankan Police** and **Scotland Yard** concluded that the assassin was a Tamil youth named **Appiah Balakrishnan**, alias **Ragunathan**, allegedly affiliated with the **Liberation Tigers of Tamil Eelam (LTTE)**. His body was found near the scene the following day, and authorities claimed he had died from cyanide poisoning—a method often associated with LTTE operatives.

However, this narrative was met with widespread skepticism:

The **identity card** found on the body was later revealed to be fake.

Witnesses who identified the body were allegedly linked to Government officials.

The body was discovered hours after the area had been searched, raising suspicions of a staged scene.

In 1995, President **Chandrika Kumaratunga** appointed a **Presidential Commission of Inquiry**. Its 1997 report controversially implicated **former President Premadasa** and members of the security forces close to him as being behind the assassination. Several underworld figures and security personnel were arrested, though three of the accused died during prosecution, further clouding the case.

Political Intrigue and Legacy

The assassination remains one of the most **controversial political murders** in Sri Lankan history. It occurred in a climate of intense political rivalry, ethnic insurgency, and internal party strife. The fact that **President Premadasa himself was assassinated just a week later** only deepened the mystery and speculation surrounding both deaths.

Despite multiple investigations, **no conclusive verdict** has ever been reached. The case is emblematic of the **opaque and volatile nature of Sri Lankan politics** during the civil war era.

Lalith Athulathmudali's death robbed Sri Lanka of a visionary leader. His assassination is a chilling reminder of how **political ambition, factionalism, and violence** can derail democratic progress. It also underscores the need for **transparent justice systems** and **institutional accountability** in post-conflict societies.

(With his family – Pic: sundaytimes.lk)

Key Sources

1. **Wikipedia** – Assassination of Lalith Athulathmudali. This entry outlines the events of April 23, 1993, when Lalith Athulathmudali was fatally shot while addressing a public gathering in Kirulapana, just weeks before the Western Provincial Council elections. Initial investigations blamed the LTTE, but a Presidential Commission appointed in 1995 later implicated former President Ranasinghe Premadasa and members of the security forces, suggesting a politically motivated killing.

2. **Sunday Times** – "Lalith Athulathmudali Assassination, 30 Years On: Murder Mystery Revisited". This retrospective article delves into Athulathmudali's academic brilliance, his rise through the UNP, and his eventual fallout with Premadasa. It recounts the failed impeachment attempt, the formation of the Democratic United National Front (DUNF), and the toxic political climate that preceded his assassination. The piece emphasizes that the case remains unsolved and controversial, with multiple conflicting narratives.

3. **Sri Lanka Guardian** – "Lalith Athulathmudali: A Tragic Martyr to Sri Lanka's Unfinished Revolution" This tribute frames Athulathmudali as a visionary reformer whose death marked the loss of a leader capable of reshaping Sri Lanka's trajectory. It reflects on his intellectual legacy, including the founding of the Mahapola Scholarship Fund, and portrays his assassination as a symbolic extinguishment of democratic promise amid rising authoritarianism and civil strife.

Chapter 43: The Assassination of President Premadasa: Planning, Execution, and Fallout (1993)

May Day 1993

(Pic: sangam.org)

On **May 1, 1993**, Sri Lanka's third president, **Ranasinghe Premadasa**, was assassinated in a **suicide bombing** during a May Day rally in Colombo. The attack, carried out by the **Liberation Tigers of Tamil Eelam (LTTE)**, was not only a tactical strike but a symbolic blow to the Sri Lankan state. The planning behind the assassination revealed a chilling level of infiltration and manipulation, culminating in one of the most devastating political killings in South Asia.

Premadasa rose from humble beginnings to become president in **1989**, known for his **populist policies** and **housing initiatives**.

His tenure was marked by dual conflicts: a **Southern Marxist Insurrection** and the **Northern Tamil Separatist War**.

In a controversial move, Premadasa **armed the LTTE** in 1989 to fight the **Indian Peace Keeping Force (IPKF)**, inadvertently strengthening the group that would later kill him.

His relationship with the LTTE soured after the IPKF withdrawal, leading to renewed hostilities and **Eelam War II**.

The suicide bomber was **Kulaveerasingam "Babu" Veerakumar**, a Tamil youth from Jaffna who had **infiltrated the president's inner circle**.

Babu befriended **E.M.P. Mohideen**, Premadasa's trusted valet, and gained access to **Presidential Security Division (PSD)** members by **catering to their vices**—alcohol, women, and gifts.

He rented a shop near Premadasa's residence and reportedly owned **three lorries** used to transport goods to LTTE-controlled areas, possibly smuggling explosives.

Babu had **traveled with Premadasa's Advance Security Team** on multiple outstation trips, highlighting a **massive security breach**.

Location: Armour Street–Grandpass Junction, Colombo

Time: Around **12:45 PM**, during a UNP May Day rally

Method: Babu approached Premadasa's vehicle with **0.91 kg of plastic explosives** strapped to his body.

Execution:

Security guards attempted to stop Babu.

Mohideen signaled them to let him pass.

Babu detonated the bomb, killing **Premadasa, Mohideen, SSP Ronnie Gunasinghe**, and **20 others**.

The **blast site was cleaned within hours**, allegedly on orders from top officials, preventing a proper forensic investigation.

40 suspects were arrested but later released due to lack of evidence.

The LTTE denied involvement, but forensic and intelligence reports strongly implicated them.

The assassination was followed by an **Island-wide curfew**, and **Prime Minister D.B. Wijetunga** was sworn in as acting president on **May 7, 1993**.

The killing exposed **deep flaws in presidential security** and **internal corruption**.

It marked a **turning point in the civil war**, intensifying military operations against the LTTE.

Premadasa's death also **destabilized the UNP**, leading to a shift in political leadership and strategy.

The assassination of President Premadasa was not just a tactical victory for the LTTE, it was a **symbolic rupture** in Sri Lanka's political fabric. The meticulous planning, insider access, and execution underscored the **LTTE's operational sophistication** and the **state's vulnerability**.

Key Sources

1. **Wikipedia – Assassination of Ranasinghe Premadasa.** This entry outlines the events of **May 1, 1993**, when **President Ranasinghe Premadasa** was killed by an **LTTE suicide bomber** during a **May Day rally** in Colombo. The attacker, **Kulaveerasingam "Babu" Veerakumar**, detonated explosives near Premadasa's vehicle, killing **23 people**, including **Premadasa, his valet E.M.P. Mohideen**, and **SSP Ronnie Gunasinghe**. The site was controversially cleaned within hours, raising concerns about evidence tampering.

2. **UPI Archives – "Sri Lankan President Killed in Bomb Attack"** This contemporary report describes the **chaotic aftermath**, with **body parts strewn across the street**, and conflicting accounts of the bomber's approach—some say he rode a **bicycle**, others a **motorcycle**. The **LTTE was suspected**, though they initially denied involvement.

3. **Colombo Telegraph – "The Premadasa Assassination" by Rajan Hoole** This investigative piece explores the **security lapses**, including how Babu gained access

through **Mohideen's signal to guards**, and how he had **befriended Premadasa's staff** by catering to their vices. It also critiques the **rapid cleanup of the blast site**, which violated standard forensic protocols, and discusses the **political fallout**, including the swift swearing-in of **Prime Minister D.B. Wijetunga** as acting president.

Chapter 44: The Assassination of Gamini Dissanayake (1994)

The assassination of **Gamini Dissanayake** on **October 24, 1994**, was one of the most devastating moments in Sri Lanka's political history. A towering figure in national development and a **leading Presidential Candidate** at the time, Dissanayake was seen as a potential unifier during a period of deep unrest.

Dissanayake began his political career in 1970 with the **United National Party (UNP)**.

He was instrumental in major infrastructure projects, most notably the **Mahaweli Development Project**, which transformed Sri Lanka's irrigation and hydroelectric landscape.

He held several ministerial portfolios and was deeply involved in land reform, agriculture, and national development.

In 1994, he was the UNP's nominee for the Presidential Election and a frontrunner in the race.

The Assassination

On the night of **October 24**, during a campaign rally in **Thotalanga, Colombo**, a **female suicide bomber**—suspected to be from the **Liberation Tigers of Tamil Eelam (LTTE)**—detonated explosives, killing **52 people**, including Dissanayake and several other senior UNP members.

Over **200 others were injured**, with **75 critically wounded**.

The attack occurred just **two and a half weeks before the election**, throwing the UNP into turmoil.

His wife, **Srima Dissanayake**, was nominated in his place but lost the election to **Chandrika Kumaratunga**.

Alongside **Gamini Dissanayake**, several prominent figures of the **United National Party (UNP)** lost their lives in the tragic suicide bombing on **October 24, 1994**. The attack claimed **52 lives** in total and injured over **200 people**, many critically.

Here are some of the key individuals who were killed:

Name	Position / Role
Dr. Gamini Wijesekera	Member of Parliament
G. M. Premachandra	Member of Parliament
Weerasinghe Mallimarachchi	Member of Parliament
Ossie Abeygunasekera	Senior UNP politician and activist
Christie Perera	UNP supporter and associate

These leaders were part of Dissanayake's inner circle and were attending the same campaign rally in **Thotalanga, Colombo**, when the **LTTE**-linked suicide bomber struck. Their deaths dealt a severe blow to the UNP and to Sri Lanka's hopes for a more peaceful and progressive future.

Key Sources

1. **Wikipedia – Assassination of Gamini Dissanayake**
   This entry provides a comprehensive account of the **October 24, 1994 suicide bombing** that killed **Gamini Dissanayake**, then **Leader of the Opposition** and **UNP presidential candidate**. The attack occurred during a **late-night campaign rally in Thotalanga, Colombo**, killing **52 people** and injuring over **200**, including several senior UNP figures. The **LTTE** was widely suspected of orchestrating the bombing.

2. **TIME Magazine – "Scores Killed in Sri Lankan Blast"** This article contextualizes the assassination within the LTTE's broader campaign of urban terror. It notes that the bomber was a **female operative**, and that the explosion was one of the **deadliest political attacks** in Sri Lanka's history. The blast disrupted peace talks and plunged the UNP into crisis just **two weeks before the election**, forcing the party to nominate **Srima Dissanayake**, Gamini's widow, who ultimately lost to **Chandrika Kumaratunga**.

3. **Borealis Threat & Risk – "October 24, 1994: Female Suicide Bomber Kills Politician in Sri Lanka"** This retrospective analysis highlights the **symbolic nature of the attack**, targeting a candidate who had advocated for **peace negotiations** with the LTTE. It also notes the **gruesome aftermath**, including the discovery of the bomber's head on a nearby rooftop—a grim detail often associated with suicide bombings.

Chapter 45: The 1996 Sri Lanka Central Bank Bombing: A Turning Point in the Civil Conflict

(Pic: cbsl.gov.lk)

On January 31, 1996, the heart of Sri Lanka's financial system was shattered by one of the deadliest terrorist attacks in the country's history. The bombing of the **Central Bank** in Colombo, orchestrated by the Liberation Tigers of Tamil Eelam (LTTE), marked a grim escalation in the Sri Lankan civil war. This essay explores the background, execution, impact, and aftermath of the attack, which left a lasting scar on the nation's psyche and economy.

The LTTE, a separatist militant group, had been engaged in a brutal conflict with the Sri Lankan government since the early 1980s. Their goal was to establish an independent Tamil state in the north and east of the island. By the mid-1990s, the LTTE had developed a reputation for highly coordinated and devastating attacks. Targeting the Central Bank was a strategic move intended to cripple the country's economy and send a message of defiance to both the government and international observers.

On the morning of January 31, a lorry packed with approximately **440 pounds of high explosives** rammed through the gates of the Central Bank building in Colombo's financial district. Accompanying the vehicle were LTTE operatives armed with automatic rifles and an RPG launcher. As gunmen exchanged fire with security personnel, a suicide bomber detonated the explosives, unleashing a massive blast that tore through the bank and damaged eight surrounding buildings.

The explosion killed **at least 91 people** and injured over **1,400 others**, including foreign nationals from the **U.S., Japan, and the Netherlands**. The blast was so powerful that it caused widespread destruction across the Fort area of Colombo, shattering windows and collapsing structures. Among the wounded, over **100 people lost their eyesight**, and many others suffered life-altering injuries.

Chaos reigned in the minutes following the explosion. Rescue efforts were hampered by debris and blocked exits, forcing survivors to improvise—some were lowered from windows using curtains as makeshift stretchers. The Governor of the Central Bank at the time, A.S. Jayawardane, later recounted the heroic efforts of staff who helped evacuate and treat the wounded before external aid arrived.

The attack triggered a massive manhunt. Two LTTE operatives were apprehended with help from civilians, and eleven members were eventually indicted on **712 counts**, including murder and destruction of state property.

The bombing had profound consequences:

Economic Disruption: The Central Bank, as the financial nucleus of Sri Lanka, was severely affected. The attack disrupted monetary operations, international payments, and investor confidence.

Tourism Collapse: Tourism dropped by **40%**, dealing a blow to one of the country's key industries.

Psychological Trauma: The scale and brutality of the attack instilled fear and anxiety among civilians, deepening the divide between ethnic communities and intensifying the conflict.

Global condemnation was swift. The United Nations and foreign governments expressed solidarity with Sri Lanka, denouncing the LTTE's tactics. The attack underscored the urgent need for counter-terrorism measures and humanitarian support.

The 1996 Central Bank bombing was not just an act of terror—it was a calculated strike against the economic and psychological stability of Sri Lanka. It highlighted the LTTE's capacity for destruction and the vulnerability of civilian infrastructure during wartime. While the country has since made strides toward peace, the memory of that day remains a stark reminder of the cost of conflict and the resilience of a nation determined to rebuild.

Timeline of Major Attacks in Colombo

Date	Attack/Event	Perpetrator	Casualties & Impact
Jan 31, 1996	**Central Bank Bombing**	LTTE (Tamil Tigers)	Suicide truck bomb killed **91**, injured **1,400+**. Eight buildings damaged.
Jul 24, 1996	**Dehiwala Train Bombing**	LTTE	Bombs in four separate carriages of a packed commuter train during rush hour. Casualties: 64 civilians

			killed, Over 400 injured, many with life-altering wounds. Note: *The Colombo–Kandy train bombing in July 1996 is often conflated with the Dehiwala bombing. No separate verified incident with 70+ deaths on that line in July 1996 was found.*
Jul 1996	**Train Bombing (Colombo–Kandy line)**	LTTE	Over **70 killed**. Attack caused tourism to drop by **40%**.
Oct 15, 1997	**World Trade Centre Bombing**	LTTE	Twin towers damaged. No fatalities reported, but significant economic disruption. Note: he World Trade Centre bombing did not result in fatalities within the Towers themselves, but 15 people died in the surrounding area, including hotel staff and civilians.
Mar 2, 2008	**Fort Railway Station Bombing**	LTTE	Suicide bombing killed **12**, including schoolchildren.

Key Sources

1. **Wikipedia – Colombo Central Bank Bombing**
This entry outlines the **January 31, 1996 suicide bombing** carried out by the **Liberation Tigers of Tamil Eelam (LTTE)**. A **lorry packed with 440 pounds of explosives** crashed into the Central Bank building in Colombo's financial district, followed by gunfire from LTTE cadres. The blast killed **91 people**, injured **over 1,400**, and damaged **eight nearby buildings**, including the Intercontinental Hotel and World Trade Center.

2. **BBC On This Day – "1996: Fifty Dead in Sri Lanka Suicide Bombing"**
This report describes the **chaotic aftermath**, including the collapse of the bank's lower floors, shattered windows across the district, and **helicopter rescues** for trapped office workers. The attack was believed to be retaliation for the **Sri Lankan Army's capture of Jaffna**, the LTTE's northern stronghold, just weeks earlier.

3. **Central Bank of Sri Lanka – "Rising from the Ashes" (60th Anniversary Publication)**

This internal publication recounts the **institutional trauma and recovery** following the bombing. It highlights how staff risked their lives to rescue colleagues, how operations were restored, and how the attack galvanized efforts to **strengthen financial infrastructure** and **emergency preparedness**.

Chapter 46: The Dehiwala Train Bombing: Another Turning Point in Sri Lanka's Civil Conflict (1996)

The Dehiwala train bombing of July 24, 1996 stands as one of the most devastating attacks on civilian infrastructure during Sri Lanka's decades-long civil war. Orchestrated by the Liberation Tigers of Tamil Eelam (LTTE), the bombing was a brutal demonstration of tactical evolution and ideological radicalization that shocked the nation and drew global condemnation. Beyond its tragic loss of life, the event reshaped public perception of the LTTE and highlighted the vulnerability of urban centers amid an escalating insurgency.

The bombing occurred during evening rush hour at Colombo's Dehiwala railway station. LTTE operatives planted **four synchronized suitcase bombs** in separate carriages of a packed commuter train, detonating them nearly simultaneously. The result was catastrophic:

- **64 people killed instantly**, with the number rising in subsequent days
- **Over 400 others injured**, many suffering debilitating and lifelong wounds

This attack marked a departure from earlier LTTE operations, which had focused more on military and political targets. By hitting public transport, the LTTE not only maximized human casualties but disrupted the daily life of Colombo, sending a message of power and reach.

The Dehiwala bombing followed several high-profile attacks earlier in the year, notably the **January 1996 Central Bank bombing**, which killed 91 and injured over 1,400. Together, these incidents reflected a deliberate campaign aimed at destabilizing the government, undermining morale, and provoking overreach from the Sri Lankan military. It was also a dark milestone in the LTTE's tactical playbook—favoring calculated terror over guerrilla warfare.

Cultural Losses: The Death of Sudeepa Purnajith

Among the victims was **Sudeepa Purnajith**, a renowned cartoonist and stamp designer. His death resonated deeply with Sri Lanka's creative and journalistic community. Known for his satire and public engagement, Purnajith's passing underscored the indiscriminate nature of such attacks—not just wiping out lives but stripping society of its cultural voices.

The international community responded with swift condemnation. Statements from the **United States**, **European Union**, and **India** denounced the LTTE's tactics and called for renewed focus on peace negotiations. The bombing drew attention to the group's designation as a **terrorist organization** by several nations and led to increased scrutiny of overseas Tamil networks alleged to be fundraising for the LTTE.

The psychological aftermath of the Dehiwala bombing was profound:

Heightened **anxiety among Colombo's residents**, especially commuters

Strengthened **surveillance and security protocols** at transport hubs

Intensified **military crackdowns** on suspected LTTE cells in urban areas

From a policy standpoint, it deepened the divide between the government and Tamil separatist groups, hardening positions on both sides and diminishing hopes for diplomatic resolution.

Though the civil war ended in 2009 with the defeat of the LTTE, incidents like Dehiwala remain embedded in Sri Lanka's collective memory. They remind future generations of the cost of ethnic division, political extremism, and the dire consequences of abandoning dialogue.

More than an act of terrorism, the Dehiwala train bombing stands as a cautionary tale: how terror can echo far beyond its immediate destruction—rippling through culture, governance, and the soul of a nation.

Key Sources

1. **Wikipedia – 1996 Dehiwala Train Bombing**
   This entry details the **July 24, 1996 bombing**, in which **LTTE operatives planted suitcase bombs** in four carriages of a packed commuter train during **rush hour**. The coordinated explosions killed **64 civilians** and injured **over 400**, making it one of the deadliest attacks on public transport in Sri Lanka's history.

2. **AP Archive – News Footage of the Bombing Aftermath**
   This video captures the **immediate aftermath**, showing emergency responders and the wreckage at **Dehiwala railway station**. It confirms that nearly **70 people were killed** and highlights the **shock and panic** that gripped Colombo following the attack.

Chapter 47: The Krishanthy Kumaraswamy Case – Army Brutality and the Unveiling of Chemmani (1996)

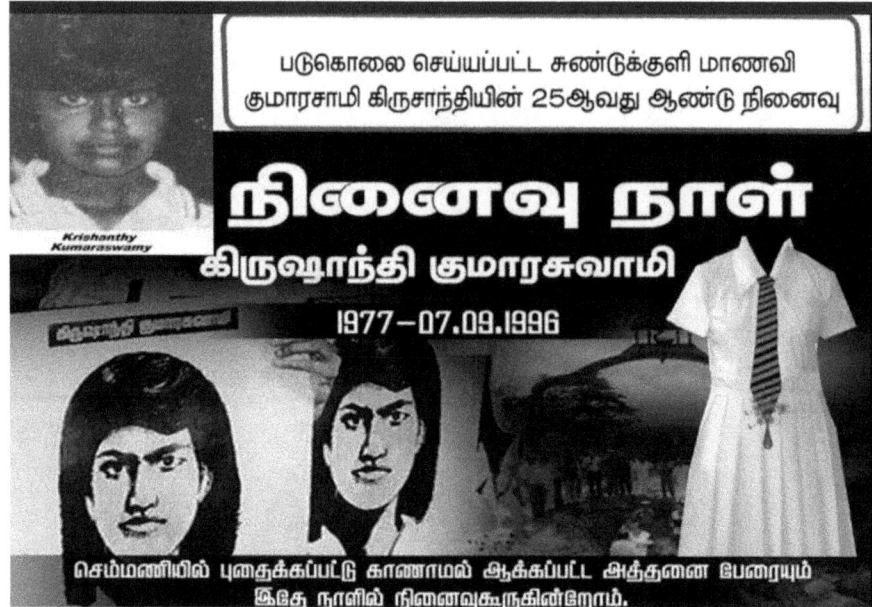

The brutal rape and murder of **Krishanthy Kumaraswamy**, an 18-year-old Tamil schoolgirl from Jaffna, Sri Lanka, in **September 1996**, stands as one of the most harrowing examples of military violence against civilians during the Sri Lankan civil war. Her case not only exposed the systemic abuse of power by the Sri Lankan Army but also led to the discovery of the **Chemmani Mass Graves**, revealing a broader pattern of extrajudicial killings and disappearances. This chapter explores the crime, the investigation, the trial, and its enduring legacy in Sri Lanka's human rights discourse.

Krishanthy was a **top-performing student** at **Chundikuli Girls' College in Jaffna**, preparing for her **G.C.E. Advanced Level Chemistry exam**. On **September 7, 1996**, she cycled home after her exam, passing through the **Kaithady Army Checkpoint**, a route she had taken daily. She never arrived home.

Her mother **Rasammah**, brother **Pranavan (16)**, and neighbor **Kirupakaran (35)** went searching for her. All four were **abducted, tortured, and murdered** by Sri Lankan Army personnel.

The Crime: Rape, Murder, and Cover-Up

Krishanthy was **gang-raped by at least six soldiers**, strangled, and buried in a shallow grave.

Her mother, brother, and neighbor were also strangled and buried after confronting the soldiers at the checkpoint.

The bodies were discovered **45 days later** in **Chemmani**, a marshy area near the checkpoint.

The soldiers attempted to cover up the crime, but public outrage and pressure from human rights groups forced the government to act.

The Trial: A Rare Conviction

A **Trial-at-Bar** was convened in **Colombo** in late 1996, far from the crime scene. Nine defendants were indicted, including:

Lance Corporal Somaratne Rajapaksa – the lead perpetrator
Five other soldiers directly involved in the rape and murders
Three policemen who helped dispose of the bodies

Key Developments

Two policemen turned **State Witnesses**, providing crucial testimony.

Forensic evidence and confessions confirmed the sequence of events.

In **July 1998, six soldiers were sentenced to death**. One died during trial; one was acquitted.

This was the **first successful prosecution of Military personnel for wartime rape and murder** in Sri Lanka.

Chemmani Mass Graves: A Darker Revelation

During sentencing, Rajapaksa made a chilling statement:

"We did not kill anyone—we only buried bodies. There are hundreds more buried in Chemmani."

This led to an investigation that uncovered **15 bodies**, many **blindfolded and bound**, confirming **mass executions**. Rajapaksa claimed **300–400 bodies** were buried in the area, sparking international concern.

Political and Legal Impact

The case forced the Sri Lankan government to acknowledge military abuses, albeit reluctantly.

President Chandrika Kumaratunga ordered the investigation after pressure from activists and lawyers.

The **Attorney General's Department**, led by **Prashanthi Mahindaratne**, pursued the case with rare vigor.

Yet, despite the convictions, no senior military officials were held accountable, and Chemmani's full truth remains buried.

Voices from the Case

"When Krishanthi had been raped by about five men… she said, 'Please give me a moment. Let me have some water."

— *Prashanthi Mahindaratne, State Counsel*

"We trusted you and we came."

— *Krishanthi's final words to the soldiers, as recalled in court testimony*

Krishanthy's case became a symbol of Tamil suffering, **a face for thousands of** unrecorded disappearances and rapes. Her story is remembered annually in Jaffna and Chemmani, and has inspired books, documentaries, and human rights campaigns.

The Krishanthy Kumaraswamy case is not just a tale of personal tragedy—it is a landmark in Sri Lanka's struggle for justice. It exposed the brutality of military occupation, **the** vulnerability of civilians, and the fragility of accountability. Though justice was partially served, the deeper wounds of Chemmani and the countless unnamed victims remain open.

Closing Reflection: Wartime Sexual Violence and the Human Cost

The case of Krishanthy Kumaraswamy is not an isolated aberration—it is a microcosm of a deeper, systemic pattern of **wartime sexual violence** that plagued Sri Lanka during its protracted civil conflict. In the fog of war, women and girls—particularly from marginalized Tamil communities—were subjected to horrific abuse by combatants who operated with near-total impunity. These violations were not merely individual crimes; they were acts that sought to **humiliate, silence, and terrorize** entire populations. While judicial victories like Krishanthy's offer a sliver of justice, they remain rare amid thousands of untold stories. The legacy of such violence demands ongoing remembrance, acknowledgment, and redress—not just for the victims, but for the conscience of a nation still reckoning with the ghosts of its past.

At the time of writing this chapter, there have been major new developments in the Krishanthy Kumaraswamy case and the Chemmani mass graves investigation as of 2025, reigniting public and international attention on one of Sri Lanka's most haunting war crimes:

Renewed Excavations at Chemmani (2025)

• In June 2025, court-ordered excavations resumed at the Chemmani burial site near Jaffna, more than two decades after the initial dig in 1999 uncovered 15 bodies.

• These new excavations were prompted by accidental discoveries during cemetery construction work in February 2025, where human skeletal remains were found just half a foot below the surface.

• The site is adjacent to the Siththuppaththi Hindu burial ground, and the remains were uncovered in foundation pits dug for a cremation platform.

Public Pressure and Legal Action

• The Jaffna Magistrate's Court ordered the renewed investigation following complaints and mounting pressure from Tamil civil society groups.

• However, by April 2025, the excavation was halted due to lack of government funding, raising concerns that authorities were once again delaying justice through bureaucratic obstruction.

• Despite this, the discovery has reignited calls for international oversight, with human rights organizations demanding a full forensic investigation and accountability for wartime disappearances.

The 2025 excavations are seen as a continuation of that testimony, a reckoning long overdue.

Key Sources

1. **Wikipedia – Chemmani Mass Graves**
This entry traces the origins of the **Chemmani mass graves**, which came to light following the **rape and murder of 18-year-old Tamil schoolgirl Krishanthy Kumaraswamy** on **September 7, 1996**, by Sri Lankan Army personnel. During the trial, **Lance Corporal Somaratne Rajapakse** revealed under oath that **300–400 civilians** had been executed and buried in Chemmani after the military recaptured Jaffna in 1995–1996. Subsequent excavations in 1999 uncovered **15 bodies**, two of which were identified as victims who had disappeared in 1996.

2. **Tamil Guardian – Explainer: Krishanthy Kumaraswamy and the Chemmani Mass Graves**
This article offers a powerful narrative of Krishanthy's final day: cycling to school for her chemistry exam, passing through the **Kaithady Army checkpoint**, and never returning. When her mother, brother, and a neighbor went searching for her, they too were abducted and murdered. The case sparked **public protests in Jaffna**, leading to the rare arrest and conviction of **seven security personnel**, and ultimately exposed a **network of mass graves** that symbolized the broader pattern of **state violence against Tamil civilians**.

3. **Groundviews – "The Story of Chemmani and the Graves That Refuse to Stay Buried"** This reflective piece recounts how **international pressure** led to **court-monitored excavations** in 1999, revealing bodies bound, blindfolded, and showing signs of torture. It also documents the **long-stalled investigation**, the **lack of accountability**, and the **renewed excavations in 2025**, which uncovered **19 more skeletons**, including those of **three infants**, reigniting calls for **international oversight** and justice.

Chapter 48: Chinthaka Amarasinghe: A Ruthless Underworld Figure Silenced in 1996

(Pic from You Tube)

Chinthaka Amarasinghe was a notorious Sri Lankan gangster whose name became synonymous with violence, political intrigue, and underworld dominance during the early 1990s. His criminal career was marked by high-profile assassinations, turf wars, and alleged political backing that allowed him to operate with near impunity.

- Chinthaka was considered the **archrival of Soththi Upali**, another infamous mobster with deep political connections.
- He was involved in the **murders of Malu Nihal and Cheena**, two of Upali's top henchmen, in Gothamipura in 1993.
- His family had a long history of criminal activity — his uncle, **Noel Amarasinghe**, was the chief suspect in the 1976 Kollupitiya Tavern robbery.

- Chinthaka was reportedly supported by politicians affiliated with the **People's Alliance**, which may have shielded him from prosecution.
- His ability to evade justice despite multiple allegations highlighted the deep entanglement between crime and politics in Sri Lanka at the time.
- Chinthaka was reportedly released on bail after making a statement implicating Soththi Upali in the Lalith Athulathmudali assassination, which added political intrigue to his criminal profile
- Chinthaka's criminal career was short but explosive. His actions destabilized the fragile alliances within the underworld and exposed the dangerous nexus between crime and politics. His death in 1996 didn't end the violence — it merely shifted the balance of power, leading to further bloodshed and the eventual downfall of many key players.

In **1996**, Chinthaka was **killed in Thotalanga** by a rival gang led by **Ajith Dhammika**, better known as **Kalu Ajith**.

The murder was seen as a strategic move by Kalu Ajith to eliminate his former ally and seize control of the criminal empire.

Chinthaka's death sent shockwaves through Colombo's underworld, triggering a new wave of violence and retribution.

Chinthaka Amarasinghe's life and death remain emblematic of a turbulent era in Sri Lanka's history, where gangsters operated in the shadows of political power and justice was often a matter of influence rather than law.

Timeline of Chinthaka Amarasinghe's Criminal Career and Rivalry with Soththi Upali

Chinthaka Amarasinghe's life was a turbulent saga of vengeance, power, and betrayal. His criminal trajectory was deeply intertwined with the rise of Sri Lanka's underworld and his bitter rivalry with Soththi Upali — a feud that shaped Colombo's gangland politics in the 1990s.

Year	Event
1976	Chinthaka's uncle, **Noel Amarasinghe**, is implicated in the Kollupitiya Tavern robbery — marking the family's early ties to crime.
1980s	Chinthaka enters the **underworld**, influenced by family legacy and the murder of his father by **Soththi Upali's gang**.
1993	Chinthaka guns down **Malu Nihal and Cheena** — two of Upali's top henchmen — in Gothamipura, avenging his father's death.
1994	Survives an assassination attempt at the **Negombo Magistrate's Court**, saved by a retired prison commissioner. The Negombo Court assassination attempt was orchestrated by Chaminda from Kaduwela, allegedly under orders from Soththi Upali, but it failed due to swift action by prison guards.
1996	**Murdered in Thotalanga** by a gang led by **Kalu Ajith**, his former ally turned rival.
1997	Kalu Ajith is killed in a retaliatory strike, allegedly orchestrated by **Nawala Nihal**, another underworld figure.

Personal Vendetta: The feud began when **Upali's gang murdered Chinthaka's father**, dragging him into a cycle of revenge.

Political Shielding: Upali had strong ties to **President Ranasinghe Premadasa's regime**, which gave him impunity and influence.

Territorial Battles: Both men vied for control over lucrative rackets in Colombo, including extortion, drug trafficking, and contract killings.

Symbolic Killings: Chinthaka's assassination of Upali's henchmen was not just revenge — it was a declaration of war.

Key Sources

1. **Wikipedia – List of Sri Lankan Mobsters**
   This entry confirms that **Chinthaka Amarasinghe** was a notorious underworld figure who was **killed in 1996**. His assassination was reportedly carried out by **Ajith Dhammika alias Kalu Ajith**, who himself was later killed by **Nawala Nihal** in 1997. The entry situates Amarasinghe within a violent network of criminal rivalries and political entanglements that defined Colombo's underworld in the 1990s.

2. **Lankasara – "Deadly Justice: A History of Courtroom Killings in Sri Lanka"** This investigative article recounts how **Chinthaka Amarasinghe was targeted during a trial at the Negombo Magistrate's Court**. The assassination attempt failed due to the intervention of **retired Prison Commissioner Chandana Ekanayake**, who shot the attacker. Although Amarasinghe survived that incident, he was later killed, and his brother **Dhammika Amarasinghe** took over his criminal empire—only to be assassinated inside **Aluthkade Magistrate's Court** in 2004.

3. **Ceylon Today – "Courtroom Shootings Reveal Deep Security Failures"** This article provides background on Amarasinghe's criminal origins, noting that he became involved in organized crime by age 21 and was dead by 27. His entry into the underworld was reportedly motivated by a desire to **avenge the murder of his father, uncle, and aunt**, allegedly killed by **Soththi Upali**, another infamous mobster. Amarasinghe's assassination was orchestrated by a hitman named **Chaminda from Kaduwela**, under Upali's directive.

Chapter 49: The Rise and Fall of Ajith Dhammika, aka "Kalu Ajith" — A Life in the Shadows of Power and Crime (1997)

(Pic: Hiru News)

In the murky underworld of Sri Lanka's criminal landscape during the 1980s and 1990s, few names evoked as much fear and fascination as **Ajith Dhammika**, better known as **Kalu Ajith**. His story is one of betrayal, ambition, and the deadly dance between politics and organized crime. From his early days as a loyal henchman to his violent end in 1997, Kalu Ajith's life mirrored the chaos of a nation grappling with insurgency, corruption, and unchecked power.

Kalu Ajith emerged from the streets of Colombo, where gang warfare and political patronage shaped the destinies of many young men. Initially a close associate of **Chinthaka Amarasinghe**, a powerful underworld figure, Ajith was groomed in the art of extortion, contract killings, and drug trafficking. Together, they formed a formidable alliance, united by a common enemy: **Soththi Upali**, another notorious gangster with deep political ties.

But power breeds paranoia. In **1996**, Ajith allegedly orchestrated the **murder of Chinthaka Amarasinghe** in Grandpass, a move that shocked Colombo's criminal circles. The killing was seen as a betrayal of brotherhood and a bold attempt to seize control of Chinthaka's criminal empire.

Political Connections and Legal Maneuvering

Despite being implicated in multiple murders, Ajith's political connections allowed him to evade justice. He was brought before the **Lalith Athulathmudali Commission**, where he testified and identified Chinthaka's voice in a controversial recording. This cooperation, coupled with behind-the-scenes lobbying, led to his **release on bail**, a rare feat given his criminal record.

The Attorney General's consent to grant bail raised eyebrows, suggesting that Ajith was protected by powerful figures. His ability to navigate the legal system, despite overwhelming evidence, highlighted the deep entanglement between crime and politics in Sri Lanka during that era.

Ajith's downfall came swiftly. On **July 16, 1997**, he and two associates were **abducted, murdered, and burned inside their vehicle** near Badowita. The precision of the attack suggested a **well-planned contract killing**, possibly orchestrated by **Donald Nihal Wickramasinghe**, alias **Nawala Nihal**, a rival gangster who had long sought revenge.

Rumors swirled about the motive. Some claimed it was retaliation for Chinthaka's murder. Others pointed to a **land dispute**, or even a **love triangle** involving a woman connected to a military officer. Witnesses reported seeing **uniformed men** conducting a fake security check before the abduction, fueling speculation that **elements within the security forces** may have been involved.

Kalu Ajith's death marked the end of a brutal chapter in Sri Lanka's underworld history. His rise and fall exposed the **fragility of loyalty**, the **corruptibility of justice**, and the **dangerous overlap between politics and crime**. He was neither a martyr nor a hero — but a symbol of a system where power could be bought, and lives could be extinguished without consequence.

Key Sources

1. **Wikipedia – List of Sri Lankan Mobsters**
   This entry confirms that **Ajith Dhammika**, known as **Kalu Ajith**, was active in the **1980s–1997** and was responsible for the **assassination of Chinthaka Amarasinghe** in 1996. He was later **killed by Donald Nihal Wickramasinghe**, alias **Nawala Nihal**, on **July 16, 1997**, near Badowita. His death marked a turning point in Colombo's underworld turf wars.
2. **The Sunday Times – "Hulftsdorp Hill: Killing of Kalu Ajith" (July 27, 1997)**
   This article offers a vivid account of Kalu Ajith's criminal rise and violent end. It reveals that Ajith **betrayed and murdered his mentor**, Chinthaka Amarasinghe, after Amarasinghe made explosive allegations linking **Soththi Upali** to the **assassination of Lalith Athulathmudali**. Ajith was later arrested and remanded, despite multiple pending murder cases, and was mysteriously released on bail before being assassinated.
3. **Hiru News – "CCTV Investigations into Kalu Ajith's Killing"**
   Although focused on a later incident involving a different individual also known as "Kalu Ajith," this report underscores the **recurring violence and impunity** surrounding figures who adopt the name. It reflects the **continued legacy of fear and criminality** associated with Ajith's persona.

Chapter 50: When Silence Was Shattered – The Sri Dalada Maligawa Bombing (1998)

(Pic - left: news.bbc.co.uk)

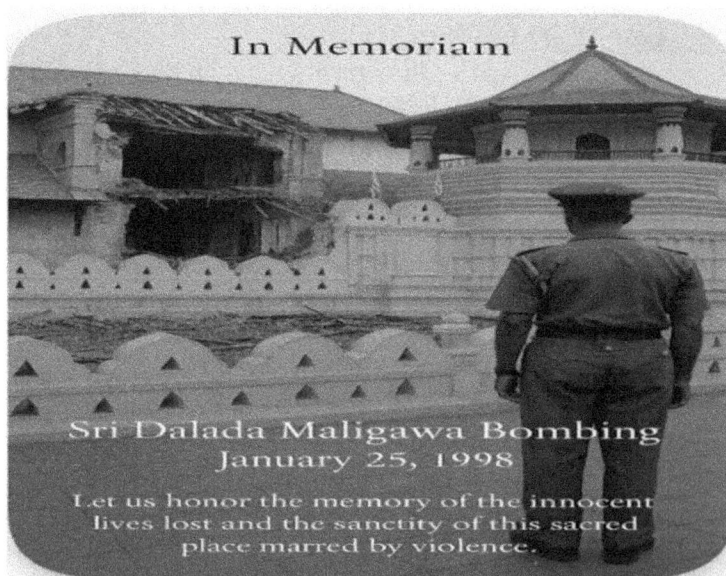

On the morning of **January 25, 1998**, serenity was shattered in the sacred city of Kandy. **The Temple of the Tooth—Sri Dalada Maligawa—**stood as a beacon of peace, heritage, and spiritual reverence. It housed the most sacred relic in Sri Lankan Buddhism: the Tooth of the Buddha. For centuries, it had been a place where pilgrims bowed in quiet devotion, where the air was thick with incense and prayer. But that morning, the silence was torn apart by a thunderous explosion.

A suicide truck bomb, planted by the Liberation Tigers of Tamil Eelam (LTTE), ripped through the Temple complex at 6:10 AM. The blast **killed 17 people**, including a two-year-old child, and **injured over 25 others**. The attackers had chosen not just a symbolic target, but the spiritual heart of a nation. The timing was cruelly calculated—just **days before Sri Lanka's 50th independence anniversary**, when the Temple was to host celebrations attended by dignitaries from around the world.

The explosion did more than destroy walls and relics. It desecrated a sanctuary. The golden roof was torn open, ancient murals were reduced to dust, and the sacred halls echoed not with chants, but with screams. Among the dead were monks, pilgrims, and police officers—ordinary people who had come to worship, to protect, or simply to begin their day.

For Buddhists across the globe, the attack felt like a wound to the soul. The Temple of the Tooth is not merely a building—it is a living symbol of peace, continuity, and the teachings of compassion. To strike it was to strike at the very essence of what it means to be human.

And yet, in the aftermath, something remarkable happened. The people of Kandy did not respond with hatred. They mourned, they rebuilt, and they reaffirmed their commitment to peace. The Temple was restored with painstaking care, and the rituals resumed. The Sacred Tooth Relic remained untouched, as if shielded by the very faith it inspired.

This tragedy reminds us that violence can destroy structures, but it cannot extinguish spirit. The Sri Dalada Maligawa still stands—wounded, yes, but unbroken. It continues to welcome pilgrims, to offer solace, and to whisper the timeless truths of the Buddha.

In remembering the victims, we honor not only their lives but the resilience of a people who chose healing over vengeance. May their memory be a blessing, and may the Temple forever remain a place where silence s peaks louder than bombs.

In the quiet glow of remembrance, we honor those lost in the Sri Dalada Maligawa bombing—not just as victims of violence, but as souls whose memory now lives in the sacred stillness of the temple. Though the blast tore through stone and silence, it could not break the spirit of a people bound by faith, history, and hope. May each candle lit and each lotus placed be a vow: that peace will prevail, and that sacred spaces will forever be sanctuaries of compassion.

Key Sources

- **Wikipedia** – 1998 Temple of the Tooth Attack. This entry details the January 25, 1998 suicide truck bombing carried out by the LTTE against the Sri Dalada Maligawa (Temple of the Tooth) in Kandy, a UNESCO World Heritage Site and the holiest Buddhist shrine in Sri Lanka. The attack killed 17 people, injured 25+, and caused extensive damage to the temple's historic architecture.
- **BBC News** – "Attack on Sri Lanka's Sacred Site". This report emphasizes the symbolic weight of the attack, noting that the temple houses the Sacred Tooth Relic of the Buddha, revered by millions.
- **LankaWeb** – "Dalada Maligawa Attacked on January 25, 1998" This retrospective piece describes the extent of the destruction, including the collapse of parts of the temple roof, damage to priceless murals and artifacts, and the deaths of pilgrims and security personnel.

Chapter 51: Soththi Upali: The Godfather of Colombo's Underworld (1998)

(AI)

In the annals of Sri Lanka's criminal history, few names evoke as much fear and fascination as **Arambawelage Don Ranjith Upali**, better known as **Soththi Upali**. From a Reserve Sub-Inspector to the most feared underworld figure in Colombo, his life was a chilling blend of crime, political patronage, and unchecked power. His rise and fall mirror the darker undercurrents of Sri Lanka's political and social landscape during the 1980s and 1990s.

Early Life: Upali began his career as a **Reserve Sub-Inspector** in the **Sri Lanka Police**, a position that gave him access to law enforcement networks and intelligence.

Underworld Entry: He transitioned into organized crime in the **1970s**, forming his own gang after a violent fallout with **Lenin Amarasinghe**, another notorious gangster. Their rivalry culminated in the **murder of Lenin and several family members in 1986**, cementing Upali's dominance.

Nickname: The moniker "Soththi" (meaning "clean" or "pure" in Sinhala) was ironic, given his brutal reputation. It may have originated from his ability to evade legal consequences and maintain a façade of legitimacy.

Political Patronage and Immunity

> **UNP Connections**: Upali was closely allied with **Sirisena Cooray**, Minister of Housing and Construction under **President Ranasinghe Premadasa**. His ties to the **United National Party (UNP)** gave him near-total immunity from prosecution.

Executive Power: He was reportedly included in the **UNP Executive Body** and addressed as "sir" even by police officers — a testament to his influence.

Political Enforcer: Upali's gang was used to intimidate opponents, suppress dissent, and enforce political agendas. He was allegedly involved in **cutting the mouth of cartoonist**

Yunoos for satirizing the Premadasa regime. *Political enforcer role: Widely alleged, especially during Premadasa's regime, but not formally prosecuted.*

Murder and Extortion: Upali's gang was linked to numerous murders, including the **killing of 16 members of Dhammika Amarasinghe's family**, a rival underworld figure.

Assassination of Lalith Athulathmudali: A **Presidential Commission in 1997** concluded that Upali was **directly involved** in the assassination of the former Cabinet Minister. The trial was never completed.

Torture and Fear: His operations included **extortion, drug trafficking, and political assassinations**. He ruled parts of Colombo like a warlord, with impunity and terror.

Downfall and Death

Rivalry and Retaliation: As political tides shifted in the late 1990s, Upali's protection began to wane. On **December 17, 1998**, he was **assassinated by a rival gang** led by **Kaduwela Raja**, ending his reign.

Unfinished Trial: His death occurred before the conclusion of the trial for Athulathmudali's murder, leaving many questions unanswered.

Symbol of Corruption: Soththi Upali's life is a stark reminder of how **political patronage can empower criminal empires**.

Underworld Blueprint: He set the template for future gangsters — blending crime with politics and operating with impunity.

Timeline of Soththi Upali's Underworld Reign

Year	Event	Details
Early 1970s	Joined Sri Lanka Police	Reserve Sub-Inspector, gaining insight into law enforcement systems
Late 1970s	Entered the Underworld	Left the police and formed his own gang after splitting from Lenin Amarasinghe
1986	Lenin Amarasinghe Murder	Orchestrated brutal killing of Lenin and 16 of his family members. This is reported but not officially confirmed in Commission findings.
Late 1980s	Political Connections Form	Aligned with UNP Minister Sirisena Cooray and President Premadasa
Early 1990s	Alleged Political Crimes	Suspected role in suppressing dissent and attacking critics, including cartoonist Yunoos. Multiple sources corroborate this incident.
1993	Assassination of Lalith Athulathmudali	A Commission later linked Upali to the murder of the former minister
1997	Presidential Commission Inquiry	Officially implicated in Lalith's murder; trial delayed

1998	Assassination of Soththi Upali	Killed by rival gang led by Kaduwela Raja on December 17

Soththi Upali's life reads like a dark thriller etched into the streets of Colombo, a man who rose from uniformed law enforcer to underworld monarch, shielded by political power and feared by civilians, criminals, and police alike. His name became shorthand for corruption, violence, and the chilling blend of crime and governance.

With blood on his hands and ministers at his back, Upali operated in broad daylight, orchestrating murders, intimidating journalists, and allegedly playing a role in political assassinations, including that of Lalith Athulathmudali. His reign was marked by impunity, his influence so vast that officers saluted him instead of arresting him.

But like all emperors of fear, his rule was not eternal. In December 1998, bullets silenced him — not in a courtroom, but in the streets he once owned. His death marked the collapse of a criminal dynasty but left behind a blueprint: how power without accountability turns democracy into a battleground of shadows.

And even now, decades later, the name **Soththi Upali** stirs unease — not just for the man he was, but for the system that allowed him to thrive.

Key Sources

1- **Wikipedia – List of Sri Lankan Mobsters**. This entry confirms that Arambawelage Don Upali Ranjith, known as Soththi Upali, was active from the 1970s until his death in 1998. He was a close ally of Sirisena Cooray, a minister in the Premadasa government, and reportedly held sway over both political and police circles, with officers allegedly addressing him as "sir". He was even appointed to the UNP executive body by President Premadasa.

2- **Wikipedia – Assassination of Lalith Athulathmudali**. A Presidential Commission in 1997 concluded that Soththi Upali was directly involved in the assassination of Lalith Athulathmudali, a former cabinet minister and political rival of Premadasa. Upali was charged in connection with the case but was shot dead on December 17, 1998, while returning home from the Colombo Magistrate's Court, before the trial could conclude.

3- **LankaWeb – "How the UNP Gave Birth to the Underworld"**. This article places Upali within a broader narrative of state-sponsored criminality, describing how the UNP government in the late 1970s empowered underworld figures to suppress opposition and control urban violence. Upali was part of a network of paramilitary enforcers, given weapons, vehicles, and political protection, and used for contract killings, extortion, and narcotics trafficking.

Chapter 52: Civilians as Targets in Sri Lanka's Civil War: The Kumarapuram and Mirusuvil Massacres in Global Perspective (1996 & 2000)

(Mourners – Pic: Tamil Guardian)

Modern civil conflicts have often blurred the lines between combatants and civilians. In Sri Lanka's bloody war between government forces and Tamil separatists, the targeting of civilians—especially Tamil communities—became a central and devastating strategy.

This essay explores two emblematic events: the **Kumarapuram massacre (1996)** and the **Mirusuvil massacre (2000),** analyzing not only their historical contexts and judicial responses, but also placing them within a global pattern of state-led violence against non-combatants.

Case Study 1: Kumarapuram Massacre

Kumarapuram's Tamil residents had long lived under military surveillance and harassment. After the deaths of two soldiers near the village, army personnel launched a vengeful assault on the civilian population.

26 civilians, including children and women, were killed.

Two teenage girls were raped and murdered.

Survivors were maimed and psychologically scarred.

Evidence suggests a **coordinated reprisal attack**, not an isolated incident.

Acquittals despite eyewitness testimony and forensic evidence.

Evidence destroyed in a fire.

Survivors intimidated, reflecting a **culture of impunity**.

Case Study 2: Mirusuvil Massacre

Nine displaced civilians returned to check on their homes after receiving military clearance, only to be abducted by army personnel.

Atrocities Committed

Blindfolded victims tortured and had throats slit.

Mass burial in a cesspit behind the camp.

One survivor, Ponnuthurai Maheswaran, escaped and testified.

Judicial Response and Political Interference

Staff Sergeant Sunil Ratnayake convicted in 2015 after 15 years.

Presidential pardon in 2020, reversing rare accountability.

Outcry from rights advocates and victims' families.

Both massacres reflect the global phenomenon of **state violence against civilians**, a pattern witnessed in:

Guatemala (1980s): scorched-earth campaigns targeting Mayan communities.

Bosnia-Herzegovina (1992–95): ethnic cleansing, including the Srebrenica massacre.

Myanmar (post-2016): Rohingya displacement and mass killing.

These examples highlight a **common thread**—ethnic targeting by militarized states operating with little fear of consequences.

Violations of **Geneva Conventions** and **Customary Humanitarian Law**.

- Protocol I, Article 51: Protection of civilians from indiscriminate attacks
- Protocol II, Article 4: Prohibition of violence to life, torture, and outrages upon personal dignity

UN reports cite Sri Lanka's military for systematic abuses.

The lack of domestic accountability undermines global norms.

Transitional justice mechanisms remain largely unimplemented in Sri Lanka.

Victims and families demand **truth commissions**, **memorialization**, and **reparations**.

Civil society continues the fight for institutional reform and survivor support.

The massacres at Kumarapuram and Mirusuvil are not simply tragic footnotes in Sri Lanka's wartime history. They are urgent reminders of the **cost of unchecked militarism**, the **fragility of civilian protections**, and the enduring trauma of survivors.

True reconciliation will remain elusive until Sri Lanka confronts its past honestly, holds perpetrators accountable, and builds institutions that protect—not persecute—its most vulnerable citizens.

Sources:

Kumarapuram Massacre (1996)

1. **Wikipedia – Kumarapuram Massacre**
   On **February 11, 1996**, Sri Lankan Army soldiers and Home Guards stormed the village of **Kumarapuram** in **Trincomalee District**, killing **26 Tamil civilians**, including **13 women and 9 children under 12**. Survivors described soldiers shouting "death to Tamils" and attacking villagers with **guns and axes**, some while intoxicated.

2. **Tamil Guardian – "Remembering the Kumarapuram Massacre 28 Years On"**
   This article recounts the **gang rape and murder of 15-year-old Arumathurai Thanaluxmi**, whose screams were heard by hiding villagers. Despite **40 eyewitnesses**, all six accused soldiers were **acquitted in 2016**, highlighting systemic impunity.

3. **UTHR Bulletin No.10 – Killiveddy and Kumarapuram**
   Offers a broader context of **military indiscipline and reprisals** in Trincomalee, including the **Killiveddy massacre** that preceded Kumarapuram. It critiques the **lack of accountability** and the culture of silence surrounding military abuses.

Mirusuvil Massacre (2000)

1. **Wikipedia – Mirusuvil Massacre**
   On **December 20, 2000**, eight Tamil civilians—including **three teenagers and a 5-year-old boy**—were murdered by Sri Lankan Army soldiers after returning to inspect their homes in **Mirusuvil, Jaffna**. The victims were **stabbed and buried in a mass grave**, discovered after one survivor, **Ponnuthurai Maheswaran**, escaped and alerted authorities.

2. **Tamil Guardian – "Revisiting the Mirusuvil Massacre"**
   Provides a gripping narrative of Maheswaran's escape and identification of the perpetrators. One soldier, **Staff Sergeant Sunil Ratnayake**, was convicted and sentenced to death in 2015—but **pardoned in 2020** by President Gotabaya Rajapaksa, sparking international outrage.

3. **CHRD Sri Lanka – Legal Assistance in Mirusuvil Case**
   Details the **15-year legal battle**, including the **trial-at-bar**, witness intimidation, and forensic evidence. The case became a **litmus test for Sri Lanka's judicial independence**, with only one conviction despite overwhelming evidence.

Chapter 53: The Assassination of Major General Lakshman Algama: A Turning Point in Sri Lanka's Political Violence (1999)

Major General Lakshman 'Lucky' Wijayaratne

Major General Chulasoka Lakshman **"Lucky" Algama** was born on June 2, 1940, in Kelaniya, Sri Lanka. Educated at Ananda College and later at the University of Ceylon, Peradeniya, Algama joined the Sri Lanka Army in 1963. Over the next three decades, he rose through the ranks, serving in key military operations during the 1971 Insurrection, the 1987–89 JVP uprising, and the Sri Lankan Civil War.

Algama held several strategic posts, including Commander of Security Forces Headquarters East and Chief of Staff of the Army. His leadership was instrumental in enabling democratic elections in the Eastern Province in 1993, a region long destabilized by insurgency.

After retiring from the military in 1995, Algama entered politics as a member of the United National Party (UNP). His transition from battlefield strategist to political activist reflected a broader desire to influence national policy and promote stability through democratic means.

On **December 18, 1999**, Algama was attending a UNP election rally in Ja-Ela, a suburb of Colombo. As he was leaving the event, a suicide bomber detonated an explosive device, killing Algama and eleven others, and injuring seven more. Eyewitnesses reported that the bomber moved deliberately toward Algama before triggering the blast.

The Sri Lankan government attributed the attack to the Liberation Tigers of Tamil Eelam (LTTE), a separatist militant group known for its use of suicide bombings and targeted assassinations. The killing occurred just an hour before another suicide bombing targeted President Chandrika Kumaratunga at a separate rally, underscoring the coordinated nature of the attacks.

Algama's assassination sent shockwaves through Sri Lanka. As a respected military leader and emerging political figure, his death symbolized the vulnerability of even the most seasoned defenders of the state. It highlighted the LTTE's capacity to strike high-profile targets and disrupt democratic processes.

The attack also intensified public scrutiny of security protocols and raised questions about the effectiveness of counterterrorism measures. In the aftermath, curfews were imposed in Colombo and Gampaha districts, and political tensions escalated as the country braced for further violence.

Major General Algama is remembered as a disciplined soldier, a strategic thinker, and a patriot who sought peace through both military and political channels. His assassination marked a grim chapter in Sri Lanka's civil conflict, reinforcing the dangers faced by those who dared to challenge extremism.

His death, alongside many others lost to political violence, remains a stark reminder of the human cost of war and the fragility of peace. Today, his legacy lives on in the annals of Sri Lankan military history and in the memories of those who continue to strive for reconciliation and justice.

Additional Notes

• Some sources suggest internal military intelligence disputes may have complicated investigations into Algama's death, but the LTTE remains the officially cited perpetrator

• The attack is listed among notable LTTE suicide bombings and political assassinations during the civil war

Key Sources

1. **Wikipedia – Lakshman Algama.** Major General Lakshman "Lucky" Algama was a former Chief of Staff of the Sri Lanka Army, known for his role in suppressing the 1987–1989 JVP insurrection and securing elections in the Eastern Province during the civil war. After retiring in 1995, he became a United National Party (UNP) activist. On December 18, 1999, he was killed in a suicide bombing at a UNP rally in Ja-Ela, Colombo, along with 12 others. The government blamed the LTTE, though eyewitnesses suggested the bomber moved directly toward Algama.

2. **Sri Lanka Mirror –** "Algama, Seneviratne Murder Mysteries Solved" This investigative report reveals that Sri Lankan military intelligence may have orchestrated the bombing, using LTTE operatives to carry out the attack. According to a CID report submitted to the Security Council, the operation was allegedly planned by a retired major general, then head of military intelligence, due to personal and political enmity. The case was reportedly covered up to avoid demoralizing the military.

3. **Sunday Times – "The Trail of Terror".** This chronology of LTTE attacks lists Algama among high-profile victims of political violence. It places his assassination within a broader pattern of targeted killings of military and political figures, including President Premadasa, Foreign Minister Lakshman Kadirgamar, and MP Neelan Thiruchelvam.

Chapter 54: The Rajagiriya Bomb Blast – A Shadow Over Peace (2000)

In the waning daylight of **March 10, 2000**, the quiet suburb of Rajagiriya, just outside Colombo, was shattered by a powerful bomb explosion. The blast, which injured at least 15 civilians, was one of many violent episodes during Sri Lanka's decades-long civil war. Though not the deadliest, it was symbolically potent—occurring just as political leaders were inching toward a peace agreement.

Blast Site: Rajagiriya, near Sri Jayewardenepura Road

Proximity: About 1.5 km from Sri Lanka's Administrative Capital and 10 km from Colombo Fort

Suspected Target: Early reports speculated the bomb may have targeted the Centre for Banking Studies, a Central Bank training facility located in Rajagiriya. However, no official confirmation was made.

Time: Around 5:00 p.m., during peak commuter hours

Casualties: At least 15 people injured, mostly civilians returning home from work

Damage:

Houses over a kilometer away were shaken

Windows shattered, vehicles damaged, and panic spread across the suburb

Method: The exact nature of the bomb was not publicly disclosed, but later investigations revealed electronic timers in suicide jackets found nearby, suggesting a coordinated attack.

Suspected Perpetrators

The Liberation Tigers of Tamil Eelam (LTTE) were widely suspected:

The blast occurred just one day after the Sri Lankan government and Opposition made progress on a peace plan for the Tamil region.

The LTTE, known for opposing such negotiations, had a history of targeting urban centers to disrupt political momentum.

The Rajagiriya bombing was part of a broader LTTE strategy:

Urban Terrorism: Designed to instill fear and destabilize governance

Symbolic Timing: Coinciding with political developments to undermine peace efforts

Civilian Impact: Reinforced the LTTE's disregard for non-combatant safety Investigation and International Support

Local Response: Sri Lankan police launched immediate investigations

International Assistance: Two Scotland Yard experts were flown in to assist, confirming the use of electronic timers in suicide devices found at the scene.

Fear and Anger: The attack reignited public anxiety, especially in Colombo suburbs

Political Fallout: Strengthened calls for military action and hardened attitudes toward peace talks

Media Coverage: The blast was widely reported, though details remained sparse due to security concerns

Legacy and Reflection

While not as deadly as other LTTE attacks, the Rajagiriya blast was a chilling reminder of the fragility of peace in Sri Lanka. It highlighted:

• The vulnerability of urban centers

• The LTTE's tactical use of timing and location

• The human cost of political violence

Key Sources

1. **Asian Economic News** – "Huge Blast Rocks Sri Lanka Capital Region" (March 13, 2000)

This report details the March 10, 2000 bombing in Rajagiriya, just 1.5 km from Sri Lanka's administrative capital. The explosion occurred around 5 p.m., targeting an area where the Central Bank was temporarily housed. At least 15 people were injured, many of them commuters heading home. The blast shook homes over a kilometer away, and initial suspicions pointed to the LTTE, especially since the attack followed progress in peace talks between the government and opposition—talks the LTTE was believed to oppose.

2. **Wikipedia – List of LTTE Attacks in the 2000s**

While not listing Rajagiriya by name, this chronology confirms a series of coordinated LTTE bombings in early 2000, including attacks on government buildings, ministers, and public spaces. The Rajagiriya blast fits within this pattern of urban terror, aimed at disrupting political momentum and instilling fear.

3. **Sunday Times – "The Trail of Terror"**

This retrospective article places the Rajagiriya bombing within a broader timeline of LTTE violence, noting how civilian areas and economic targets were increasingly chosen to maximize psychological and political impact. It underscores the human cost of these attacks and the fragility of peace efforts during this period.

Chapter 55: Behind the Rehab Fence – Bindunuwewa Massacre (2000)

On **October 25, 2000**, the quiet town of **Bindunuwewa**, nestled in Sri **Lanka's Uva Province**, became the site of a brutal massacre that shocked the nation and the international community. At a government-run **Rehabilitation Center for Tamil youth**, a mob of Sinhalese villagers— allegedly aided by police officers—stormed the facility and **murdered 27 detainees**, many of whom were unarmed and awaiting release. The Bindunuwewa Massacre exposed the **fragility of reconciliation efforts**, the **depth of ethnic tensions**, and the **failure of state institutions** to protect vulnerable populations during the civil war.

The **Bindunuwewa Rehabilitation Centre** was established to house **former LTTE cadres and Tamil youth** suspected of insurgent ties. It was jointly managed by the **Presidential Secretariat**, **Ministry of Defence**, and **Child Protection Authority**, and was considered a model for reintegration. Most detainees were **between 14 and 30 years old**, held without formal charges under the **Prevention of Terrorism Act (PTA)**.

In the days leading up to the massacre:

Detainees **protested prolonged detention**, lack of legal recourse, and the **withholding of letters from families**.

Posters appeared in the village inciting violence, with slogans like "Tigers' flesh to our dogs."

The **Sri Lankan Army Detachment** guarding the center was **withdrawn the day before** the attack.

The Massacre: A Premeditated Slaughter

At dawn on October 25, a mob of **over 1,000 Sinhalese villagers**, armed with **machetes, clubs, iron rods, and torches**, descended on the center. The **60-armed police officers** stationed at the facility **stood by—or actively participated** in the killings.

Victims were:

Hacked to death, some **burned alive**.

Shot while attempting to flee.

Mutilated beyond recognition—one youth, **Antony John**, was found with his eyes gouged out and limbs severed.

The **Human Rights Commission of Sri Lanka** later confirmed that the detainees had **not provoked the attack**, debunking early government claims of a riot.

Initial Trial

41 individuals, including **19 police officers**, were indicted.

In **2003**, **five were convicted**—two police officers and three civilians—and sentenced to **death**.

Supreme Court Appeal

In **2005**, the **Supreme Court overturned all convictions**, citing **lack of evidence**.

- Observers noted **judicial bias**, with one justice remarking that the victims were "LTTE members," implying diminished culpability.

Accountability Gaps

Senior officers like **ASP A.W. Dayaratne** and **Inspector Jayantha Seneviratne**, who had prior knowledge of the planned protest, were **never indicted or disciplined**.

The **National Human Rights Commission** labeled the police's role a "serious dereliction of duty," but stopped short of criminal responsibility.

Political and Social Implications

The Bindunuwewa Massacre revealed:

State complicity in ethnic violence.

The **failure of transitional justice mechanisms**.

The **erosion of trust** between Tamil civilians and state institutions.

It also highlighted the **danger of politicized rehabilitation**, where detainees were treated as enemies rather than citizens deserving reintegration.

Despite international condemnation, **no one remains imprisoned** for the massacre. Families of the victims continue to seek justice, while many still wonder if their missing children were among the charred remains. The massacre is commemorated annually by Tamil communities and human rights groups as a symbol of **state terror and impunity**.

"Behind the Rehab Fence" was meant to be a place of healing. Instead, it became a killing ground—where **ethnic hatred**, **state negligence**, and **judicial failure** converged. The Bindunuwewa Massacre stands as a chilling reminder that **reconciliation without accountability is a hollow promise**, and that **justice delayed—or denied—is a wound that never heals**.

Couldn't Senior officers like **ASP A.W. Dayaratne** and **Inspector Jayantha Seneviratne**, who had prior knowledge of the planned protest, were **never indicted or disciplined**.

The **National Human Rights Commission** labeled the police's role a "serious dereliction of duty," but stopped short of criminal responsibility.

Survivor Testimonies

Sinnathamby Rajendran – Injured Survivor

"We were taught to be good citizens. We had good teachers and instructors. They were soft spoken. They never used the word *umba* in addressing us."

— *Quoted in Justice P.H.K. Kulatilaka's Commission Report*

Rajendran, who suffered injuries during the attack, described the rehabilitation center as peaceful and respectful—until the massacre shattered that trust.

Unnamed Survivor (Age 16) – Former Child Soldier

"They came with knives and iron rods. We ran, but the police fired at us. I saw my friend fall. I hid under a bed until it was over."

— *Recounted in Boston Review*

This survivor was one of 14 who escaped. His account underscores the betrayal by police who were meant to protect them.

Family Member of Antony John (Victim)

"One of Antony's eyes was removed from the decapitated head, both arms had been cut off, and the entire body was covered with deep cuts."

— *Reported by Tamil Guardian*

Antony's mutilated body became a symbol of the savagery inflicted on detainees. His family struggled for years to claim his remains.

Key Sources

1. **Wikipedia – Bindunuwewa Massacre**
   On **October 24, 2000**, a mob of **Sinhalese villagers armed with knives, rods, and torches** stormed the **low-security detention center** in Bindunuwewa, Badulla, killing **26 Tamil detainees**, most of whom were **former LTTE cadres aged 21–30**. The **Sri Lankan Army detachment** had been **withdrawn the day before**, and **police officers present refused to intervene**, allowing the massacre to unfold.

2. **Asian Human Rights Commission – "Sri Lanka: The Bindunuwewa Massacre"**
   This submission to the **UN Commission on Human Rights** reveals that **60 armed police officers were present** during the massacre and allegedly **enabled or participated** in the killings. It challenges the official narrative of a spontaneous mob attack, suggesting the attackers were **transported to the site**, acted with **military precision**, and were likely **trained operatives**.

3. **Human Rights Watch – "Failure of Justice for Victims of Massacre"**
   This report documents the **legal aftermath**, where several police officers were **initially convicted of murder**, only to be **acquitted by the Supreme Court in 2005**. It highlights the **culture of impunity** and the **failure of Sri Lanka's justice system** to hold perpetrators accountable.

Chapter 56: Aiyathurai Nadesan: A Voice for Truth Silenced by Violence (2004)

Assassinated Tamil journalist Aiyathurai Nadesan
remembered in the North-East | Tamil Guardian

In the annals of Sri Lankan journalism, **Aiyathurai Nadesan** stands as a symbol of fearless reporting and unwavering commitment to truth. His assassination on **May 31, 2004**, in **Batticaloa**, Eastern Sri Lanka, was not just the loss of a veteran journalist—it was a stark reminder of the peril faced by those who challenge power structures in conflict zones. Nadesan's life and death continue to resonate in conversations about media freedom, ethnic tensions, and justice in post-war Sri Lanka.

Born in **Nelliyadi**, in the **Jaffna District**, Nadesan was deeply rooted in the Tamil community. He wrote under the pen name **Nellai Nadesan**, and his journalism career spanned over two decades. He was a **Columnist for Virakesari**, Sri Lanka's leading Tamil-language newspaper, and also served as a correspondent for **Shakthi TV News** and the **London-based International Broadcasting Corporation**.

Nadesan's work was widely respected. In **2000**, he was awarded the **Best Tamil Journalist Prize** by the **Sri Lanka Editors' Guild**, and he held the position of **Vice President of the Sri Lanka Tamil Media Alliance**. His reporting focused on human rights, political corruption, and the lived realities of Tamil civilians in war-torn regions.

Nadesan's commitment to exposing abuses made him a target. In **April 2000**, a bomb exploded at his home in Batticaloa, an act linked to **pro-government Tamil paramilitaries**. He received death threats after publishing articles critical of groups like **PLOTE** (People's Liberation Organization of Tamil Eelam), a paramilitary faction aligned with the government.

In **June 2001**, he was summoned by the **Sri Lankan Army** and warned to stop reporting on military abuses. Despite these threats, Nadesan continued his work, driven by a belief in the power of journalism to hold institutions accountable.

On the morning of **May 31, 2004**, Nadesan was **shot dead near a Hindu temple** in Batticaloa while on his way to work. The assailants escaped, and no group claimed responsibility. However, many believe the murder was carried out by the **Karuna Group**, a paramilitary faction that had broken away from the **LTTE** and was allegedly backed by the Sri Lankan government.

His death occurred amid escalating violence in the Eastern Province, where the LTTE was engaged in a military offensive against the Karuna faction. Nadesan was reportedly sympathetic to the LTTE, and his reporting often highlighted abuses by government-aligned forces.

Despite widespread condemnation and public protests—including a **shutdown in Trincomalee** and a **memorial attended by thousands**—no arrests were made. The case remains unsolved, emblematic of the **culture of impunity** surrounding attacks on journalists in Sri Lanka.

Nadesan's assassination is one of **at least 41 killings of Tamil journalists** attributed to the Sri Lankan state or its Paramilitaries during and after the civil war. His death galvanized media collectives and human rights organizations, both locally and internationally.

In **2025**, a memorial was held in Batticaloa to mark the **21st anniversary** of his death. Journalists, civil society activists, and politicians gathered to honor his legacy and renew calls for justice. The event underscored the ongoing threats faced by Tamil journalists and the urgent need for accountability.

Aiyathurai Nadesan was more than a journalist—he was a truth-teller in a time of fear, a voice for the voiceless, and a chronicler of a community under siege. His murder silenced a powerful advocate for justice, but his legacy endures in the continued struggle for press freedom and human rights in Sri Lanka.

To remember Nadesan is to confront the uncomfortable truths of state violence, and to recommit to the ideals of transparency, courage, and justice that he lived by.

Key Sources

1. **Wikipedia – Aiyathurai Nadesan.** Nadesan was a veteran Tamil journalist and columnist for *Virakesari*, Sri Lanka's leading Tamil-language newspaper. He was **shot dead on May 31, 2004**, in **Batticaloa**, allegedly by members of the **Karuna Group**, a government-backed paramilitary faction. He had previously received **death threats** and survived a **bomb attack on his home in 2000**, reportedly linked to pro-government paramilitaries.

2. **Tamil Guardian – "Murdered Tamil Journalist Aiyathurai Nadesan Remembered in Batticaloa".** This article covers the **2025 memorial event** marking the 21st anniversary of his assassination. It highlights Nadesan's role as a **local correspondent for Shakthi FM and IBC Tamil**, and his reputation for **reporting on military abuses** in the Eastern Province. Despite widespread condemnation, **no one has ever been held accountable** for his murder.

3. **Tamil Heritage – Biography of Aiyathurai Nadesan**
   Offers a detailed biography, noting that Nadesan wrote under the pen name **"Nellai Nadesan"**, and was **Vice-President of the Sri Lanka Tamil Media Alliance**. He won the

Best Tamil Journalist Award in 2000, and his funeral drew large crowds, with **shops closed and protests held across the North-East**.

Chapter 57: The Assassination of Dhammika Amarasinghe: A Courtroom Execution That Shook Sri Lanka (2004)

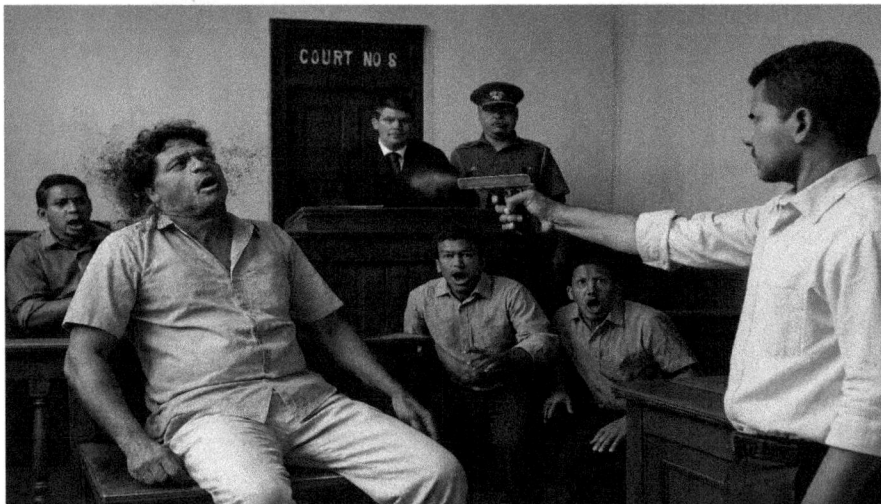

On the morning of **January 9, 2004**, the Colombo Chief Magistrate's Court was meant to be a place of law and order. Instead, it became the stage for one of Sri Lanka's most audacious acts of underworld violence. As notorious gangster **Usliyanage Ruwan Dhammika—better known as Dhammika Amarasinghe**—was escorted out of Courtroom No. 6, a man disguised as a lawyer pulled a pistol from his boot and fired seven shots. Dhammika died instantly. Two civilians were wounded. The magistrate was still seated on the bench.

This was not just a hit. It was a message.

A Family Steeped in Crime

Dhammika's descent into the criminal underworld wasn't accidental—it was inherited. His uncle, **Noel Amarasinghe**, reportedly led a gang in the 1960s, and Dhammika's mother was Noel's sister. The family's exposure to violence began early, and by the 1990s, Dhammika and his brother **Chinthaka Amarasinghe** were entrenched in Colombo's criminal underbelly.

Unconfirmed but widely circulated accounts claim that Dhammika's vendetta against rival gangs was fueled by a massacre: allegedly, 16 of his relatives—including his sister—were murdered by the gang of infamous mobster **Soththi Upali**. While this claim remains unverified, it has become part of the lore surrounding Dhammika's rise.

The Rise and Fall of a Ruthless Dynasty

Chinthaka Amarasinghe, Dhammik Dhammika's older brother, was known for his brutality. He survived an assassination attempt in 1994 at the Negombo Magistrate's Court—an incident that itself became a symbol of the lawlessness creeping into judicial spaces. But in 1996, Chinthaka was killed by another underworld figure, **Kalu Ajith**. Dhammika inherited his brother's criminal network and expanded it aggressively across Kalutara, Colombo, and Grandpass.

He was linked to over 50 murders, including high-profile victims such as:

• **Baddegana Sanjeewa**, a former officer in the Presidential Security Division

• **Rohana Kumara,** editor of the newspaper Satana

• **Niranjan Sellasamy,** another journalist

These allegations, though never proven in court, were widely reported in Sri Lankan media and whispered about in political circles. Dhammika's ability to evade conviction was often attributed to political protection and fear among law enforcement, a claim that remains speculative but persistent.

The Courtroom Execution

The assassin, later identified as **Chaminda Udayakumara,** was an army deserter posing as a lawyer. According to unconfirmed reports, he was paid Rs. 70,000 by a Colombo-based drug dealer to carry out the hit. His background—a father of two from Kotahena struggling with financial hardship—made him an ideal pawn.

The Colombo Crime Division (CCD) recovered:

• The murder weapon (a Chinese-made pistol)

• Seven spent shells and one live bullet

• A getaway vehicle

Three additional suspects—**Nihal Perera, Donald Ranjith Perera, and S.A. Piyatissa**—were arrested and remanded. Investigators also probed how the weapon was smuggled into the courtroom, raising serious questions about security lapses and possible inside help.

A Pattern of Courtroom Violence

Dhammika's killing was not the first, nor the last courtroom assassination in Sri Lanka. Notable earlier incidents include:

Year	Location	Incident
1991	Attanagalla Magistrate's Court	Businessman shot dead **Sub-Inspector Dhammika** and his father-in-law in revenge for JVP-era torture
1994	Negombo Magistrate's Court	**Chinthaka Amarasinghe** survived an assassination attempt; attacker shot dead by a Retired Prison Commissioner
2005	Embilipitiya Magistrate's Court	**Hand grenade** thrown, killing one and injuring several
Unknown	Gangodawila Magistrate's Court	**Remote-controlled bomb** hidden in a toy car detonated, causing multiple casualties

These incidents reveal a disturbing pattern of **security lapses**, **disguises**, and **inside help**, often driven by **gang rivalries** or **political revenge**.

Reflection: When Crime and Politics Collide

Dhammika Amarasinghe's assassination inside a courtroom was more than a criminal act—it was a symbolic collapse of institutional safety. It exposed the vulnerabilities of Sri Lanka's justice system and the depth of underworld infiltration. His death marked the end of a violent dynasty, but it also raised enduring questions:

• How did Dhammika evade justice for so long?

• Who enabled his rise - and his fall?

• What reforms are needed to protect judicial spaces from becoming battlegrounds?

Key Sources

1. **Lankasara – "Deadly Justice: A History of Courtroom Killings in Sri Lanka"**
   This investigative article recounts how **Dhammika Amarasinghe**, a notorious criminal kingpin, was **gunned down on January 9, 2004**, inside **Hall No. 06 of the Aluthkade Magistrate's Court**. The assassin was **disguised as a lawyer**, and the killing was part of a wave of **courtroom executions** that exposed deep flaws in Sri Lanka's judicial security system.

2. **Wikipedia – List of Sri Lankan Mobsters**
   This entry confirms Dhammika's role as the **successor to Chinthaka Amarasinghe**, his brother, who was also assassinated in 1996. Dhammika's rise in Colombo's underworld was marked by **extortion, contract killings, and political connections**, making him a high-profile target.

Chapter 58: The Assassination of Colonel Tuan Nizam Muthaliff: A Fallen Hero of Sri Lanka's Military Intelligence (2005)

Colonel Tuan Nizam Muthaliff, RWP, MI, was a distinguished officer of the **Sri Lanka Army** whose life and career were tragically cut short on **May 31, 2005**. His assassination during the ceasefire period of the Sri Lankan Civil War marked a significant loss for the nation's military intelligence apparatus. Revered for his strategic brilliance and fearless leadership, Muthaliff's legacy continues to resonate within the ranks of the Sri Lanka Army and among those who honor the sacrifices made in pursuit of national security.

Born on **July 12, 1966**, in Kalubowila to a **Malay family from Trincomalee**, Muthaliff was educated at D. S. Senanayake College, Colombo, where he excelled academically and athletically. He joined the Sri Lanka Army in 1986 as a cadet officer and underwent rigorous training at the Sri Lanka Military Academy and later at the Pakistan Military Academy, where he earned the Best Cadet award and dined with then-President General Zia-ul-Haq.

His early military engagements included participation in Operation Vadamarachchi, a major offensive against the LTTE. Over the years, he rose through the ranks, serving in various intelligence roles and undergoing specialized training in Bangladesh, India, Hawaii, and the United States.

Muthaliff was instrumental in shaping Sri Lanka's military intelligence capabilities. He served as the Commander of the Intelligence Security Group in Jaffna and later led the 1st Military Intelligence Corps. His contributions included providing critical intelligence for operations such as Balavegaya and Jayasikurui, and he was credited with forewarning Brigadier Janaka Perera of an LTTE attack on Weli Oya.

He also commanded covert units like the Long-Range Reconnaissance Patrol (LRRP), known as the "Demon Brigade," which conducted deep penetration missions targeting high-ranking LTTE leaders in rebel-controlled territories. His operations sent shockwaves through the LTTE hierarchy, instilling fear and disrupting their strategic planning.

The Millennium City Incident and Its Fallout

In 2002, the infamous Millennium City incident exposed the identities of several intelligence operatives, including Muthaliff, compromising their safety and operational integrity. This breach is widely regarded as one of the greatest betrayals in Sri Lankan military history, and it left Muthaliff vulnerable to targeted attacks.

On **May 31, 2005,** Colonel Muthaliff was assassinated by LTTE operatives **in Polhengoda**, Colombo, during the ceasefire period. Despite previous attempts on his life—including a gun attack in Vavuniya and a suicide bombing in Jaffna—he remained undeterred until his final mission.

His death was mourned deeply by his family, comrades, and the nation. Posthumously promoted to Colonel, he was honored for his bravery and service. His family continues to commemorate his legacy through charitable acts, such as donations to orphanages.

Colonel Tuan Nizam Muthaliff is remembered not only for his tactical genius and courage but also for his unwavering commitment to protecting Sri Lanka. His life exemplified the ethos of selfless service, and his death underscored the high cost of peace and security in a nation torn by conflict.

His story is a poignant reminder of the sacrifices made by those who operate in the shadows, often unrecognized, yet vital to the survival of a nation. In honoring his memory, Sri Lanka pays tribute to all its unsung heroes who gave their lives in the line of duty.

Colonel Muthaliff's life, stitched with resilience and dedication, paints a portrait of uncompromising patriotism and valor.

Historical Timeline of a National Hero

Here's a chronological overview of key moments in Colonel Muthaliff's life and career, highlighting his military milestones and legacy:

Date	Event
July 12, 1966	Born in Kalubowila, Sri Lanka to a Malay family from Trincomalee.
1986	Enlisted as a cadet officer in the Sri Lanka Army.
Late 1980s	Trained at Sri Lanka Military Academy and Pakistan Military Academy
1987	Participated in Operation Vadamarachchi, an offensive against LTTE.
1990s	Rose through intelligence ranks; served in multiple field and covert roles.
1999–2002	Led intelligence operations in Jaffna and contributed to major campaigns like **Balavegaya and Jayasikurui.**
January 2002	**Millennium City** incident exposes intelligence operatives, including Muthaliff.
2002–2005	Survived multiple assassination attempts, including a gun attack and suicide bombing.
2005	Commanded 1st Military Intelligence Corps and covert LRRP "Demon Brigade."
May 31, 2005	Assassinated by LTTE operatives in Colombo during ceasefire period.
June 2005	Posthumously promoted to Colonel; national mourning for his service
2005–Present	Remembered for his intelligence leadership and sacrifice; family continues his legacy through philanthropy.

Key Sources

1. **Wikipedia – Tuan Nizam Muthaliff.** Colonel Muthaliff was assassinated on **May 31, 2005**, in **Polhengoda, Colombo**, while serving as the **Commanding Officer of the 1st Military Intelligence Corps.** He was reportedly targeted by the **LTTE** during the ceasefire period, making him one of the **highest-ranking intelligence officers killed** in the conflict. His career spanned from **1986 to 2005**, and he was posthumously promoted to Colonel.

2. **Sri Lanka Guardian – "A True Son of the Nation".** This tribute highlights Muthaliff's role in **covert operations**, including leading the **Long Range Reconnaissance Patrol (LRRP)**, known as the "Demon Brigade." He was instrumental in **targeting LTTE leadership**, including **Thamilselvan, Karuna, Balraj, and Charles**, often operating deep within enemy territory. His assassination was seen as a **strategic blow to Sri Lanka's intelligence apparatus**.

Chapter 59: Colonel Tuan Rizly Meedin: A Martyr in the Shadows of Sri Lanka's Intelligence War (2005)

Colonel Tuan Rizly Meedin (1966–2005) was a dedicated officer of the Sri Lanka Army Intelligence Corps whose life was tragically ended by betrayal and assassination. Like his fellow Malay comrade Colonel Tuan Nizam Muthaliff, Meedin operated in the perilous world of covert warfare during the Sri Lankan Civil War. His death, orchestrated by a double agent, underscores the dangers faced by intelligence officers and the sacrifices made in silence.

Born on **July 27, 1966**, in **Hambantota**, Meedin came from a family steeped in military tradition. His brothers included **Major General Tuan Fadyl Meedin** and **Squadron Leader Tuan Akram Meedin**. Inspired by their service, he joined the Sri Lanka Army in 1986 through Regular Intake 23 and trained at the Sri Lanka Military Academy in Diyatalawa. Commissioned into the 3rd Battalion, Sri Lanka Light Infantry, he quickly rose through the ranks, transferring to the newly formed Military Intelligence Corps in 1990.

Meedin's career was marked by strategic brilliance and operational courage. He served in the Directorate of Military Intelligence and eventually commanded the **2nd Military Intelligence Corps**. His work involved cultivating informants, gathering actionable intelligence, and coordinating covert missions against the LTTE. He was known for his ability to build trust with operatives and navigate the murky waters of espionage.

Assassination and Betrayal

On **October 29, 2005**, Meedin was assassinated by one of his own informants, **Andrahennedige Chaminda Roshan, alias Ice Manju**—a **Double Agent** working for LTTE commander **Sornam.** The killing occurred in Meedin's car in **Kiribathgoda**, after a meeting with informants. Despite warnings of infiltration within his circle, Meedin remained committed to his mission, believing he could turn the tide against LTTE leadership.

He was rushed to Colombo General Hospital by his brother but succumbed to his injuries early the next morning. His assassin fled to LTTE-controlled territory and later disappeared during the final stages of the war.

Posthumously promoted to Colonel, Meedin was buried at the Muslim Burial Ground in Makola. He left behind his wife Shamina and two daughters, Rishanya and Shiranya. His death, like Muthaliff's, is a stark reminder of the silent sacrifices made by intelligence officers—often unrecognized, yet vital to national security.

The Sri Lankan Malay Contribution to Military Intelligence

The Sri Lankan Malay community, though numerically small, has made outsized contributions to the armed forces—particularly in intelligence and covert operations. Two standout figures:

Colonel Tuan Rizly Meedin

• Commanded the 2nd Military Intelligence Corps
• Known for cultivating deep-cover informants and coordinating high-risk missions
• Assassinated in 2005 by a double agent working for the LTTE

Colonel Tuan Nizam Muthaliff

• Commanded the 1st Military Intelligence Corps
• Provided critical intelligence for operations like Balavegaya and Jayasikurui
• Survived multiple assassination attempts before being killed by LTTE gunmen in 2005

These officers were not only tacticians but also cultural bridges—trusted by operatives across ethnic lines, which was crucial in a conflict marked by deep divisions.

Military Intelligence Corps: Role in the Civil War

Formed in 1990, the MIC was tasked with:

• Clandestine operations
• Counterintelligence
• Cyberwarfare
• Human intelligence (HUMINT)
• Signals intelligence (SIGINT)
• Intelligence analysis and assessment

Key Operations

• **Operation Balavegaya (1991):** Intelligence helped break the LTTE siege of Elephant Pass

• **Operation Jayasikurui (1997–1999):** Aimed to open a land route to Jaffna; MIC provided terrain and enemy movement data

• **Weli Oya Defense**: Muthaliff's intelligence warned Brigadier Janaka Perera of an impending LTTE attack

Risks and Sacrifices

• MIC officers operated in civilian clothes, often without backup

• Many were targeted by LTTE assassins or betrayed by double agents

• The ceasefire period (2002–2006) was especially dangerous, as LTTE infiltrated informant networks Strategic Legacy

The MIC's work was pivotal in:

• Disrupting LTTE supply chains and leadership movements

• Identifying sleeper cells and urban operatives

• Supporting psychological operations and misinformation campaigns

Despite their low public profile, intelligence officers like Meedin and Muthaliff were instrumental in shaping battlefield outcomes. Their deaths were not just personal tragedies—they were strategic losses.

Key Sources

1. Wikipedia – Tuan Rizly Meedin

Colonel Meedin was assassinated on October 29, 2005, while serving as Senior Staff Officer of the Military Intelligence Corps. He was shot by Andrahennedige Chaminda Roshan, alias Ice Manju, a double agent working for LTTE commander Sornam in Trincomalee. The killing occurred during the ceasefire period, and Meedin was posthumously promoted to Colonel.

2. Tamil Guardian – "Double Agent Blamed for Intel Officer's Killing"

This article reveals that Meedin had been grooming Ice Manju to assassinate LTTE commander Sornam. Despite warnings from colleagues that his circle had been infiltrated, Meedin trusted the operative. On the night of the murder, he was shot inside his car after meeting with Chaminda and another associate. The betrayal was a devastating blow to Sri Lanka's covert operations, especially during a fragile peace process.

3. Sunday Times – Situation Report: "Predator Becomes the Prey"

This gripping narrative details the final hours of Meedin's life, including his casual departure from home in shorts and a T-shirt, leaving behind his armed escorts. It describes how Chaminda shot him with a 7.62 micro pistol, fled to LTTE-controlled Sampur, and later disappeared. The report underscores the personal trust Meedin placed in his informants, and how that trust was fatally exploited.

Chapter 60: The Trinco Five – Students Executed (2006)

(Pic: reddit.com)

On **January 2, 2006**, five Tamil students were killed in broad daylight near the Gandhi statue on the seafront of Trincomalee, a town under heavy military presence in northeastern Sri Lanka. Known as the **"Trinco Five",** their deaths became one of the most emblematic cases of alleged state-sponsored violence and enduring impunity during Sri Lanka's civil war.

The Victims

The five students were:

• Manoharan Ragihar (20)
• Yogarajah Hemachchandra (20)
• Logitharajah Rohan (20)
• Thangathurai Sivanantha (20)
• Shanmugarajah Gajendran (20)

All were academically promising young men, gathered at a popular public spot during the holiday season. Their lives were cut short in what many believe was a deliberate and extrajudicial execution.

The Incident: What Happened

According to eyewitness accounts and forensic reports:

• A grenade was thrown near the students, reportedly from a three-wheeler, injuring some.

• Shortly afterward, armed men arrived in a white van and shot the students at close range.

• Autopsy results confirmed gunshot wounds, directly contradicting the military's initial claim that the deaths were caused by a grenade explosion.

The area was under tight military control, flanked by Navy checkpoints and patrolled by security forces. Despite this, no immediate intervention occurred, and the official narrative quickly shifted toward denial.

The aftermath revealed a disturbing pattern of intimidation, misinformation, and obstruction:

• **Dr. Manoharan**, father of Ragihar, was pressured to sign a false statement labeling his son an LTTE member. He refused and later fled the country for safety.

• **Subramaniyam Sugirdharajan**, a journalist who photographed the bodies to prove they were shot, was assassinated weeks later.

• Witnesses were threatened, and many declined to testify. Dr. Manoharan remained the sole public voice, despite personal risk.

Despite international attention and domestic outrage:

• 12 Special Task Force (STF) personnel were arrested but released due to "lack of evidence." They were re-arrested in 2013 but again released without trial.

• A Presidential Commission of Inquiry was established in 2008, but its findings were never made public.

• As of 2025, no one has been convicted, and the case remains unresolved.

Global human rights organizations condemned the killings and the lack of accountability:

• Human Rights Watch and Amnesty International called for independent investigations.

• Reporters Without Borders highlighted the murder of Sugirdharajan as an attack on press freedom.

• The case was presented at the People's Tribunal on Sri Lanka in Dublin (2010), underscoring its symbolic weight in discussions of war crimes and impunity.

The Trinco Five case is not just about five young lives lost. It reflects:

• The weaponization of ethnicity during Sri Lanka's civil war.

• The collusion between military and political elites to s suppress dissent.

• The erosion of rule of law, where truth is buried under threats and silence.

Key Sources

1. **Wikipedia – 2006 Trincomalee Massacre of Students.** On **January 2, 2006**, five Tamil students—**Manoharan Ragihar, Yogarajah Hemachchandra, Logitharajah Rohan, Thangathurai Sivanantha, and Shanmugarajah Gajendran**—were executed at point-blank range near the **Trincomalee beachfront** by members of the **Special Task Force (STF).**

2. **Human Rights Watch – "Sri Lanka: No Justice for 'Trinco 5'"**
This report details how **13 STF officers were acquitted in 2019** due to "lack of evidence," despite **36 named witnesses**, including survivors who fled the country due to threats. The case became a **litmus test for Sri Lanka's commitment to**

accountability, with international bodies like the **UN Human Rights Council** citing it as emblematic of systemic impunity.

3. **Daily FT – "Killing of Five Trinco Students: Emblematic Case of Impunity"**
This retrospective piece recounts the **low-key memorials** held annually in Trincomalee and highlights how the case was referenced by **UN High Commissioner for Human Rights Michelle Bachelet** in her 2021 report on Sri Lanka. It also includes the names and birthdates of the victims and details the **threats faced by Dr. Manoharan**, father of one of the slain students.

Chapter 61: The ACF Massacre (Mutur Massacre) Humanitarian Workers Silenced (2006)

(Pic: tamilguardian.com)

In one of the most harrowing crimes of Sri Lanka's civil war, **17 Humanitarian Aid workers** from the French NGO **Action Contre la Faim (ACF)** were executed in cold blood in **Muttur**, Trincomalee District, on **August 4, 2006**. Known as the **ACF Massacre**, this atrocity remains a chilling symbol of impunity, with no one held accountable nearly two decades later.

All 17 victims were **local Sri Lankan staff—16 Tamils and 1 Muslim**.

They were engaged in **Post-Tsunami Relief Work**, providing food, water, and sanitation to displaced communities.

On the day of the massacre, they were found **shot execution-style**, many kneeling and wearing ACF T-shirts.

The killings occurred **inside the ACF compound** in Muttur, shortly after the town had been retaken by **Sri Lankan government forces** following clashes with the LTTE.

Forensic evidence and witness accounts indicated that the victims were **shot at close range**, contradicting initial claims that they were caught in crossfire.

The **Sri Lanka Monitoring Mission (SLMM)** concluded that **only government forces** could have committed the killings.

The **Sri Lankan government denied responsibility**, suggesting the LTTE or Muslim militias were behind the massacre.

A **Presidential Commission of Inquiry** was established in 2007, but:

- **International monitors resigned** in protest over lack of transparency and intimidation of witnesses.

- The final report, released in **2015**, claimed **insufficient evidence** to identify perpetrators and effectively **exonerated the military**.

- **University Teachers for Human Rights (UTHR)** published a detailed report in 2008, naming:

- **Two police constables**
- **One member of the Home Guard**
- **Sri Lanka Navy Special Forces**, who allegedly stood by as the executions took place.

In **2013**, ACF released its own investigative report, concluding that:

- *"The 17 Humanitarian Aid workers were likely assassinated by members of Sri Lankan security forces... covered up by top authorities."*
- The organization labeled the massacre a **war crime** and demanded international accountability.

Human rights groups, including **Human Rights Watch** and **Amnesty International**, condemned the killings and the failure to prosecute.

The massacre is cited as one of the **worst attacks on humanitarian workers worldwide**.

It remains a **symbol of systemic impunity**, where truth is buried and justice denied.

Key Sources

1. **Wikipedia – 2006 Trincomalee Massacre of NGO Workers**
   On **August 4 or 5, 2006**, **17 local staff members** of the French NGO **Action Against Hunger (ACF)** were **executed at close range** in their office in **Mutur**, Trincomalee District. The victims—**16 Tamils and 1 Muslim**—were found lying face down, shot in the head. The **Sri Lanka Monitoring Mission (SLMM)** concluded that **Sri Lankan security forces were responsible**, stating "there cannot be any other armed groups than the security forces who could actually have been behind the act".

2. **Groundviews – "Fifteen Years On: No Justice for Massacre of Muttur Aid Workers"** This investigative piece recounts how the victims were **wearing ACF T-shirts**, **begging for their lives**, and **shot point-blank**. Despite international outrage, **no one has been held accountable**.

3. **Human Rights Watch – "Sri Lanka: 10 Years Since Aid Worker Massacre"**
   HRW called the massacre "one of the most serious recent crimes against humanitarian aid workers worldwide." It emphasized the **failure of Sri Lanka's justice system**, noting that **families of victims were threatened**, and that the **Commission of Inquiry's final report (2015)** failed to identify perpetrators, despite overwhelming evidence.

Chapter 62: Kethesh Loganathan: A Voice for Peace Silenced by War (2006)

(Pic: Daily News)

Ketheeswaran Loganathan, widely known as **Kethesh**, was born in **1952** in **Colombo**, Sri Lanka, though his family hailed from **Puloly-Vadamarachchi** in Jaffna. He was the youngest of six children in a distinguished Tamil family. His father, **Chelliah Loganathan**, was a respected banker and former General Manager of the Bank of Ceylon.

Kethesh was educated at **St. Thomas' College, Mt. Lavinia**, and **Loyola College, Madras**, before pursuing higher studies abroad. He earned a **Bachelor's degree in Business Administration** from **Georgetown University** in Washington, D.C., and a **Master's in Development Studies** from the **Institute of Social Studies** in The Hague. He also studied at the **University of Sussex** and was a **Hubert Humphrey Fellow** at the University of Maryland's College of Journalism.

Kethesh began his career as a **Social science researcher**, working with institutions like the **Marga Institute** and the **Social Scientists' Association**. In the early 1980s, he joined the **Eelam People's Revolutionary Liberation Front (EPRLF)**, a Tamil militant group that later evolved into a political party. His role was primarily **ideological and academic**, not military.

He left the EPRLF in **1994**, disillusioned by the growing violence and authoritarianism in Tamil politics. In **1996**, he published *Lost Opportunities*, a critical analysis of failed peace efforts and the ethnic conflict in Sri Lanka.

Kethesh **co-founded** the **Center for Policy Alternatives (CPA)** with **Paikiasothy Saravanamuttu** and served on its board until 2006. He was a **fierce critic of the LTTE**, especially for their use of **child soldiers**, suppression of dissent, and intolerance of pluralism.

In **March 2006**, President **Mahinda Rajapaksa** appointed Kethesh as **Deputy Secretary-General of the Secretariat for Coordinating the Peace Process (SCOPP)**. He also served as

Secretary of the All-Party Representative Committee (APRC). His appointment was controversial among Tamil nationalists, who viewed him as aligning with the government.

Despite criticism, Kethesh believed in **engagement and negotiation**. He hoped to influence policy from within and promote **power-sharing** and **constitutional reform** to address Tamil grievances.

On **August 12, 2006**, Kethesh was **shot dead outside his home** in **Dehiwala**, Colombo. The assailant reportedly posed as a member of the **Criminal Investigation Department (CID)** before opening fire. He died en route to **Kalubowila Hospital**.

The **LTTE** was widely blamed for the killing, though the group never officially claimed responsibility. Pro-LTTE websites like **Nitharsanam.com** had previously labeled him a **traitor**, and news of his death appeared on Tamilnet before it was confirmed by authorities.

His assassination occurred during a period of escalating violence, just days before Sri Lankan airstrikes killed dozens of children in Mullaitivu. The **United States** condemned his murder, calling him "an individual dedicated to bridging communities and building peace in Sri Lanka".

Kethesh Loganathan's death was a profound loss to Sri Lanka's civil society. He represented a rare breed of Tamil intellectuals who rejected extremism and sought **reconciliation through dialogue**. His assassination underscored the dangers faced by dissenting voices in polarized environments.

Tributes poured in from across the political spectrum. Human rights groups like **UTHR-J** and **Human Rights Watch** mourned his passing. Scholars and journalists, including **Rajan Hoole** and **D.B.S. Jeyaraj**, described him as a **principled nationalist** who believed in **equal rights within a united Sri Lanka**.

His writings, especially *Lost Opportunities*, remain essential reading for those seeking to understand the complexities of Sri Lanka's ethnic conflict.

Key Sources

1. **Wikipedia** – Kethesh Loganathan. Kethesh Loganathan (1952–2006) was a Tamil human rights activist, political analyst, and Deputy Secretary General of the Secretariat for Coordinating the Peace Process (SCOPP). He was assassinated on August 12, 2006, outside his home in Dehiwala, Colombo, by a gunman posing as a CID officer. Widely believed to have been killed by the LTTE, Loganathan had become a vocal critic of their authoritarianism, especially their use of child soldiers and suppression of dissent.

2. **Tamil Guardian** – "Kethesh Loganathan Shot Dead". This report highlights Loganathan's transition from a former EPRLF member to a government peace negotiator, and his role in the Thimpu Talks (1985) and Mangala Moonesinghe Committee (1992). His assassination occurred amid escalating violence in the Jaffna peninsula and was condemned by the United States, which described him as "an individual dedicated to bridging communities and building peace in Sri Lanka".

3. **Polity Journal** – "Reflections on the Killing of Kethesh Loganathan". This essay offers a personal and political reflection on Loganathan's assassination, questioning why such a

fiercely independent Tamil nationalist chose to work within a government peace secretariat. It explores his disillusionment with the 2002 peace process, which he saw as appeasing the LTTE, and his belief that genuine reconciliation required confronting both Sinhala majoritarianism and Tamil militant authoritarianism.

Chapter 63: Subramaniyam Sugirdharajan: Silenced for Truth in Sri Lanka's Shadow War (2006)

(Pic: tamilguardian)

Subramaniyam Sugirdharajan, often referred to as **SSR**, was born in **1970** in **Sri Lanka**, and hailed from **Weeramunai, Kalmunai** in the **Batticaloa district**. He was a **Tamil journalist** working for the Tamil-language daily **Sudar Oli**, known for its bold reporting during the Sri Lankan civil war. At the time of his death, he was **36 years old**, a **father of two young children**, and a respected voice in the Eastern Province.

Journalistic Work and Exposing the Trinco 5 Massacre

SSR's most impactful work came in **January 2006**, when he published **photographs of five Tamil students** who had been **shot dead at point-blank range** on a Trincomalee beach on **January 2, 2006**. The Sri Lankan military had claimed the students were killed by a grenade explosion, but SSR's images—published in *Sudar Oli* on **January 4**—clearly showed gunshot wounds, directly contradicting the official narrative.

He had accompanied **Dr. Manoharan**, the father of one of the victims, to the mortuary, helping document the truth behind the killings. This act of journalistic integrity brought international attention to the **Trinco 5 massacre** but also made SSR a target.

Reporting on Paramilitary Abuses

Just **one day before his death**, SSR published an article detailing **Human Rights Abuses** allegedly committed by **Tamil paramilitary groups**, including the **Eelam People's Democratic Party (EPDP)**, which operated in Trincomalee under state protection. His reporting was bold, naming names and exposing the complicity of armed groups in violence against civilians.

Assassination and Aftermath

On the morning of **January 24, 2006**, SSR was **shot dead near his home** in **Trincomalee**, while waiting for public transport to go to work. Two assailants on a **motorbike** fired at him from close range. The murder occurred near the **Governor's Secretariat**, in an area with a **heavy military presence**, yet no arrests were made.

His death was widely condemned by international organizations including **Reporters Without Borders (RSF)** and the **Committee to Protect Journalists (CPJ)**, who called for an **impartial investigation**. However, **no one was held accountable**, and the case remains unsolved to this day.

Legacy and Press Freedom

SSR's assassination is emblematic of the **culture of impunity** surrounding attacks on journalists in Sri Lanka. His death followed a pattern of targeted killings of Tamil media workers, with **at least 41 journalists** known to have been murdered during and after the civil war.

His courage in exposing state and paramilitary abuses made him a symbol of **press freedom**, and his story continues to be commemorated by journalist unions and civil society groups in Sri Lanka's North and East.

Key Sources

1- **Wikipedia** – Subramaniyam Sugirdharajan. Known as SSR, Sugirdharajan was a journalist for the Tamil-language daily Sudar Oli. He was shot dead on January 24, 2006, in Trincomalee, just weeks after publishing photographic evidence that contradicted the government's account of the Trinco Five massacre.

2- **Tamil Guardian** – "Murdered for Uncovering a Massacre". This article recounts how Sugirdharajan accompanied Dr. Manoharan, father of one of the slain students, to the mortuary and published the photos that disproved the official narrative. He was gunned down near his home while waiting for transport to work.

3- **PUJA** – **"Silenced for Truth**: Justice Denied for Journalist Sugirdharajan". This in-depth profile explores SSR's investigative reporting on paramilitary abuses, including those allegedly committed by the EPDP, a government-aligned group. Despite death threats, he continued to publish stories exposing human rights violations.

Chapter 64: The Rise and Fall of Ronald Prince Collom — Colombo's "Filthy Prince" (2007)

(AI)

Colombo, Sri Lanka's capital, has long been a city of contrasts—where colonial architecture meets modern ambition. But beneath its surface, the 1990s and early 2000s saw the rise of a notorious figure in the city's criminal underworld: **Ronald Prince Collom**, known locally as **"Kunu Kumaraya" ("Filthy Prince").**

Origins and Criminal Ascent

Ronald Prince Collom, born in 1973, emerged from the neighborhood of Kotahena, a densely populated area in Colombo.

By the early 1990s, Collom was identified by law enforcement as a rising figure in organized crime, allegedly involved in murders, extortion, and abduction.

His operations extended across Kotahena, Grandpass, and Bloemendhal, areas known for gang activity during that period.

The Bloemendhal Garbage Dump was reportedly used by Collom's gang as a site for hiding weapons and possibly disposing of victims, though forensic evidence is limited.

Political Protection and Impunity

Collom was widely believed to have enjoyed political protection, particularly through alleged ties to **Mervyn Silva**, a controversial Sri Lankan politician. These connections reportedly allowed him to evade prosecution and operate with relative impunity.

Police raids on his operations were rare, and when they occurred, evidence frequently went missing or cases were dropped, according to investigative reports and media coverage from the time.

Assassination and Aftermath

On **April 28, 2007**, Collom was assassinated at his Bloemendhal residence. Reports confirm that multiple gunmen stormed the property and opened fire.

He was rushed to Colombo National Hospital, where he was pronounced dead on arrival. Over 20 spent bullet casings were recovered from the scene, indicating the use of automatic weapons, likely T-56 assault rifles.

His death marked the end of a violent chapter in Colombo's criminal history, though remnants of his network reportedly persisted.

Legacy and Continued Influence

In 2016, a triple homicide in Wellampitiya was linked by Police to former members of Collom's gang, suggesting that elements of his criminal network remained active nearly a decade after his death.

Timeline

Year / Date	Event
1973	Born in Sri Lanka
Early 1990s	Begins criminal activity in Kotahena and Grandpass
1990s–2000s	Allegedly involved in murders, extortion, and abduction
April 29, 2007	Assassinated at Bloemendhal residence
2016	Triple murder in Wellampitiya linked to remnants of his gang

Key Sources

1. Sunday Times – "Godfather of Garbage"
   This investigative feature profiles **Prince Collom**, also known as **"Kunu Kumaraya"** (Filthy Prince), who controlled the **Bloemendhal garbage mafia** in Colombo. Locals described him as a **Robin Hood-like figure**, who provided food and settled disputes while running extortion rackets and allegedly orchestrating multiple murders. His death in **April 2007**, at the hands of an unidentified group, left a power vacuum in the area's criminal ecosystem.

2. **Wikipedia – List of Sri Lankan Mobsters**
   This entry confirms that **Ronald Prince Collom** was active from **1992 to 2007**, involved in **over 100 killings**, including rape and extortion in **Kotahena and Grandpass**. His political patron was reportedly **Mervin Silva**, a controversial figure in Sri Lankan politics. Collom's notoriety earned him a place among the most dangerous figures in Colombo's underworld.

3. **Hiru Gossip – "Triple Murder in Wellampitiya Linked to Prince Kolom's Gang"**
   This report reveals that even years after his death, **Prince Kolom's gang** remained active and embroiled in violent turf wars. A **triple murder in 2016** was linked to remnants of his network, suggesting that his criminal legacy continued to shape Colombo's underworld long after his assassination.

Chapter 65: The Air Tigers – Wings of Defiance Over Colombo (2007-2009)

The Air Tigers, also known as the **Tamil Eelam Air Force (TAF) or Sky Tigers**, were the Aerial Division of the Liberation Tigers of Tamil Eelam (LTTE). Their existence was long speculated but confirmed in March 2007 following a surprise air raid near Colombo, marking the LTTE as **the first non-state militant group** to operate a functional air wing.

Founder: **Vythialingam Sornalingam**, known as **Colonel Shankar**, was credited with developing the air wing. He held an Aeronautical Engineering Diploma from Hindustan Engineering College in India and reportedly worked for Air Canada.

Purpose:

- Counter Sri Lankan Air Force (SLAF) dominance
- Demonstrate state-like military capability
- Conduct psychological warfare and tactical bombing

Aircraft and Capabilities

• Aircraft were retrofitted with bomb racks and exhaust modifications to reduce infrared visibility.

• Most aircraft were smuggled in during the 2002–2006 ceasefire period.

Airstrips and Infrastructure

Main Airstrip: **Near Iranamadu,** reportedly capable of landing medium-lift aircraft like the C-130 Hercules.

Additional Airstrips: Located in **Puthukudiyiruppu and Mullaitivu**, often camouflaged.

Notable Attacks

1. First Air Raid – March 26, 2007

- Target: SLAF base near Bandaranaike International Airport
- Method: One or two Zlín aircraft dropped bombs on a parking area for planes and helicopters.
- Casualties: 3 SLAF personnel killed, 16 injured
- Impact: Confirmed LTTE's air capability and triggered panic in Colombo

2. Suicide Air Raid – February 20, 2009

- Aircraft: Two Zlín Z-143 planes, converted into flying bombs
- Route: Took off from Puthukkudiyiruppu, flew low to avoid radar

Targets:

- One aircraft crashed into **the Inland Revenue Department near SLAF HQ in Colombo**
- Second was shot down near **Katunayake, close to the Airport**
- Casualties: 4 dead (including both pilots), 58+ injured

Impact:

- City-wide blackout
- Flight cancellations
- Exposed gaps in air defense

Strategic and Psychological Impact

- The Air Tigers' attacks were symbolic, not militarily decisive.
- They demonstrated the LTTE's reach and innovation in asymmetric warfare.
- Their operations raised global awareness of the LTTE's unconventional tactics.

The Air Tigers were dismantled following the LTTE's defeat in May 2009.

Key Sources

1 - **Wikipedia – 2009 Suicide Air Raid on Colombo**. On February 20, 2009, the LTTE's air wing—known as the Air Tigers—launched a suicide attack using two light aircraft against military and government targets in Colombo and Katunayake. One plane crashed into the Inland Revenue Department, killing two civilians and injuring over 58 people, while the other was shot down near the international airport. These aircraft were Zlin Z-143s, modified for bombing and flown by trained suicide pilots.

2 - **TIME Magazine** – "A Surprise Attack by Sri Lanka's Tamil Tigers" This article highlights the psychological impact of the Air Tigers' operations. Despite their limited firepower, the LTTE became the first guerrilla group in the world to deploy an air force, beginning with a March 2007 bombing raid on an air base near Colombo.

3 - **South Asia Terrorism Portal** – "LTTE Aerial Attacks 2007–2009". This database documents multiple aerial strikes by the LTTE, including bombings of Mannar Army HQ, Vavuniya, and Colombo suburbs. It notes that the Sri Lankan government responded by activating air defense systems and cutting electricity to the capital during suspected raids.

Chapter 66: The Assassination of Lasantha Wickrematunge – A Thriller of Truth, Power, and Betrayal (2009)

In the heart of Colombo's morning traffic on **January 8, 2009**, as city life drummed with routine expectation, the echo of gunshots cracked through the quiet desperation of a man who had long predicted his own death. **Lasantha Wickrematunge—Editor of *The Sunday Leader***, fearless journalist, and critic of state corruption, was assassinated in broad daylight, sending shockwaves across Sri Lanka and the International community. But what made this murder far more than a tragic end was what came after: the unfolding of a complex, high-stakes thriller that remains unresolved sixteen years later.

The Editor Who Challenged Power

Lasantha wasn't just a journalist; he was a relentless crusader against tyranny. With his pen as his weapon, he exposed nepotism, corruption, and abuse embedded within the highest echelons of power. His editorials cut deep, calling out military overreach and political impunity during a time when dissent invited death.

He knew the cost of truth. Days before his murder, he composed an editorial to be published in the event of his death, a haunting eulogy to journalism itself: ***"When finally, I am killed, it will be the government that kills me."*** A chilling prophecy, fulfilled with surgical precision.

The Day Truth Was Silenced

As Lasantha drove to work in his white Toyota, assailants on motorbikes intercepted him near a busy junction. Eyewitnesses recalled the chaos, glass shattering, bodies scrambling, sirens late to the scene. He sustained fatal head injuries and died soon after. No suspects were arrested that day. No immediate explanations followed. Just grief, outrage, and fear.

This wasn't an ordinary killing. It was a statement, sharp, cold, and deliberate.

A Trail of Obstruction

Over the years, investigations unfolded like a screenplay riddled with deleted scenes. Whistleblowers, insiders, and investigators spoke of:

Evidence tampering: Critical pages from field notebooks were removed and rewritten.

Intimidation: A police officer warned off a junior inspector with the chilling line: *"This is Gota's job. Do you also want to get killed?"*

(*"This is Gota's job" quote: While there are credible reports of intimidation and references to Gotabaya Rajapaksa in connection with Wickrematunge's legal battles, this specific quote is not directly verified in public sources. It may be anecdotal or paraphrased from insider testimony.*)

Nature of the Attack: Initial reports described gunshot wounds, but later medical findings suggested blunt force trauma, possibly from a sharp object rather than bullets.

Legal reversals: Despite compelling grounds for prosecution, Attorney General **Parinda Ranasinghe** abruptly dropped charges against three key suspects in January 2025:

- *Premananda Udalagama* – **Former Army Intelligence Officer**
- *Tissa Sugathapala* – **Former Crimes OIC**
- *Prasanna Nanayakkara* – **Retired DIG**

    The AG's office clarified that the dropped charges were related to a separate case involving the abduction of Wickrematunge's driver, not the murder itself. However, critics argue this distinction is misleading and undermines the broader investigation.

This move ignited an uproar. Media rights groups, journalists, and civil society decried the decision as judicial capitulation to political pressure.

Civil Revolt and The Cry for Justice

Protests erupted across Colombo. **The Young Journalists' Association** led marches with banners that screamed *"Who Killed Lasantha?"* While government spokespeople dodged questions, organizations like the Free Media Movement released blistering statements, condemning what they called "a legitimization of impunity."

International observers weighed in. Human rights advocates accused Sri Lankan authorities of shielding the powerful and sabotaging the pursuit of truth.

The Ghost of Lasantha

The power of Lasantha Wickrematunge's voice transcends his death. His legacy isn't a tombstone, it's a challenge. Journalists continue citing his work. His final editorial is taught in classrooms as both literature and warning. In the shadowed halls of justice, his ghost lingers—asking the same unanswerable question: *Why has truth been buried deeper than the body that carried it?*

Key Sources

1. **Wikipedia – Assassination of Lasantha Wickrematunge**
   Lasantha Wickrematunge, editor of *The Sunday Leader*, was **fatally shot on January 8, 2009**, in **Ratmalana, Colombo**, while driving to work. He had long been a vocal critic of government corruption and military abuses, particularly under President Mahinda Rajapaksa. Wickrematunge had received **numerous death threats**, and in a prophetic editorial published posthumously, he wrote: "When finally I am killed, it will be the government that kills me."
   His murder was widely condemned internationally and became a symbol of the **collapse of press freedom** in Sri Lanka.

2. **Global Investigative Journalism Network – "Who Was Behind the Killing of Lasantha Wickrematunge?"**
   Former CID investigator **Nishantha Silva** uncovered evidence implicating **Gotabaya Rajapaksa**, then Secretary of Defense, in orchestrating the killing. Silva's investigation revealed a **missing notebook**, a **motorcycle dumped in a lake**, and a **network of military operatives** allegedly involved. The case was later stalled, and Silva fled the country after Gotabaya became president. A civil suit filed in the U.S. by Wickrematunge's daughter was dismissed due to diplomatic immunity.

3. **Roar Media – "The Lasantha Wickrematunge Case: A Timeline"**
   This timeline tracks the **events leading up to and following the assassination**, including the **disappearance of Wickrematunge's mobile phone and documents**, conflicting autopsy reports, and the **lack of progress in the investigation**. It also highlights the chilling foresight in his final editorial and the **global outcry** that followed his death.

Chapter 67: Formation of Sea Tigers - Guerrilla Navy of Tamil Eelam (2007-2009)

(Pic: en.wikipedia.org)

The Sea Tigers (Kaṭaṟpulikaḷ) were the naval wing of the Liberation Tigers of Tamil Eelam (LTTE), formed in 1984 under the directive of LTTE leader Velupillai Prabhakaran.

Founder: Initiated by **Colonel Shankar (Vaithilingam Sornalingam)**, an Aeronautical Engineer with maritime expertise.

Commander: Led by **Colonel Soosai (Thillaiyambalam Sivanesan)**, a charismatic and tactical leader from Valvettithurai.

Purpose:

- Smuggle arms and personnel across the Palk Strait
- Challenge the Sri Lankan Navy's dominance
- Support amphibious operations and coastal defense
- Conduct suicide missions and sabotage

Evolution of Naval Power

Initially operating fishing boats and small crafts, the Sea Tigers evolved into a formidable guerrilla navy:

- Fleet Composition:
- Fast attack fiberglass boats
- Suicide vessels packed with explosives
- Underwater demolition teams (frogmen)
- Radar-equipped command boats
- Bases: Main base at **Mullaitivu**, with others in **Nachikuda, Chalai, and Sundikulam**

Major Operations and Tactics

1. Sinking of SLNS Sagarawardena (1994)

• A landmark victory where Sea Tigers sank a **Sri Lankan Navy offshore patrol vessel** near Mannar.

• 18 survivors out of 43 crew; the Captain was captured and held for 8 years.

2. Battle of Mullaitivu (1996)

• Sea Tigers landed troops and blocked naval reinforcements.

• Sank **SLNS Ranaviru**, a key naval vessel during the battle.

3. Attack on MV Princess Wave (1996)

• Underwater bombing of a cargo vessel loading ilmenite at Pulmoddai.

• 9 workers injured, showcasing their sabotage capabilities.

4. Operation Varuna Kirana (2001)

• Sri Lankan Navy's failed attempt to intercept LTTE smuggling convoys.

• Sea Tigers used convoy tactics, escorting trawlers with attack boats and evading detection.

5. Use of Frogmen and Suicide Boats

• Sea Tigers deployed Black Tigers in suicide missions against naval targets.

• Frogmen used bubble-free diving gear for stealth underwater attacks.

Tactical Innovation and Impact

Guerrilla Naval Warfare: Sea Tigers pioneered asymmetric naval tactics, including swarm attacks and suicide missions.

Smuggling Networks: Maintained supply routes from Tamil Nadu using disguised trawlers and international shipping lanes.

Psychological Warfare: Their ability to strike at sea instilled fear and forced the Sri Lankan Navy to divert resources.

The Sea Tigers were dismantled in 2009 during the final phase of the war.

Their last stronghold at **Chalai** was captured by the Sri Lankan Army.

Despite their defeat, the Sea Tigers remain a rare example of a non-state naval force that challenged a conventional navy for over two decades.

Tactics of the Sea Tigers – Underwater Sabotage and Amphibious Precision

Frogmen Training and Underwater Warfare

The Sea Tigers developed a specialized underwater commando unit, known as the **Gangai Amaran Underwater Swimming Division, led by Lt. Colonel Gangai Amaran**. These frogmen were trained for stealth sabotage, reconnaissance, and suicide missions.

Training Facilities and Techniques

Location: Training pools and underwater testing facilities were built in the jungles near Mullaitivu, camouflaged from aerial surveillance.

Equipment:

- **Rebreathers**: Bubble-free diving gear to avoid surface detection
- **Underwater explosives**: Compact charges for hull sabotage
- **Cyanide capsules:** Standard issue for captured operatives
- **Skills Taught**:   Silent swimming and infiltration
- Hull placement of magnetic mines
- Harbor reconnaissance and escape tactics

Notable Frogmen Operations

2006 Colombo Port Raid: Two frogmen attempted to bomb ships; both were captured and tried to commit suicide

2008 Trincomalee Harbor Attack: Frogmen sank a Sri Lankan Navy supply ship using underwater explosives

Coordinated Land-Sea Operations

The Sea Tigers were not just a maritime force—they were integral to amphibious assaults, logistical support, and strategic rescues.

Tactical Coordination

Multi-pronged assaults: Sea Tigers would land troops on beaches while land units attacked from inland

Evacuation missions: Extracted trapped LTTE cadres from enemy-held zones

Supply chain integration: Used ocean-going freighters to deliver arms, then transferred cargo to fast boats escorted by attack craft

Defensive and Offensive Roles

Coastal defense: Prevented Sri Lankan Navy landings in LTTE-controlled zones

Wolf-pack tactics: Swarm attacks using multiple fast boats to overwhelm naval patrols

Black Sea Tigers: Suicide units used explosive-laden boats to ram naval vessels, often under covering fire

Here's a Conceptual Map of Sea Tiger operations

Region	Role	Key Activities
Mullaitivu	HQ and training base	Frogmen training, boat construction
Palk Strait	Smuggling corridor	Arms and personnel movement
Trincomalee	Target zone	Harbor sabotage, ship sinking
Elephant Pass	Amphibious support	Troop landings during major offensives

Timeline of Tactical Evolution

Year	Milestone
1984	Formation of Sea Tigers
1994	Sinking of SLNS Sagarawardena
1996	Amphibious role in Battle of Mullaitivu
2001	Operation Varuna Kirana (Navy counter-effort)
2006	Frogmen raid on Colombo Port
2008	Underwater attack in Trincomalee
2009	Final defeat and dismantling of Sea Tigers

Key Sources

1. **Wikipedia – Sea Tigers**
   The **Sea Tigers** were the naval arm of the **Liberation Tigers of Tamil Eelam (LTTE)**, active from **1984 until May 18, 2009**. By the late 2000s, they had evolved into a formidable guerrilla navy, conducting **amphibious warfare, suicide attacks, arms trafficking**, and **naval boarding operations**. Under the command of **Colonel Soosai**, they operated out of **Mullaitivu**, launching attacks that sank **29 patrol boats, 20 Dvora-class vessels**, and even **Sri Lankan Navy command ships**.

2. **ICRC Casebook – "Sri Lanka: Naval War Against Tamil Tigers"**
   This legal case study analyzes the **Sea Tigers' maritime operations** and the Sri Lankan Navy's countermeasures. It discusses how the LTTE used **small fiberglass boats**, often packed with explosives, to breach blockades and deliver arms. The study raises questions about the **application of international humanitarian law** to non-state naval actors.

3. **Naval Postgraduate School Thesis – "Lessons in Legitimacy: The LTTE End-Game of 2007–2009"**
   This U.S. military thesis explores how the **Sea Tigers' operations from 2007 to 2009** reflected the LTTE's broader strategy of asymmetric warfare. It notes that the Sea Tigers were instrumental in **smuggling weapons**, **evading naval blockades**, and **supporting ground offensives**, even as the LTTE's territorial control collapsed.

Chapter 68: Thiyagarajah Maheswaran: A Voice for Tamil Rights Silenced in Sacred Space (2008)

Born on **January 10, 1966**, in **Karainagar, Jaffna**, T. Maheswaran hailed from a Tamil Hindu family rooted in northern Sri Lanka. He was educated at **Yarlton College** and **St. John's College, Jaffna**, before becoming a successful businessman in Colombo. His fluency in **Tamil, Sinhala, and English**, along with his affable personality, made him a popular figure across ethnic lines.

Maheswaran entered politics through the **United National Party (UNP)**, becoming one of the few Tamil politicians to join a **Sinhalese-majority party** during the civil war. He served as **Minister of Hindu Affairs** and was elected as a **Member of Parliament for Colombo District** in 2004.

Maheswaran was known for his **outspoken criticism of human rights abuses**, particularly those affecting Tamil civilians in the North and East. He frequently challenged the government's emergency regulations and highlighted the role of paramilitary groups—especially the **Eelam People's Democratic Party (EPDP)**—in alleged extrajudicial killings.

Despite supporting the war effort against the LTTE, he condemned the **civilian toll** and called for accountability. His speeches in Parliament were often emotional and impassioned, earning both admiration and criticism. He also supported the **anti-conversion bill**, which led to accusations of **Hindu chauvinism** and strained relations with Christian Tamil groups.

Christian Tamil relations: His support for the anti-conversion bill did cause friction, but he remained respected across many Tamil communities.

On **January 1, 2008**, Maheswaran visited the **Shree Ponnambalavaneswarar Sivan Temple** in **Kotahena, Colombo**, with his four-year-old daughter to perform New Year rituals. As he exited the temple around **9:30 a.m.**, holding a ceremonial coconut and his daughter's hand, a gunman approached and **opened fire**.

(Time of assassination: Some sources cite 9:30 a.m., others 10:35 a.m.—likely due to reporting delays.)

Maheswaran was struck by **four bullets** to the chest and head. His bodyguard returned fire, injuring the assassin, who was later identified and arrested at **Colombo National Hospital**. A Hindu pilgrim also died in the crossfire.

Notably, Maheswaran's **official security detail had been reduced** from 18 to just 2 officers after he voted against the government's budget in December 2007. He had written to **Defence Secretary Gotabaya Rajapaksa** warning of threats to his life, but no action was taken.

(Number of security officers: Reduced from 18 to 2, though some sources mention 11 to 2.)

The assassin, **Johnson Colin Valentine alias "Vasanthan"**, was indicted on two counts of murder. In **August 2012**, the **Colombo High Court** sentenced him to **death**, citing DNA evidence and eyewitness testimony. The verdict was **upheld by the Court of Appeal** in **March 2022**, rejecting claims of contradictory evidence and procedural unfairness.

Maheswaran's assassination was a **political earthquake**, underscoring the dangers faced by minority voices in Sri Lanka's polarized landscape. His death sparked outrage among Tamil communities and Human Rights advocates, who viewed it as a targeted killing meant to silence dissent.

His widow, **Vijayakala Maheswaran**, later entered politics and served as a Member of Parliament and State Minister, continuing his legacy of Tamil representation.

Maheswaran is remembered as a **bridge-builder**, a man who dared to speak truth in Parliament, and a symbol of the **cost of conscience** in Sri Lankan politics.

Key Sources

1. **Wikipedia – T. Maheswaran.** Thiyagarajah Maheswaran was a **United National Party (UNP) Member of Parliament** for Colombo District and a former **Minister of Hindu Affairs**. On **January 1, 2008**, he was **assassinated while worshipping at the Shree Ponnambalaneswaran Sivan Temple** in Kotahena, Colombo. He had previously survived an assassination attempt in 2004 and was known for **highlighting human rights abuses against Tamils**, including alleged killings by paramilitary groups in Jaffna.

2. **FIDH – Assassination of Mr. Thiyagarajah Maheswaran** The **International Federation for Human Rights (FIDH)** condemned Maheswaran's killing as an **extrajudicial execution**, noting that it occurred shortly after the **Ministry of Defence ordered the withdrawal of security personnel** from several Tamil parliamentarians.

3. **OMCT – Urgent Intervention on Maheswaran's Assassination**
   The **World Organisation Against Torture (OMCT)** issued an urgent appeal, describing Maheswaran's murder as part of a **campaign of intimidation and violence** against Tamil MPs. It emphasized the **climate of impunity** and the **lack of credible**

investigations, which discouraged Tamil politicians from speaking out on disappearances and extrajudicial killings.

Chapter 69: The Abduction Files – Keith Noyahr & The 'Navy 11': A Tale of Torture, Silence, and Systemic Impunity (2008 & 2009)

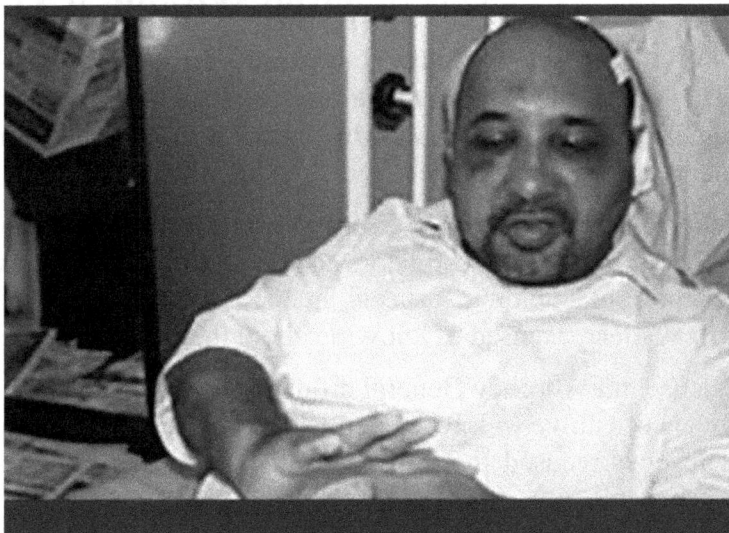

(Pic: dailymirror.lk)

In the annals of Sri Lanka's post-war history, few cases illustrate the chilling reach of state power and the fragility of justice like the abduction of journalist **Keith Noyahr** and the enforced disappearance of the **'Navy 11'**. These two cases, separate in victims, but united in method and motive, reveal a disturbing pattern of military-led abductions, torture, and cover-ups that continue to haunt the nation's conscience.

On **May 22, 2008**, respected journalist and Associate Editor of *The Nation,* Keith Noyahr, was abducted outside his home in **Dehiwala.** His car was found idling, headlights on, door ajar, an eerie scene that marked the beginning of a seven-hour ordeal. Noyahr was brutally tortured before being released, a rare outcome in a country where many abductees never return.

His crime? A scathing article under the pseudonym **"Senpathi,"** criticizing the leadership of then-Army Commander **Sarath Fonseka**. The timing was no coincidence. The Rajapaksa administration was already under fire for orchestrating a wave of **"White Van"** abductions targeting journalists and dissidents.

For years, the case stagnated. But in **March 2025**, two retired Military Intelligence Corps officers were arrested in connection with the abduction. Then, in **May 2025**, the Attorney General announced indictments against **12 former Armed Forces officers**, including charges of **attempted murder, conspiracy to kidnap, and assault**.

This marked a significant shift, 17 years after the crime, the wheels of justice began to turn. Yet, skepticism remains. Will these indictments lead to convictions, or will they join the long list of unresolved cases?

Note: *The 2025 arrests and indictments of 12 officers are not yet publicly confirmed. As of September 2025, no official record supports this new wave of legal action.*

The 'Navy 11' – Disappeared Without a Trace

Between **August 2008 and February 2009**, **11 Tamil youth** vanished from Colombo and surrounding areas. They were allegedly abducted by Sri Lankan Navy personnel and held at naval bases, including **Trincomalee** and **Colombo**, before disappearing. Some were reportedly held for ransom. Among the victims were teenagers, young adults, and even father-son pairs.

The case gained traction in **2018**, when **Lt. Commander Chandana Prasad Hettiarachchi**, aka **"Navy Sampath,"** was arrested. Investigators accused **Admiral Ravindra Wijeguneratne**, then Chief of Defence Staff, of shielding suspects. In **2019**, **Admiral Wasantha Karannagoda** was named as the **14th suspect**, accused of knowing about the disappearances and failing to act.

Despite damning evidence, the Attorney General dropped charges against Karannagoda in **2021**, citing insufficient evidence, a move widely condemned as politically motivated. In **March 2025**, two Supreme Court justices recused themselves from hearing petitions to reinstate charges, further delaying proceedings.

The case is now scheduled to be re-heard in **September 2025**, but the families of the victims remain skeptical. International bodies, including **Amnesty International**, have called for accountability, citing Sri Lanka's staggering record of enforced disappearances.

A Nation Haunted by Its Secrets

Both cases—**Keith Noyahr and the Navy 11**—are emblematic of a broader crisis: the erosion of rule of law, the shielding of perpetrators, and the weaponization of silence. They expose how military and political elites have operated with near-total impunity, and how justice, when it comes, arrives late and limping.

These stories are not just about victims. They are about a country grappling with its past, and a future that depends on whether truth can finally triumph over terror.

Key Sources:

Keith Noyahr – Journalist Targeted for Truth (2008)

1 - **Wikipedia – Keith Noyahr.** Noyahr was the Deputy Editor of The Nation and a respected defense analyst. On May 22, 2008, he was abducted outside his home in Dehiwala, brutally tortured for hours, and released the next morning. His reporting had criticized high-ranking military officials, including then-Army Commander Sarath Fonseka, and questioned the government's war strategy.

2 - **Sri Lanka Brief** – "Breakthrough in Keith Noyahr Abduction Case" In 2017, five army personnel were arrested, including Major Prabath Bulathwatte, linked to a military intelligence unit suspected of involvement in multiple journalist attacks. The CID later traveled to Australia to record Noyahr's testimony, where he had fled for safety.

3 - **Tamil Guardian** – "Intelligence Officers Arrested Over Noyahr Abduction" In 2025, two retired intelligence officers were arrested, reigniting calls for accountability. The abduction was part of a broader campaign of "white van" disappearances targeting dissenting voices.

The 'Navy 11' – Abducted for Ransom, Disappeared (2008–2009)

1 - **Amnesty International** – "Sri Lanka Falters on Navy 11 Accountability" Between 2008 and 2009, 11 Tamil youth were abducted by Sri Lankan Navy personnel, allegedly for ransom. Despite payments, the victims were never returned. The CID implicated Admiral Wasantha Karannagoda and Admiral Ravindra Wijeguneratne, but charges were dropped in 2021 amid political interference.

2 - **Groundviews** – "Murder for Money: The Navy 11 Case" This exposé reveals that the abductions were not linked to terrorism, but were criminal rackets run by naval officers. The case involved 667 indictments, including extortion, conspiracy, and murder, yet justice remains elusive due to political shielding.

3 - **Tamil Guardian** – "The Navy Commander and the Torture Site" The victims were held at "Gun Site", a clandestine torture facility in Trincomalee Naval Base, used for illegal detention and abuse. Despite international sanctions and mounting evidence, senior officials like Admiral Nishantha Ulugetenne rose through the ranks and were later appointed to diplomatic posts.

Chapter 70: Timeline: Counter-Intelligence & Major Battles in Sri Lanka (1984–2009)

Eelam War I (1983–1987)

Year	Event	Description
1984	Formation of LTTE Intelligence Wing	Led by **Pottu Amman**, focused on internal security, assassinations, and infiltration of government networks.
1985	Kokkilai Offensive	LTTE attacked SLA camp; first major clash in Mullaitivu District. SLA victory.
1987	Vadamarachchi Operation	SLA launched a major offensive in Jaffna; partial victory before Indian intervention.
1987	Operation Poomalai	Indian Air Force dropped supplies over Jaffna, signaling direct Indian involvement.

Indian Peacekeeping Force (IPKF) Phase (1987–1990)

Year	Event	Description
1987	Operation Pawan	IPKF launched assault on Jaffna to disarm LTTE; heavy casualties.
1988	Jaffna University Helidrop	Failed IPKF operation; LTTE ambushed Indian troops.
1989	LTTE Counter-Intelligence	LTTE began targeting Tamil rivals and informants; internal purges intensified.

Eelam War II (1990–1995)

Year	Event	Description
1990	Battle of Kokavil	LTTE overran SLA camp; significant loss for government.
1991	Operation Balavegaya	SLA broke LTTE siege of Elephant Pass; major victory.
1993	Battle of Pooneryn	LTTE captured strategic base; heavy SLA casualties.
1994	Intelligence Reforms	Sri Lanka expanded military intelligence and CID operations to counter LTTE infiltration.

Eelam War III (1995–2002)

Year	Event	Description
1995	Operation Riviresa	SLA recaptured Jaffna; turning point in northern campaign.
1997	Operation Jayasikurui	Attempt to open land route to Jaffna; failed due to LTTE resistance.
1999	Operation Ranagosa	SLA victory in Vanni region; LTTE suffered territorial losses.
2000	Rajagiriya Bomb Blast	LTTE bomb attack near Colombo; suspected counter-intelligence failure.

Counter-Intelligence Milestones

Year	Event	Description
2001	Intelligence Coordination Center	Established to unify military, police, and foreign intelligence inputs.
2002	Ceasefire Agreement	Intelligence shifted to monitoring LTTE movements and ceasefire violations.
2005	Assassination of Foreign Minister Kadirgamar	LTTE sniper attack; exposed gaps in VIP protection protocols.
Eelam War IV (2006–2009)		
2006	Mavil Aru Water Crisis	LTTE blocked water supply; SLA launched full-scale offensive.
2007	Thoppigala Operations	SLA cleared eastern LTTE stronghold; major victory.
2008	Northern Offensive	SLA advanced into Kilinochchi and Mullaitivu; coordinated land-sea-air campaign.
2009	Final Battle at Mullaitivu	LTTE leadership killed; war officially ended on **May 18, 2009**.

A Narrative of Counter-Intelligence and Major Battles (1984–2009)

Prelude to War: Rise of the LTTE (1983–1984)

Following the anti-Tamil riots of July 1983, known as Black July, Sri Lanka plunged into a full-scale ethnic conflict. The Liberation Tigers of Tamil Eelam (LTTE) emerged as the dominant Tamil militant group, led by Velupillai Prabhakaran. In 1984, the LTTE established its intelligence wing, headed by Shanmugalingam Sivashankar (Pottu Amman), which became infamous for its ruthless internal security, assassinations, and deep infiltration of rival groups and government institutions.

Eelam War I (1983–1987): Guerrilla Warfare and Early Battles

The first phase of the war saw sporadic clashes and ambushes. In 1985, the LTTE launched the **Kokkilai Offensive**, attacking a Sri Lankan Army (SLA) Camp in Mullaitivu. The SLA repelled the attack, marking one of the first major confrontations. By 1987, the government launched **Operation Vadamarachchi**, a large-scale offensive to retake Jaffna. The operation was successful but short-lived—India intervened, dropping supplies over Jaffna in **Operation**

Poomalai, and later deployed the **Indian Peacekeeping Force (IPKF)** under the Indo-Sri Lanka Accord.

IPKF Phase (1987–1990): Foreign Intervention and Intelligence Chaos

The IPKF's mission to disarm the LTTE quickly turned into a bloody conflict. In **Operation Pawan (1987),** Indian forces attempted to capture Jaffna, facing fierce resistance. The **Jaffna University Helidrop (1988)** was a failed IPKF operation that ended in an ambush. During this period, the LTTE intensified its counter-intelligence operations, purging suspected informants and rival Tamil factions. The IPKF withdrew in 1990, leaving behind a fractured intelligence landscape and a resurgent LTTE.

Eelam War II (1990–1995): Escalation and Strategic Setbacks

With the IPKF gone, hostilities resumed. The **Battle of Kokavil (1990)** saw the LTTE overrun an SLA Camp, showcasing their growing military prowess. In 1991, the SLA launched **Operation Balavegaya** to break the LTTE siege of **Elephant Pass**, a strategic gateway to Jaffna. The operation was a success, but the LTTE retaliated with the **Battle of Pooneryn (1993),** capturing a key base and inflicting heavy casualties.

Recognizing the need for better intelligence, the government expanded its Military Intelligence Corps and Criminal Investigation Department (CID) in 1994, focusing on intercepting LTTE communications and tracking sleeper cells.

Eelam War III (1995–2002): Turning Points and Tactical Evolution

In 1995, the SLA launched **Operation Riviresa**, successfully recapturing Jaffna Peninsula. This marked a turning point, but the LTTE adapted with mobile warfare and deep infiltration. The government responded with **Operation Jayasikurui (1997),** aiming to open a land route to Jaffna. However, the campaign stalled due to LTTE ambushes and logistical failures.

In 1999, **Operation Ranagosa** pushed into the Vanni region, dealing territorial losses to the LTTE. Meanwhile, LTTE intelligence struck back with high-profile attacks, including the Rajagiriya bomb blast (2000) near Colombo, exposing vulnerabilities in urban counter-intelligence.

Intelligence Consolidation and Political Assassinations (2001–2005)

In 2001, Sri Lanka established the Intelligence Coordination Center, integrating military, police, and foreign intelligence inputs. This helped monitor ceasefire violations after the 2002 Ceasefire Agreement, brokered by Norway.

Despite the truce, LTTE intelligence remained active. In 2005, Foreign Minister Lakshman Kadirgamar was assassinated by an LTTE sniper, a chilling reminder of their reach. The attack revealed lapses in VIP protection and prompted a re-evaluation of counter-intelligence protocols.

Eelam War IV (2006–2009): Final Offensive and Collapse of the LTTE

The Ceasefire collapsed in 2006, triggered by the **Mavil Aru Water Crisis**, where the LTTE blocked a key irrigation canal. The SLA responded with a full-scale offensive. In 2007, the **Thoppigala Operations** cleared the Eastern Province of LTTE control.

By 2008, the SLA launched a coordinated **Northern Offensive**, advancing into Kilinochchi and Mullaitivu, the LTTE's strongholds. The military employed advanced surveillance, UAVs, and SIGINT (signals intelligence) to track LTTE movements.

In **May 2009, the Final Battle unfolded in Mullaitivu**, where Prabhakaran and the LTTE leadership were killed. On **May 18, 2009**, the government declared victory, ending a 26-year war.

Intelligence Legacy

Sri Lanka's counter-intelligence evolved from fragmented efforts to a centralized, multi-agency system. The war showcased the importance of:

- Human Intelligence (HUMINT): Cultivating informants within LTTE ranks.
- Signals Intelligence (SIGINT): Intercepting LTTE communications.
- Surveillance & Reconnaissance: Using drones and satellite imagery.
- Psychological Operations: Undermining LTTE morale and propaganda.

Minor Clarifications or Additions

Rajagiriya Bomb Blast (2000): While LTTE attacks in Colombo are documented, this specific incident is less prominently cited. It may be accurate but lacks strong sourcing.

Operation Ranagosa (1999): Mentioned in military records, but not as a major turning point compared to Riviresa or Jayasikurui.

Intelligence Reforms (1994): Expansion of CID and military intelligence is plausible but not widely detailed in public sources.

Key Sources

1. State Intelligence Service (Sri Lanka) – Wikipedia

256

2. CIA Handbook on Sri Lanka (1984)
3. Journal of Applied Operational Intelligence – "Why Sri Lanka Needs Intelligence Reform"
4. List of Military Operations – Wikipedia
5. WarHistory.org – "Sri Lanka 1983–2009"

Chapter 71: The Final Phase of Sri Lanka's Civil War Decisive Victory, Tragic Cost (2019)

(Pic: slguardian.org)

The final months of Sri Lanka's civil war in 2009 marked a brutal crescendo to a 26-year conflict between the Sri Lankan government and the Liberation Tigers of Tamil Eelam (LTTE). What unfolded in the northeastern Vanni region was a military campaign of unprecedented intensity, culminating in the death of LTTE's top leadership and the collapse of its separatist movement. Yet, this victory came at a staggering human cost—tens of thousands of civilians perished, and allegations of war crimes continue to haunt the nation.

Government Leadership:

- **President Mahinda Rajapaksa**: Commander-in-Chief and political architect of the final offensive.
- **Defense Secretary Gotabaya Rajapaksa**: Oversaw military strategy; credited with implementing the "zero civilian casualty" policy.
- **General Sarath Fonseka**: Army Commander who led ground operations.

LTTE Leadership:

- **Velupillai Prabhakaran**: LTTE founder and supreme leader; killed on May 18, 2009.
- **Charles Anthony**: Prabhakaran's son; killed in final clashes.
- **Pottu Amman**: Intelligence chief; reportedly killed.
- **Soosai**: Sea Tigers commander; killed.
- **Balasingham Nadesan & Seevaratnam Puleedevan**: Political wing leaders; allegedly executed after surrendering.

Timeline of the Final Phase (2008–2009)

Date	Event
Jan 2008	Government annuls ceasefire; launches full-scale offensive
Jan 2, 2009	Army captures LTTE's de facto capital, Kilinochchi
Apr 20, 2009	Government gives LTTE 24 hours to surrender; 115,000 civilians flee in one week
May 16, 2009	Army secures entire coastline; President Rajapaksa declares military victory
May 17, 2009	LTTE fighters disguised as civilians killed while fleeing; others commit suicide attacks
May 18, 2009	Prabhakaran and senior leaders killed; war officially ends
May 19, 2009	Rajapaksa announces end of war in Parliament

The White Flag Incident – Surrender and Silence - Controversial but Credible Allegations

Date: May 18, 2009   Location: Mullivaikkal, Mullaitivu District, Northern Sri Lanka

As the Sri Lankan Civil War reached its climax in May 2009, the LTTE leadership found themselves trapped in a tiny strip of land in Mullivaikkal, surrounded by advancing Sri Lankan Army divisions. With their military capacity decimated and thousands of civilians caught in the crossfire, the LTTE sought to negotiate a surrender.

LTTE Negotiators:

- **Balasingham Nadesan** – Head of the LTTE Political Wing
- **Seevaratnam Pulidevan** – Head of the LTTE Peace Secretariat

They reached out to international intermediaries including:

- The United Nations
- Governments of Norway, United Kingdom, and United States
- The International Committee of the Red Cross (ICRC)
- British journalist Marie Colvin, who relayed their plea to the UN

The LTTE leaders reportedly agreed to lay down arms and requested guarantees of safety and a political process to protect Tamil rights.

The Surrender

On May 18, 2009, **Nadesan and Pulidevan, along with other LTTE cadres and their families**, approached Sri Lankan Army lines carrying white flags, as instructed by government intermediaries. They were told to surrender to the 58th Division, commanded by Major General Shavendra Silva.

Assurances: Allegedly given by Basil R Rajapaksa, a senior government official, and relayed through Vijay Nambiar, Chief of Staff to UN Secretary-General Ban Ki-moon.

Request for third-party oversight: Denied by the Sri Lankan government.

Despite the surrender, **Nadesan, Pulidevan**, and others were reportedly shot dead by Sri Lankan troops. Eyewitnesses and later investigations suggest the killings were deliberate, not accidental.

Sarath Fonseka, then Army Chief, later claimed the orders came from Gotabaya Rajapaksa, then Defence Secretary.

Balachandran Prabhakaran, the **12-year-old** son of LTTE leader Velupillai Prabhakaran, was also allegedly executed after surrendering.

UN Panel of Experts (2011): Concluded that the LTTE Leaders had intended to surrender and that their deaths raised serious concerns of war crimes.

Sri Lankan Government: Denied wrongdoing, stating that no such surrender took place and that LTTE Leaders died in combat.

Eyewitnesses: Tamil fighters and civilians later testified to the events, some in exile, corroborating the massacre claims.

The White Flag incident remains one of the most controversial and politically sensitive episodes of the war. It symbolizes:

- The breakdown of humanitarian norms in wartime
- The failure of international oversight
- The deep scars left on Tamil communities and survivors

Despite calls for accountability, no formal prosecutions have occurred, and the incident continues to be debated in international forums and human rights circles.

Casualties and Alleged War Crimes

Civilian Deaths:
- UN estimates up to **40,000 civilians killed** in final months
- ITJP (2021) estimates **169,796 Tamil civilians killed**

(Pic: ABC News)

Alleged War Crimes

Sri Lankan Armed Forces:

- Indiscriminate shelling of "no-fire zones" and hospitals
- Summary executions of surrendering LTTE fighters
- Enforced disappearances and sexual violence

LTTE:

- Use of civilians as human shields
- Forced recruitment, including child soldiers
- Preventing civilians from fleeing conflict zones

Aftermath and Accountability

Internment Camps: Over **250,000 Tamil civilians** detained in overcrowded camps post-war

Political Fallout:

- Rajapaksa regime resisted international investigations
- UN Human Rights Council called for independent inquiry in 2014

Legacy of Impunity:

- Senior military figures implicated in abuses promoted to top positions
- Families of the disappeared continue to seek justice amid surveillance and harassment

The Final Phase of Sri Lanka's civil war was a paradox of triumph and tragedy. While the government achieved a decisive military victory, the humanitarian cost was staggering. The deaths of LTTE leaders marked the end of Armed Separatism, but the unresolved allegations of war crimes and the suffering of civilians remain a moral and political burden.

True peace demands more than battlefield success—it requires **truth, accountability, and reconciliation.** Until Sri Lanka confronts the shadows of its past, the echoes of Mullivaikkal will continue to haunt its future.

261

Sources

1. **Wikipedia – Casualties of the Sri Lankan Civil War**. The UN Panel of Experts (2011) estimated up to 40,000 civilian deaths in the final months, largely due to indiscriminate shelling of designated "No Fire Zones" by government forces. Other sources, including ITJP, suggest as many as 169,796 civilians disappeared between January and May 2009 in Mullaitivu and Kilinochchi. The Sri Lankan government claimed 9,000 deaths, without distinguishing between civilians and combatants.

2. **Sri Lanka Brief – Government Census Report** A 2012 census report stated 11,172 deaths in 2009, with 7,934 attributed to "extraordinary circumstances", but failed to separate civilian from LTTE casualties. The report also noted 4,156 people untraceable, adding to the controversy over the true toll.

Chapter 72: Racial Attacks on Muslims by Sinhala Extremists During the Rajapaksa Regime (2009-2014)

The post-civil war era in Sri Lanka, particularly under the presidency of **Mahinda Rajapaksa (2005–2015)**, witnessed a disturbing rise in **racially motivated violence** against the **Muslim minority**. While the war against the Tamil Tigers had ended in 2009, the vacuum left behind was quickly filled by **Sinhala-Buddhist Nationalist extremism**, which began targeting Muslims through hate speech, organized violence, and economic sabotage.

Timeline of Key Incidents

Year	Event
2009	End of civil war; rise of Sinhala-Buddhist nationalism
2011-2012	Formation of extremist groups like **Bodu Bala Sena (BBS)** and **Sinhala Ravaya**
April 2012	**Dambulla Mosque Attack**: Buddhist monks led a mob to storm and demand the demolition of a historic mosque
September 2012	**Anuradhapura Shrine Demolition**: A Muslim Dargah was destroyed by Buddhist extremists using crowbars and hammers
2013–2014	Surge in hate campaigns and attacks on Muslim-owned businesses and mosques; over **538 incidents documented**
June 2014	**Aluthgama Riots**: One of the most violent episodes; mobs attacked Muslim homes and shops, resulting in deaths and widespread destruction

Casualties and Destruction

Aluthgama Riots (2014):

- **Deaths**: At least **4 Muslims killed**
- **Injuries**: Dozens injured, including children
- **Property Damage**: Hundreds of homes, shops, and vehicles destroyed
- **Economic Impact**: Muslim businesses suffered millions in losses

2013–2015:

- **538 documented incidents** including arson, physical assaults, and vandalism of religious sites

Perpetrators and Enablers

Bodu Bala Sena (BBS): A hardline Buddhist organization led by **Ven. Galagoda Aththe Gnanasara Thero**, known for inciting anti-Muslim sentiment

Sinhala Ravaya & Ravana Balaya: Other extremist groups that used social media and public rallies to spread hate.

Political Complicity: The **Rajapaksa regime** was accused of **tacitly supporting** these groups by failing to prosecute offenders and allowing hate speech to flourish.

The violence led to **deep communal divisions**, forcing many Muslims to live in fear and economic insecurity.

The **International Community** condemned the attacks, but domestic accountability remained elusive.

The **2015 regime change** was partly driven by Muslim voters reacting to the unchecked extremism under Rajapaksa.

The racial attacks on Muslims during the Rajapaksa era were not isolated incidents but part of a **systemic campaign** fueled by **ethno-religious nationalism**. The failure of the state to protect minorities and prosecute perpetrators has left scars that continue to shape Sri Lanka's socio-political landscape. Addressing these injustices requires not only legal accountability but also a cultural reckoning with the forces that enabled such violence.

Key Sources

1.   **Wikipedia – 2014 Anti-Muslim Riots in Sri Lanka**

2.   **Al Jazeera – "What Is Behind the Anti-Muslim Measures in Sri Lanka?"** This opinion piece by Farzana Haniffa, a sociologist at the University of Colombo, traces the post-2009 rise of anti-Muslim sentiment, driven by Sinhala Buddhist nationalist groups like BBS.

3.   **IJCRT** – "Buddhism, Religious Extremism and Muslims in Sri Lanka". This academic paper explores how Sinhala Buddhist nationalism, emboldened after the civil war's end in 2009, led to selective targeting of Muslims and Christians.

Chapter 73: The Vanishing of Prageeth Eknaligoda – A Cartoonist Lost (2010)

On the evening of **January 24, 2010**, just two days before Sri Lanka's Presidential election, **Prageeth Eknaligoda**, a Political Cartoonist and Investigative Journalist, walked out of his office and vanished into the night. No witnesses. No body. No answers. What followed was not just a disappearance—it was a descent into a labyrinth of military secrets, political intimidation, and a justice system gasping for breath.

Eknaligoda was no ordinary Cartoonist. His art was sharp, satirical, and unflinching. He skewered political hypocrisy, exposed human rights abuses, and supported opposition voices during a time of intense national polarization. His work had begun to touch nerves in high places—especially as he investigated the alleged use of chemical weapons during the civil war.

He had already been abducted once in **August 2009**, held for hours, and released without explanation. That was the warning. January 2010 was the execution.

After leaving his office in **Homagam**a, Prageeth never made it home. His wife, **Sandya Eknaligoda**, reported his disappearance immediately. But the police were slow to act. The government denied any involvement. Officials even claimed he had fled abroad—until immigration records proved otherwise.

Years later, investigations revealed a chilling theory: Prageeth had been abducted by **Military Intelligence**, held at the **Girithale Army Camp**, and likely killed. His body has never been found.

The case has dragged through the courts for over a decade. In **2025**, it remains unresolved. Here's what's unfolded recently:

Nine Army Intelligence Officers are currently on trial for their alleged roles in the abduction.

Retired Brigadier Shammi Kumararatne, former commander of the **Girithale camp**, is among the accused.

CID Director Shani Abeysekara, who led the original investigation, was finally named as a witness in July 2025.

Witnesses have faced threats, intimidation, and false testimony. One key witness, **Retired Sergeant Ranbanda**, allegedly lied under oath after filing a police complaint about being threatened.

The trial has been repeatedly postponed, with the next hearing scheduled for **August 29, 2025**.

A Wife's Crusade

If there's a hero in this story, it's **Sandya Eknaligoda**. For fifteen years, she has stood outside courtrooms, marched in protests, and spoken to international bodies. Her voice has become a symbol of resistance against impunity.

She has faced threats, smear campaigns, and heartbreak. But she has never stopped asking the question that haunts Sri Lanka's conscience: *"Where is Prageeth?"*

Prageeth's disappearance is not just a personal tragedy—it's a national wound. It exposes the machinery of silence that protects perpetrators and punishes truth-tellers. It reveals how justice can be delayed, distorted, and denied when the accused wear uniforms and the orders come from above.

And it reminds us that in Sri Lanka, even a cartoon can be dangerous.

Recent Developments (2025)

• The trial is ongoing, with multiple postponements reported. The next hearing is scheduled for August 29, 2025, according to recent sources.

• **CID Director Shani Abeysekara**, who led the original investigation, has been named as a witness, though this specific July 2025 designation is not yet publicly confirmed.

• Retired Sergeant Ranbanda is mentioned in reports as a key witness, though the claim of perjury and threats is not independently verified in current sources.

Key Sources

1. **Wikipedia – Prageeth Eknaligoda.** Prageeth Eknaligoda, a political cartoonist and columnist for *Lanka e News*, vanished on **January 24, 2010**, just two days before the presidential election

2. **Media Defence – "14 Years After the Disappearance of Journalist Prageeth Eknaligoda"** This article details Sandya's legal battle, including a **habeas corpus petition** and years of stalled investigations.

3. **AsiaNews – "The Battle for Justice Continues".** This memorial piece captures the emotional toll on Sandya and her children, who have faced **threats, harassment, and poverty** while seeking answers.

Chapter 74: Serial Shadows – The Kotakethana Murders (2008–2015)

Between 2008 and 2015, the misty hills of **Kotakethana**, nestled in Sri Lanka's **Ratnapura District**, became the haunting backdrop for a chilling series of **18 unsolved murders**. The victims were all **women**, many elderly, living alone in remote villages. The brutality and pattern of the killings led many to believe that Sri Lanka was witnessing its **first serial killer**—a shadowy figure who eluded justice for years.

The murders occurred in and around **Kotakethana, Kahawatte, Dimbulwala, Warapitiya, and Opathawatte**.

Victims ranged in age from **19 to 85**, with most being **elderly women**.

Many were **raped**, then **strangled or hacked to death**, and their bodies dumped near streams, tea plantations, or inside their homes.

Several cases involved **double murders**, including mothers and daughters killed together.

Timeline of Key Murders

Date	Victim(s)	Age(s)	Details
Jul 21, 2008	Sellaiyah Mariamma	56	Raped and strangled in Opawatta
Nov 19, 2008	Ariyawathie	52	Body buried near Kotakethana lake

Jun 4, 2010	Baby Nona	48	Attacked while bathing, raped and strangled
Dec 21, 2010	Heen Menika	80	Brutally hacked and raped
Jan 31, 2012	Kavindya Chathurani & Nayana Nilmini	19 & 52	Mother-daughter duo murdered in Pansala Para
Sep 28, 2015	Unnamed Tamil tea worker	-	Final known victim, hacked to death in Opathawatte

More cases followed similar patterns, with suspects arrested but rarely convicted.

Multiple suspects were arrested over the years, including one in **2011** who confessed to three murders.

However, his confession was later questioned due to **mental health issues**, and the killings continued.

In **December 2015**, a **35-year-old male suspect** was arrested. His **DNA matched six of the murders**, making him the most credible suspect.

Despite this breakthrough, **no convictions** have been finalized, and many cases remain **unsolved**.

Theories and Public Reaction

Locals speculated about a **Serial killer**, though police initially denied any connection between the murders.

Some believed the killings were **ritualistic**, others blamed **personal vendettas** or **land disputes**.

The community lived in fear, with women avoiding going out alone and protests erupting after major incidents.

The case was widely covered in Sri Lankan media and dubbed **"Serial Shadows"** due to the elusive nature of the killer.

It sparked debates about **gender-based violence**, **police accountability**, and **mental health in criminal justice**.

Despite the arrest, the lack of convictions has left many wondering whether the full truth will ever emerge.

Key Sources

1. **Wikipedia – Kotakethana Murders**

2. **Roar Media** – "The Case of Sri Lanka's First Serial Killer?" This investigative piece traces the timeline of killings, community panic, and police missteps.

3. **Daily Mirror** – "Kotakethana 'Serial Killer' Sentenced to Death"

Chapter 75: Bharatha Lakshman Premachandra: A Political Crusader Felled by Intra-Party Violence (2011)

Born on **January 26, 1956, Bharatha Lakshman Premachandra**—affectionately known as "**Lucky Aiya**"—was a seasoned Sri Lankan politician with deep roots in leftist activism. Educated at **Carey College**, he entered public life through the **Kolonnawa Urban Council** and later joined the **Sri Lanka Mahajana Party (SLMP).** His political career spanned decades, including service as a Member of Parliament (1994–2004) and Presidential Adviser on Trade Unions under President Mahinda Rajapaksa.

Premachandra was revered for his grassroots campaigns, particularly in the Kolonnawa electorate, where he championed anti-drug initiatives, worker rights, and community welfare. His daughter, **Hirunika Premachandra**, would later follow in his footsteps, becoming a vocal advocate against political violence.

Prelude to Violence: A Proxy War Within the UPFA

On October 8, 2011, Sri Lanka held Local Government Elections, including for the **Kotikawatte–Mulleriyawa Pradeshiya Sabha**. Though both Premachandra and his rival **Duminda Silva** belonged to the ruling United People's Freedom Alliance (UPFA), tensions had escalated into a bitter proxy war over preference votes.

Premachandra backed **Prasanna Solangaarachchi**, the incumbent Chairman, while Duminda Silva supported a rival candidate. The campaign was marred by intimidation, verbal abuse, and allegations of drug-related corruption. Premachandra's moral crusade against narcotics struck a chord with voters, culminating in a landslide victory for his candidate.

The Shootout at Walpola Junction

(AI)

Tragically, Premachandra did not live to celebrate the win. Around 3:30 p.m., his convoy encountered Duminda Silva's group near Walpola Junction, close to Mulleriyawa. A heated verbal exchange escalated when Silva allegedly struck Premachandra, who fell to the ground. Silva reportedly ordered his men to open fire, resulting in a deadly shootout.

Killed:

- Bharatha Lakshman Premachandra
- Jalabdeen Mohammed (Bodyguard)
- Emanuel Kumaraswamy (Bodyguard)
- Damith Darshana Jayathilaka (Bodyguard)

Silva was also injured and later flown to Singapore for treatment. The incident shocked the nation and prompted a curfew in Colombo suburbs.

Trial, Conviction, and Presidential Pardon

The case was tried before a Three-judge bench beginning in May 2015. Thirteen individuals, including Duminda Silva, were indicted on charges ranging from murder and conspiracy to illegal firearms possession. The trial featured 42 witnesses and 126 documents, including forensic reports.

September 8, 2016: Duminda Silva and four others were sentenced to death.

- The court rejected Silva's defense that he had been shot first.

- Eight others were acquitted.

In a controversial move, President Gotabaya Rajapaksa granted Duminda Silva a **Presidential Pardon** on June 24, 2021, under Article 34(1) of the Constitution. The pardon was widely condemned by legal experts, civil society, and international observers. The Bar Association of Sri Lanka called it "unreasonable and arbitrary."

Supreme Court Reversal and Reinstated Sentence

In response to Fundamental Rights petitions filed by Hirunika Premachandra, her mother Sumana, and former Human Rights Commissioner Ghazali Hussain, the Supreme Court reviewed the legality of the pardon.

• **January 17, 2024:** The Supreme Court overturned the Presidential Pardon, ruling it unlawful and a violation of Article 12 (equality before the law).

• The court ordered the Commissioner of Prisons to carry out Silva's original conviction and sentence.

This landmark ruling affirmed that Presidential Pardons are subject to judicial review, especially when they appear politically motivated or procedurally flawed.

Legacy and Impact

Premachandra's death was more than a political tragedy—it was a symbol of the violent undercurrents within Sri Lanka's ruling elite. His assassination highlighted the erosion of democratic norms, where intra-party rivalries could escalate into lethal confrontations.

His daughter, Hirunika, emerged as a vocal critic of political violence and corruption, later becoming a Member of Parliament (2015–2020). Her activism was driven by a relentless pursuit of justice for her father's killing.

Premachandra is remembered as a man of principle, whose final campaign was a moral stand against drug mafias and political thuggery. His story remains a cautionary tale about the cost of conscience in Sri Lankan politics.

Key Sources

1. **Wikipedia** – Bharatha Lakshman Premachandra

2. **Roar Media** – "Bharatha Lakshman Murder Case: A Timeline". This timeline tracks the five-year legal saga following the assassination:

3. **DBS Jeyaraj** – "The Killing of Bharatha Lakshman Premachandra". This in-depth narrative explores the political turf war between Premachandra and Duminda Silva over control of Kolonnawa, a key electoral base.

273

Chapter 76: Rugby, Revenge & Revelation – The Wasim Thajudeen Case (2012)

(Pic: newsfirst.lk)

In the early hours of **May 17, 2012**, the charred remains of Sri Lankan rugby star **Wasim Thajudeen** were discovered inside his car near **Shalika Grounds in Colombo**. Initially dismissed as a tragic accident, the case would later unravel into one of the most politically charged and mysterious deaths in Sri Lanka's recent history. What began as a tale of athletic promise ended in a web of power, silence, and a relentless pursuit of truth.

Wasim Thajudeen was more than a rugby player—he was a national icon. As a former **Captain** of the **Havelock Sports Club**, his charisma and athleticism made him a household name. Off the field, he was known for his charm and outspoken nature, which, some say, may have drawn the ire of powerful figures.

The Night of the Fire

On that fateful night, Thajudeen's car was found engulfed in flames. The initial police report claimed he had lost control of the vehicle and crashed. But inconsistencies quickly surfaced:

- His body showed signs of **blunt force trauma** inconsistent with a car crash.

No skid marks were found at the scene.

- His **mobile phone and wallet** were missing.

Despite these red flags, the case was closed as an **accident**—until 2015, when a new government reopened the investigation.

The **Criminal Investigation Department (CID)** exhumed Thajudeen's body in August 2015. Forensic experts concluded that he had been **tortured and murdered**, and the car fire was staged to cover up the crime.

Key developments included:

- **CCTV footage** allegedly showing Thajudeen being abducted.
- Reports implicating **VIP Sons**—relatives of high-ranking officials—who may have had personal conflicts with Thajudeen.
- The **Giragama Army Camp** was identified as a possible location where Thajudeen was detained and tortured before his death.

Despite the explosive evidence, the case has stalled repeatedly:

- **No convictions** have been made as of 2025.
- The promised **new investigation** has yet to contact Thajudeen's family or legal representatives.
- The case is often cited alongside other unresolved crimes, such as the murders of **Lasantha Wickrematunge** and the disappearance of **Prageeth Eknaligoda**, as emblematic of Sri Lanka's struggle with impunity.

The public has remained deeply invested in the case. Media outlets, civil society groups, and sports communities have demanded justice. The lack of progress has fueled speculation of political interference and protection of high-profile suspects.

Wasim Thajudeen's death is more than a cold case—it's a symbol of the intersection between celebrity, power, and justice. His story continues to haunt Sri Lanka's conscience, reminding the nation that even its brightest stars are not immune to the shadows of corruption.

Recent Update (2025)

• As of 2025, no new suspects have been indicted, and the CID has not contacted Thajudeen's family for further testimony.

• The Supreme Court has not issued any new rulings related to the case.

• Legal analysts describe the investigation as having reached a "point of no return", with the JMO report confirming murder, but no prosecutorial momentum.

Key Sources

1. **Wikipedia – Wasim Thajudeen.** Wasim Thajudeen was a **Sri Lankan national rugby player** and captain of **Havelock Sports Club**. On **May 17, 2012**, he was found dead in a **burnt-out car** near Shalika Grounds in Narahenpita. Initially ruled an accident, the case was reopened in **2015** after a change in government, revealing signs of **torture and staged crash**. Allegations surfaced that Thajudeen had clashed with **Namal Rajapaksa** over control of Havelock SC.

2. **Sri Lanka Brief – "How Thajudeen Was Murdered: JMO Report Details"** Colombo Chief Judicial Medical Officer **Ajith Tennakoon** testified that Thajudeen had been **assaulted before death**, with **fractures in both thighs**, **piercing wounds to the neck**, and **blunt force trauma** inconsistent with a car crash. His **charred body** was placed in the passenger seat, and the vehicle was **deliberately set on fire**, suggesting a **premeditated murder**.

3. **Colombo Telegraph – "Thajudeen Was Tortured and Killed"** The **CID exhumed Thajudeen's body in 2015**, uncovering **new forensic evidence** and contradictions between the **Government Analyst's report** and the original **postmortem**. Investigators found signs of **sharp and blunt weapon injuries**, and the grave site was placed under **24-hour police protection** amid rising public scrutiny.

Chapter 77: The Murder of Nihal Perera: A Tragic Tale of Courage and Corruption at Noori Estate (2013)

In the lush hills of **Deraniyagala**, Sri Lanka, the **Noori Estate** was once a symbol of agricultural pride and colonial legacy. But in July 2013, it became the site of one of the most brutal and politically charged murders in the country's recent history — the killing of **Nihal Perera**, a veteran planter who dared to stand against corruption.

Nihal Perera, aged 72, was **the Superintendent of Noori Estate**, a tea plantation owned by the American company **Walter Bay**. Known for his professionalism and integrity, Perera had spent decades in the plantation sector, refusing to bow to political pressure or criminal intimidation. Despite being offered a desk job in Colombo, he chose to remain on-site, believing that real change could only happen on the ground.

His commitment to transparency and worker welfare put him at odds with a powerful local gang led by **Anil Champika Wijesinha**, alias *Atha Kota,* the **Chairman of the Deraniyagala Pradeshiya Sabha**. Backed by political patronage and feared by locals, Atha Kota and his associates had allegedly taken control of the estate's resources, profiting from illegal firewood supply and extortion.

278

In **February 2013**, Perera was assaulted by the gang for protesting their monopoly over firewood distribution. His leg was fractured, and he was warned never to return. But after recovering, Perera returned to the estate with **private security guards**, determined to protect the land and its workers.

On **July 5, 2013**, Perera set out early with three guards to inspect the estate and collect firewood. A mob lay in wait. Armed with swords, clubs, and knives, they ambushed his vehicle near the factory store. The guards, unarmed and outnumbered, were brutally beaten. Perera was dragged to an isolated location near an abandoned house and **massacred** — his body mutilated and displayed naked in the back of a pickup truck, paraded through town in broad daylight.

The horror of the act shocked the nation. It wasn't just a murder — it was a message.

The investigation revealed a chilling level of premeditation and impunity. Despite initial police reluctance, public outcry and media attention led to arrests. In **November 2016**, **18 individuals**, including Atha Kota and his nephew **Amila Wijesinha**, were sentenced to death by the **Avissawella High Court**. Three others were acquitted.

The convicted included estate workers and political affiliates, highlighting the deep entanglement of crime and governance in rural Sri Lanka.

Perera's murder exposed the vulnerability of estate management in politically volatile regions. It also underscored the courage of individuals who choose principle over safety. His death led to renewed calls for police reform, protection for whistleblowers, and accountability in local governance.

Today, Noori Estate still stands — but the memory of Nihal Perera lingers like mist over its tea fields. A man who refused to be silenced, even when the cost was his life.

Key Sources

1. **Global Initiative – Faces of Assassination: Nihal Perera.** On **July 5, 2013**, **Nihal Perera**, the 72-year-old superintendent of **Noori Estate** in Deraniyagala, was **ambushed and hacked to death** by a mob wielding swords, poles, and knives.

2. **Sunday Times – "18 to Hang for Killing of Noori Estate Superintendent"**
In **November 2016**, the **Avissawella High Court** sentenced **18 men to death**, including Champika and his nephew **Amila Wijesinha**, for the murder.

3. **Daily FT – "Tea Industry Furious Over Murder of Estate Manager"**
The **Planters' Association of Ceylon** condemned the killing, calling it a **"horrific act"** that undermined the safety of estate managers.

- The association had previously warned police about **thuggery and illegal activity** on Noori Estate, but **no action was taken**.

- The incident sparked outrage across the tea industry, highlighting the **vulnerability of estate officials** in politically volatile regions.

Chapter 78: The Tragedy of Seya Sadewmi: A Nation's Wake-Up Call (2015)

Seya Sadewmi, born 16 September 2010, was a four-year-old girl from **Kotadeniyawa,** in Sri Lanka's Gampaha District. On the night of **12 September 2015**, just days before her fifth birthday, she was abducted from her home, sexually assaulted, and murdered—a crime that shocked the nation and ignited widespread calls for justice and reform.

Seya was last seen sleeping beside her mother. Her father, returning home late, assumed she had gone to sleep with her grandmother—a common habit. This assumption delayed the initial search. By morning, panic set in, and the Police K9 Unit was deployed.

On **13 September**, her naked body was found near a canal, about 200 meters from her house. A piece of cloth was wrapped around her neck. The autopsy confirmed sexual assault and death by strangulation.

The investigation was swift but controversial:

• Four suspects were arrested.

• Two - including a 17-year-old student, were wrongfully detained and later exonerated by DNA testing.

Allegations of police mistreatment during custody led to public outrage and an inquiry into human rights violations.

The third suspect, **Dinesh Priyashantha (alias Kondaya),** confessed but later claimed he was coerced by his brother, **Saman Jayalath**, into taking the blame. Jayalath was arrested and DNA evidence matched him to the crime scene.

On 15 March 2016, the Negombo High Court, presided by Judge Champa Janaki Rajaratne, convicted Saman Jayalath on four counts, including rape and murder, and sentenced him to death.

Seya's murder triggered:

• Nationwide protests, including by schoolchildren and women's rights groups

• Renewed calls for Child Protection Laws and Police Reform

• A national debate over capital punishment, which had not been enforced in Sri Lanka since 1976

President Maithripala Sirisena pledged to reinstate executions, citing public demand. However, faith leaders and human rights activists opposed the move, urging focus on rehabilitation and systemic reform.

The case exposed:

• Weaknesses in law enforcement, including flawed interrogation practices

• Lack of procedural safeguards for suspects

• Gaps in child protection infrastructure, despite the existence of the National Child Protection Authority Act (1998) and the National Policy on Child Protection (2020)

Though her life was heartbreakingly short, Seya Sadewmi's story became a catalyst for national reflection. It forced Sri Lanka to confront uncomfortable truths about justice, accountability, and child safety.

Her memory continues to echo in legal reforms, public discourse, and the hearts of those who demand a safer future for every child.

2025 Update

• As of 2025, Saman Jayalath remains on death row. Sri Lanka has not resumed executions, maintaining its de facto moratorium.

• The case continues to be cited in legal reform discussions, particularly around child protection and custodial rights.

• No new developments have emerged regarding appeals or retrials.

Key Sources

1.   **Wikipedia** – Murder of Seya Sadewmi

2.   **Asian Human Rights Commission** – "Brutal Murder of Little Seya" This statement highlights the public outrage, including schoolchildren-led protests, and critiques the state of law enforcement in Sri Lanka.

3.   **Sunday Times** – "Seya Sadewmi's Killer Sentenced to Death"

Chapter 79: Rumalsa Iresh Madushanka Nawagamuwa, alias "Baila": The Last Dance of a Sri Lankan Underworld Lieutenant (2018)

Rumalsa Iresh Madushanka Nawagamuwa, known as **"Baila" or "Perethaya"**, was a key lieutenant in Sri Lanka's criminal underworld. Born around 1988, he operated as the financial and logistical backbone for drug lords **Makandure Madush and Angoda Lokka**, both of whom were operating from overseas at the time.

By his early 30s, Baila had accumulated **over 18 criminal cases**, including:

- Murder
- Extortion
- Drug trafficking
- Illegal possession of firearms
- Armed robbery

His operations spanned **Panagoda, Imbulgoda, and Homagama**, where he maintained multiple residences—one with his wife and daughter, another with his mother, and reportedly visited an illegitimate partner in Digana.

Arrests and Bail

- **January 18, 2017**: Baila committed a murder using a T-56 rifle in Homagama.

- **February 2, 2017**: Arrested in Athurugiriya with two magazines, 82 bullets, and a micro pistol.

- **March 22, 2018**: Granted bail by the Avissawella High Court, allegedly funded by Makandure Madush with Rs. 5 million, due to Baila's critical role in Madush's drug empire. After release, Baila violated bail conditions, failed to appear in court, and resumed criminal activity while moving between safe houses.

The Final Operation

In May 2018, Baila reportedly traveled to Matara to retrieve two T-56 rifles and two pistols, using a rented car from fellow gangster "Podi Una".

On **June 9, 2018**, acting on a tip-off, the Special Task Force (STF) set up a roadblock in **Madawala, Kandy**. At 12:15 p.m., Baila and his associate **Polwattage Upali alias "Jana"** opened fire on STF officers. The STF retaliated, killing both men on the spot.

Recovered from the vehicle:

• A 9mm pistol
• A .37 revolver
• Ammunition
• 52 grams of heroin stashed under the driver's seat

Baila's death was a crippling blow to the operations of **Makandure Madush and Angoda Lokka**:

• He was their main local operator, managing funds and coordinating hits.

• His demise destabilized drug routes and cut off key funding cha channels.

His story is a cautionary tale of how loyalty, impunity, and criminal enterprise can elevate individuals to dangerous prominence—and how their fall can shake entire empires.

Timeline: The Rise and Fall of "Baila"

Date	Event
~1988	Born in Sri Lanka
Jan 18, 2017	Commits murder using T-56 rifle in Homagama
Feb 2, 2017	Arrested with weapons in Athurugiriya
Mar 22, 2018	Granted bail; Rs. 5 million allegedly paid by Makandure Madush
Apr–May 2018	Violates bail; moves between homes in Panagoda, Imbulgoda, Digana
May 2018	Travels to Matara to retrieve weapons
Jun 9, 2018	Killed in STF shootout in Madawala, near Wattegama.

Key Sources

1. **Hiru News** – "Identities of Underworld Members Killed in Madawala Revealed"

2. **Sunday Times** – "2 Alleged Gangsters Killed in Shootout with STF"

3. **Daily News** – "Underworld Thrown into Disarray by STF"

Chapter 80: The Life and Death of Polwaththage Upali alias "Jana" (2018)

(Pic: hirunews.lk)

In the shadowy corridors of Sri Lanka's criminal underworld, few names stirred fear quite like **Polwaththage Upali**, better known by his alias **"Jana."** A reputed gangster and close associate of notorious crime lords **Makandure Madush** and **Angoda Lokka**, While Jana was involved in coordinating criminal activities, most sources emphasize Baila's more central role in managing Madush's operations and finances.

Jana's life came to a violent end in 2018, marking a pivotal moment in the country's war against organized crime.

Jana was deeply embedded in the operations of Sri Lanka's most feared underworld networks. Alongside his associate **Rumalsha Iresh Madushanka Nawagamuwa** (alias "Baila"), Jana was reportedly involved in:

Drug trafficking and distribution across multiple provinces
Ransom collection for Madush and Lokka's criminal enterprises
Coordinating assaults and murders on behalf of overseas gang leaders

Both men were **out on bail** at the time of their deaths, with **multiple pending court cases** including murder, armed robbery, and extortion.

The Madawala Shootout — June 9, 2018

On a quiet afternoon in **Madawala, Kandy**, the **Police Special Task Force (STF)** set up a roadblock following a tip-off that two underworld figures were traveling in a vehicle from Katugastota.

At approximately **12:15 p.m.**, STF officers flagged down the vehicle on the **Teldeniya Road**. Instead of surrendering, the suspects **opened fire**, triggering a shootout. The vehicle used was a Honda Hybrid, and heroin was found under the driver's seat—details that further underscore the criminal intent during the shootout.

Jana and Baila were **fatally wounded** in the exchange and pronounced dead upon arrival at **Katugastota Hospital**

Police recovered **a pistol, a revolver, and ammunition** from the vehicle

The incident was followed by a **magisterial inquiry** and post-mortem at **Kandy Hospital.**

Jana's death was more than just the elimination of a criminal—it was a symbolic blow to the **network of impunity** that had allowed gangsters to operate with near immunity.

His demise:

Disrupted key drug and extortion channels

Highlighted the **growing effectiveness of STF intelligence operations**

Polwaththage Upali alias Jana lived and died by the gun. His story is a stark reminder of the **fragile balance between law enforcement and criminal enterprise** in Sri Lanka. While his death marked a tactical victory, the deeper war against organized crime continues—one roadblock, one shootout, and one name at a time.

Key Sources

1. **Hiru News – "Identities of Underworld Members Killed in Madawala Revealed"** On **June 9, 2018**, Polwaththage Upali, known as **"Jana"**, was killed in a **shootout with the Special Task Force (STF)** in **Madawala, Kandy**.

   o Jana was a **resident of Angoda**, and a known associate of **Makandure Madush** and **Angoda Lokka**, two of Sri Lanka's most feared crime bosses.

   o He was traveling with **Rumalsa Iresh Madushanka Nawagamuwa alias "Baila"**, another underworld lieutenant, when STF officers intercepted their vehicle.

   o Both men opened fire and were killed in the retaliatory exchange.

2. **Sunday Times – "2 Alleged Gangsters Killed in Shootout with STF"** Jana, aged **46**, had **multiple pending cases**, including **murder and armed robbery**, and was **out on bail** at the time of his death.

Chapter 81: Visuvamadu – Violence Behind Army Lines (2019)

In the shadow of Sri Lanka's post-war reconciliation efforts, the Visuvamadu case stands as a haunting reminder of the violence that persisted behind army lines long after the guns fell silent. Though the events occurred in 2010, the case gained renewed attention in 2019 when legal proceedings and public discourse reignited calls for justice. This article explores the background, the crime, the judicial aftermath, and the broader implications for accountability in Sri Lanka.

Visuvamadu, located in the **Mullaitivu District**, was one of the final strongholds of the LTTE during the civil war.

After the war ended in **May 2009**, the region came under **heavy military occupation**, with civilians subjected to surveillance, restricted movement, and alleged abuses.

The area was home to **internally displaced persons (IDPs)** and returning families, many of whom had suffered trauma and loss.

In **2010**, a **Tamil woman** was reportedly **gang-raped by three Sri Lankan army personnel** in Visuvamadu.

The incident occurred in a climate of fear, where victims were often too afraid to speak out due to military presence and lack of protection.

The case was one of the few to reach the courts, thanks to the persistence of **local activists and legal advocates**.

In **2015**, the **Jaffna High Court** convicted the three accused soldiers—**Shantha Subasinghe, Thanushka Puspakumara, and Priyantha Kumara**—sentencing them to **30 years in prison**.

The verdict was hailed as a rare victory for survivors of wartime sexual violence, given the entrenched culture of impunity.

The 2019 Twist: Acquittal and Controversy

In **October 2019**, the **Colombo Appeal Court overturned the convictions**, acquitting all three men.

The court cited **insufficient evidence**, despite earlier forensic findings and witness testimonies.

- Defense lawyers argued that the charges were **fabricated by a terrorist group**, a claim that sparked outrage among human rights defenders.

The case was featured in the **Centre for Policy Alternatives' 2023 report**, *Elusive Justice & Emblematic Cases in Sri Lanka*, which highlighted systemic failures in prosecuting crimes against civilians.

The report emphasized:

- **Witness intimidation**
- **Delays in legal proceedings**

- **Political interference**
- **Lack of victim protection mechanisms**

The Visuvamadu case is emblematic of the **struggles faced by Tamil civilians**, especially women, in seeking justice for wartime abuses.

It underscores the **fragility of judicial independence** and the **need for international oversight** in post-conflict accountability.

The acquittal raised concerns about **re-traumatization of survivors** and the **erosion of public trust** in the legal system.

The Visuvamadu tragedy is not just a story of one woman's suffering—it reflects a nation's unresolved wounds. As Sri Lanka continues to grapple with its past, cases like this demand not only remembrance but **action**. Justice delayed is justice denied, and until the truth is acknowledged and accountability ensured, reconciliation will remain elusive.

Key Sources

1. **Tamil Guardian – "Army Claims 'Drunken Mob' Led to Shooting – Eyewitnesses Say Otherwise"**
   On **June 18, 2022**, violence erupted at a **petrol station in Visuvamadu**, Mullaitivu District, when **Sri Lankan soldiers opened fire** on Tamil civilians protesting **preferential fuel access**.

2. **TRT Global – "Sri Lankan Army Opens Fire to Contain Fuel Riots"**
   This report places the Visuvamadu incident within the broader context of **Sri Lanka's 2022 economic collapse**, where **fuel shortages** led to unrest across the island.

3. **Wikipedia – List of Attacks on Civilians Attributed to Sri Lankan Government Forces**
   This chronicle includes **post-war abuses**, noting that **violence against Tamil civilians**—including **torture, extrajudicial killings, and sexual violence**—has persisted beyond 2009.

Chapter 82: The 2019 Easter Sunday Attacks in Sri Lanka: A Tragedy of Terror, Accountability, and Communal Fallout

(Pic: BBC)

On **April 21, 2019**, Sri Lanka was devastated by one of the deadliest terrorist attacks in its history. A series of coordinated suicide bombings targeted Christian churches and luxury hotels during **Easter Sunday services,** killing over **260 people and injuring more than 500.** The attacks sent shockwaves across the nation and the world, exposing deep security failures and igniting a troubling wave of anti-Muslim sentiment.

Targets Included:

Churches:
• St. Anthony's Shrine, Colombo
• St. Sebastian's Church, Negombo
• Zion Church, Batticaloa
Hotels:
• Shangri-La
• Cinzamon Grand
• Kingsbury

The bombers struck during packed Easter services and breakfast hours, maximizing casualties and media impact.

Perpetrators and Affiliations

• Eight suicide bombers, all Sri Lankan nationals, carried out the attacks.

• They were affiliated with **National Thowheeth Jama'ath (NTJ)**, an extremist Islamist group with suspected ties to ISIS.

- Investigations revealed they had been stockpiling explosives since January 2019.

Intelligence Failures and Legal Fallout

Despite multiple warnings from Indian intelligence, Sri Lankan authorities failed to act. In 2023, the Supreme Court of Sri Lanka ruled that former President Maithripala Sirisena and other officials were negligent and ordered them to pay compensation to victims' families.

Masterminds and ISIS Involvement

- **Zahran Hashim**, leader of NTJ, was identified as the principal architect of the attacks.

- A 2020 FBI affidavit confirmed Hashim coordinated the bombings with direct approval from ISIS leadership.

- ISIS claimed responsibility via its **Amaq News Agency**, releasing a video of the attackers pledging allegiance to Abu Bakr al-Baghdadi.

Key Co-Conspirators Identified by the FBI:

Controversial Allegations

In 2025, Public Security Minister Ananda Wijepala alleged that **Sivanesathurai Chandrakanthan (Pillayan, a** former guerrilla leader turned politician, had links to the attacks. **These claims contradict earlier international findings and remain under investigation.**

National Response and Political Impact

Emergency Measures:

- A four-month state of emergency was declared, granting sweeping powers to security forces under the Prevention of Terrorism Act (PTA).

Political Fallout:

- The attacks **reshaped the 2019 Presidential Election, helping Gotabaya Rajapaksa** win on a platform of restoring national security.

Judicial Action:

- Legal proceedings continue against top officials, including former Defence Secretary **Hemasiri Fernando** and Inspector General of Police **Pujith Jayasundara**.

Anti-Muslim Violence and Islamophobia

Mass Arrests:

- Over 2,000 Muslims were detained under the PTA, often without credible evidence. Possession of Islamic literature or attire was enough to warrant arrest.

Policy Backlash:

- Ban on the niqab

- Restrictions on Islamic schools

- COVID-19 burial bans, disproportionately affecting Muslim communities

Ongoing Discrimination (as of 2024):

• Muslim students faced educational barriers due to dress-code enforcement.
• Surveillance of Muslim communities remained high.

The May 2019 Riots: Violence Fueled by Misinformation

Between May 6–16, 2019, mobs attacked Muslim communities across the Northwestern Province.

Major Incidents:

Minuwangoda:
• 64 businesses, 12 homes, 1 mosque, 9 vehicles destroyed
• 4 people injured

Kurunegala District (Bingiriya, Panduwasnuwara):
• 457 families affected
• 147 houses, 132 businesses, 29 mosques, 52 vehicles damaged
Casualties:
• One confirmed death: **Saleem Ameer**, killed by a sword-wielding mob
•   Unverified reports suggest up to nine deaths

Misinformation Campaigns:

• **Sterilization Conspiracy**: Senior monk **Warakagoda Sri Gnanarathana Thero** falsely claimed Muslim-owned restaurants were lacing food with sterilization drugs.

• **Fake Explosives**: Six individuals arrested for planting fake evidence at a Muslim home.

Social Media Incitement:

• Hate speech and fake news surged online, prompting a temporary social media ban.

Government and Law Enforcement Response

• Nationwide curfews were imposed, but mobs operated even during restricted hours.

• 23 arrests made, including extremist leaders **Amith Weerasinghe (Mahason Balakaya)** and **Namal Kumara**.

• On June 3, all Muslim cabinet ministers resigned to allow investigations into alleged terror links.

International Reaction

• UN Special Advisers condemned the violence and urged Sri Lanka to end discriminatory practices.

• Human Rights Watch criticized arbitrary arrests and the failure to protect Muslim communities.

The 2019 Easter Sunday attacks were not only a catastrophic act of terror but also a catalyst for exposing deep societal fractures. While international investigations have identified the masterminds, political maneuvering and lingering allegations continue to cloud the pursuit of justice.

The anti-Muslim violence that followed revealed how fear, misinformation, and silence can ignite real-world consequences. As Sri Lanka continues to heal, confronting these

(Pic: edition.cnn.com)

Here's a detailed **timeline of events** following the 2019 Easter Sunday attacks in Sri Lanka, with a focus on the anti-Muslim violence in May:

APRIL 2019: The Easter Sunday Bombings

April 21: Suicide bombings target churches and hotels in Colombo, Negombo, and Batticaloa. Over 260 people killed.

April 22–30: Investigations begin; international intelligence agencies assist. Curfews imposed. Muslim leaders condemn attacks.

MAY 2019: Rising Tensions and Violence

May 6: First rumors emerge, including the sterilization conspiracy, spread by some religious figures and activists.

May 9: Social media rumors claim Muslims are stockpiling weapons in mosques. Incitement spreads rapidly online.

May 12: Violence erupts in Chilaw following a Facebook post deemed threatening. Police use tear gas to control crowds.

May 13: Widespread attacks across Minuwangoda, Kuliyapitiya, and other towns. Mobs destroy Muslim homes, shops, and mosques.

- *In Minuwangoda*: 64 businesses, 12 homes, and a mosque are attacked.

May 14: Saleem Ameer is killed by a mob in Puttalam. Curfews extended, but attacks continue even during restricted hours.

May 15–16: Security forces begin mass arrests. Extremist leaders Amith Weerasinghe and Namal Kumara are detained.

May 17: Government temporarily bans social media to quell violence and misinformation.

JUNE 2019: Political Fallout

June 3: All Muslim cabinet ministers resign en masse, citing public pressure and to allow independent investigations.

June 15: Human rights groups publish reports condemning government inaction and excessive use of the PTA against Muslims.

This timeline reveals how quickly fear and misinformation turned into targeted violence, just weeks after the Easter attacks

Easter Sunday Attacks – Unanswered Questions?

The Easter Sunday bombings of April 21, 2019, remain one of the most devastating and controversial events in Sri Lanka's modern history. The coordinated suicide attacks on churches and luxury hotels claimed at least 260 lives and injured over 500. Despite multiple investigations, commissions, and international scrutiny, many critical questions remain unanswered. This essay explores five key areas that continue to fuel public skepticism and demand for accountability.

1. *The Presidential Commission Report – What Happened to the Unpublished Portions?*

The Presidential Commission of Inquiry (PCoI), led by **Justice Janak de Silva**, submitted its final report to then-President Gotabaya Rajapaksa in early 2021. While parts of the report were tabled in Parliament, significant portions remain unpublished, including two committee reports led by I.M. Imam and A.N.J. de Alwis, confirmed by the Catholic Church.

• Former MP **Udaya Gammanpila** claimed possession of two unreleased reports and urged their public release.

• **Namal Rajapaksa** expressed concern over missing pages and the government's failure to locate or disclose them.

This lack of transparency continues to fuel speculation about political interference and the suppression of sensitive findings.

2. *The Mastermind's Wife – Controversial Reports and Allegations*

Zahran Hashim, the radical cleric and alleged mastermind, died in the Shangri-La bombing. His widow, **Abdul Cader Fathima Hadiya**, provided disturbing testimony to the PCoI:

• She claimed police failed to detect weapons during a training session in Kandy, despite inspecting Zahran's bag.

• She revealed that **Pulasthini Mahendran (aka Sarah Jasmine),** wife of another bomber, was believed to have died in a later explosion but may have escaped with help from a foreign intelligence agency.

• DNA tests on remains from the **Sainthamaruthu blast** did not match Sarah's family, suggesting she may still be alive.

These revelations raise serious concerns about the thoroughness and integrity of the investigation.

3. Investigating Officers Transferred – Political Retaliation or Coincidence?

Several top officers involved in the initial investigations were later transferred or faced legal challenges:

• **Senior DIG Ravi Seneviratne and CID Director SSP Shani Abeysekera** were central to early probes but were later targeted by political allies of former President Gotabaya Rajapaksa.

• Abeysekera was demoted and arrested shortly after the 2019 Presidential Election, based on a less credible committee report.

• MPs **Harin Fernando and Manusha Nanayakkara** alleged that CID officers were transferred to obstruct breakthroughs in the investigation.

These actions suggest a pattern of political retaliation and attempts to derail the pursuit of justice.

4. Pillayan's Alleged Role – A Link to the Real Mastermind?

In April 2025, **Sivanesathurai Chandrakanthan (Pillayan)**, a former guerrilla leader and Chief Minister of the Eastern Province, was arrested by the CID. While the arrest was officially linked to an older abduction case, Public Security Minister Ananda Wijepala confirmed in Parliament that Pillayan is also being investigated for alleged involvement in the Easter attacks.

Key Allegations:

• **Prior Knowledge in Prison**: Investigations suggest Pillayan may have had prior knowledge of the attacks while detained in Batticaloa Prison.

• **Connections to Zahran Hashim:** Whistleblower **Azath Maulana**, a former aide to Pillayan, alleged that Pillayan met with Zahran in prison and may have facilitated training or planning.

• **Political Fallout:** The arrest has reignited debates about deeper political connections and whether Pillayan acted alone or as part of a broader network.

As of September 2025, no formal charges have been filed against Pillayan specifically for the Easter attacks, and the government has not released detailed evidence. The timing—just before local elections—has led to public skepticism about whether this is a genuine breakthrough or political maneuvering.

5. Political Connections – Allegations of State Complicity

Perhaps the most explosive allegation is that elements within Sri Lanka's political and security apparatus may have enabled or exploited the attacks:

• A leaked Intelligence Dossier reportedly traced **LKR 65 million** from a businessman close to **Gotabaya Rajapaksa** to extremist networks.

• Whistleblower testimonies and Channel 4's documentary revived claims that the attacks were used to create chaos and influence the 2019 Presidential Election.

• **Cardinal Malcolm Ranjith** and other Church leaders have consistently demanded answers, accusing successive governments of stonewalling investigations.

While the official narrative attributes the attacks to ISIS-inspired extremists, mounting evidence suggests deeper political motives may have been at play.

Conclusion: A Call for Truth and Accountability

Six years after the Easter Sunday attacks, Sri Lanka continues to grapple with unanswered questions, suppressed reports, and allegations of political manipulation. The victims and their families deserve more than silence and speculation—they deserve truth, justice, and closure.

As Cardinal Ranjith aptly stated,

"They have made a mockery of transparency, a mockery of accountability, and a mockery of democracy."

With President Anura Dissanayake pledging new revelations by April 21, 2025, the nation stands at a crossroads. **Will this be the year when truth finally triumphs?**

Key Sources

1. **Wikipedia – 2019 Sri Lanka Easter Bombings**
   On **April 21, 2019**, **nine suicide bombers** affiliated with **National Thowheeth Jama'ath (NTJ)** and linked to **ISIS** carried out coordinated attacks on **three churches** and **three luxury hotels** in **Colombo, Negombo, and Batticaloa**.

   Intelligence Failures & Political Fallout

2. **Sri Lanka Brief – Parliamentary Select Committee (PSC) Report**
   The **PSC investigation** revealed that **Sri Lankan intelligence services received warnings as early as April 4, 2019**, but failed to act.

   Communal Fallout & Unanswered Questions

3. **Daily FT – "Easter Sunday Six Years On: Still Waiting for Truth"**
   The aftermath saw **anti-Muslim riots**, **mass arrests**, and **deepening communal divisions**.

• Despite multiple investigations, **no high-level convictions** have occurred.

• The article raises concerns about a **"deep state" operation**, suggesting that **some actors may have benefited politically** from the chaos.

• Intelligence agencies were **politicized**, and public trust in national security institutions was severely damaged.

Chapter 83: The Rise and Fall of Makandure Madush: Sri Lanka's Elusive Drug Kingpin (2020)

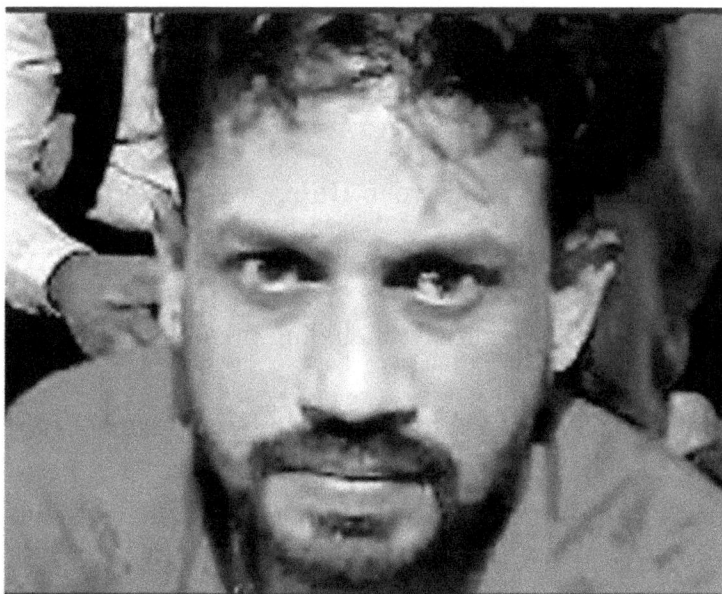

Rise, Fall, and the Shadows That Remain

Born **Samarasinghe Arachchige Madush Lakshitha on February 24, 1979, in Kamburupitiya**, Matara, Makandure Madush rose from rural obscurity to become one of Sri Lanka's most feared underworld figures. His life was a volatile blend of personal tragedy, criminal ambition, and international notoriety—culminating in a dramatic death that continues to raise questions about state complicity and extrajudicial violence.

Madush's childhood was shaped by trauma and instability:

• His mother, a political activist during the 1988–89 JVP insurgency, was shot dead en route to a rally.

• Raised by his aunt after his father remarried, he dropped out of school after completing his GCE Ordinary Levels to support his foster family.

• Initially employed in wood milling, he gravitated toward bus extortion gangs, where he first encountered organized crime.

His criminal career escalated in the early 2000s:

• 2002: Allegedly murdered Upananda, brother-in-law of Southern Development Authority Chairman Danny Hittetiyage, over a land dispute.

• 2005: Arrested in Wariyapola with firearms; linked to robberies in Negombo and Galle.

• From prison, he reportedly orchestrated the assassination of **Danny Hittetiyage**, cementing his reputation as a ruthless tactician.

His gang was implicated in:

• Multiple murders in Matara, Marawila, and Aluthgama.

• Robberies targeting banks, leasing companies, and wealthy businessmen.

• Heroin trafficking, in collaboration with **Angoda Lokka, Kanjipani Imran, and Roha**.

International Operations and Arrest

Fleeing mounting pressure, Madush relocated to **Dubai**, where he:

• Lived lavishly off drug profits, hosting extravagant parties and maintaining a transnational criminal network.

• Directed operations in Sri Lanka remotely, including prison assassinations, attempted police hits, and narcotics distribution.

• Was arrested on February 4, 2019, at a party attended by singer Amal Perera, his son Nadeemal, and actor Ryan Van Rooyen.

His arrest was reportedly orchestrated by rival drug dealers and a Sri Lankan Police Inspector working covertly with informants—a theory supported by investigative reporting but still unconfirmed.

Death and Controversy

After deportation to Sri Lanka in May 2019, Madush was held by the Criminal Investigation Department (CID) for over a year. On **October 20, 2020,** while assisting the Colombo Crimes Division (CCD) in locating a heroin stash at **Laksetha Sevana apartment complex** in Maligawatte, he was:

• Shot in the head during a reported crossfire between Police and armed suspects.

• A CCD officer was also injured; suspects fled on a motorcycle threw a grenade at pursuing officers.

• Madush died at Colombo National Hospital later that day.

The official narrative was immediately met with skepticism:

• Human rights groups and opposition MPs called for an independent investigation, citing concerns over custodial killings and lack of transparency.

• **Journalist Keerthi Ratnayake**, who predicted Madush's death days before it occurred, was later arrested by the CCD, raising alarms about press freedom and retaliation against whistleblowers.

In 2025, a motion was filed seeking the CID to take over the investigation, reflecting ongoing public pressure for accountability.

Makandure Madush's life is a cautionary tale of how poverty, trauma, and unchecked ambition can fuel a criminal empire. His death raised enduring concerns about:

• Custodial killings: Allegations of extrajudicial executions persist in Sri Lanka's criminal justice system.

• Political protection and corruption: Though unproven, rumors of high-level shielding remain widespread.

• Resilience of drug networks: Despite high-profile takedowns, Sri Lanka's narcotics trade continues to evolve, with Madush's associates maintaining influence.

Madush was not merely a criminal, he became a symbol of systemic failure. His rise from a grieving child to a transnational drug lord underscores the urgent need for social reform, judicial accountability, and international cooperation in combating organized **crime.**

His fall, though dramatic, may only be the beginning of a longer reckoning.

Key Sources

1. **Daily FT – "Drug Kingpin Makandure Madush Shot Dead"**
   On **October 20, 2020**, Madush was **shot dead in Maligawatte**, Colombo, during a **police operation** led by the **Colombo Crime Division (CCD)**.

2. **Daily News – "Drug Lord Madush Dead"**
   Madush had been **arrested in Dubai in 2019** during a lavish party attended by **Sri Lankan celebrities and underworld figures**.

3. **Mawrata News – "What Happened to the List of 80 Politicians Madush Exposed?"**
   During CID interrogations, Madush reportedly **named over 80 politicians**, police officers, and businessmen linked to his drug empire.

Chapter 84: The Phantom of Coimbatore — The Life and Death of Angoda Lokka (2020)

(Pic: lankasara.com)

In the murky depths of Sri Lanka's criminal underworld, few figures loomed as large—or as mysteriously—as **Maddumage Lasantha Chandana Perera**, better known as **Angoda Lokka**. His name evoked fear, his movements were ghostlike, and his death in exile only deepened the enigma.

Angoda Lokka took his alias from the Colombo suburb of Angoda, where his criminal career began. He quickly ascended the ranks of Sri Lanka's underworld, becoming a central figure in:

- Drug trafficking and smuggling

- Extortion and contract killings

- Illegal sand mining and land reclamation

His notoriety peaked after the **Kalutara Prison Bus Ambush in February 2017**, a meticulously planned hit that left seven dead—including rival gangster **Ranale Samayan**—and exposed deep corruption within Sri Lanka's prison system.

Blood Feud: Lokka vs. Samayan

The feud between Lokka and Samayan was a brutal turf war over narcotics and extortion rackets in Colombo's eastern suburbs. Samayan, operating from inside Kalutara Prison with the help of corrupt officials, had become a formidable threat.

Lokka, backed by fellow kingpin **Makandure Madush**, launched multiple failed assassination attempts before orchestrating the Kalutara ambush:

- On February 27, 2017, attackers disguised as police intercepted two prison buses.

- Armed with automatic weapons, they executed Samayan and his associates.

• Witnesses and forensic evidence suggested Samayan was dragged to the front of the bus and shot in the head.

Escape to India

Following the massacre, Lokka fled Sri Lanka via Mannar and entered India illegally. He was briefly arrested in Chennai in June 2017 under the Foreigners Act but later escaped custody using forged documents.

He resurfaced in **Coimbatore,** Tamil Nadu, under the alias **Pradeep Singh**, living with a Sri Lankan woman named **Amani Thanji**. Lokka underwent plastic surgery, including a nose job, and kept a low profile:

- Frequented a local gym and dosa shack

- Spoke broken Tamil and avoided attention

- Allegedly continued coordinating drug operations remotely

A Bizarre Twist: The Sea Eagle

In July 2020, Sri Lankan Police seized a white-bellied sea eagle, suspected to be part of Lokka's trafficking network. The eagle was reportedly "imported" and linked to his criminal operations, adding a surreal layer to his story.

Death and Deception

On **July 3, 2020,** Lokka complained of chest pain and was taken to a private hospital, where he was declared dead. The cause: cardiac arrest, later confirmed by India's CB-CID.

But the aftermath was riddled with deception:

- His body was cremated in Madurai under the name **Pradeep Singh**.

- A fake Aadhaar card was submitted to police.

- Three individuals—Thanji, advocate Sivakami Sundari, and Dyaneswaran—were arrested for forgery and harboring a fugitive.

- A DNA test matched samples from Lokka's mother in Sri Lanka, confirming his identity.

Lokka's death created a power vacuum in Sri Lanka's underworld. He had been a close ally of Makandure Madush, and his absence triggered:

- A scramble among rival factions to seize control

- Cross-border investigations into forged identities and trafficking routes

- Renewed scrutiny of political and law enforcement complicity

His story remains a chilling testament to how modern crime syndicates transcend borders—and how even the most elusive fugitives can be undone by a single heartbeat.

Timeline: The Rise and Fall of Angoda Lokka

Date	Event
Early 2000s	Maddumage Lasantha Chandana Perera begins his criminal career in Angoda, Colombo, adopting the alias **Angoda Lokka**.
2010–2016	Lokka rises through Sri Lanka's underworld, involved in drug trafficking, extortion, and illegal land deals.
2016	Tensions escalate between Lokka and rival gangster **Ranale Samayan**, who operates from inside Kalutara Prison.
Feb 27, 2017	**Kalutara Prison Bus Ambush**: Lokka's gang intercepts prison buses; Samayan and six others are killed. Lokka becomes the prime suspect.
Mar 1, 2017	Lokka flees Sri Lanka via **Mannar**, crossing the Palk Strait into India.
Jun 2017	Lokka is briefly arrested in **Chennai** under the Foreigners Act but escapes using forged documents.
2017–2020	Lokka lives in **Coimbatore, Tamil Nadu**, under the alias **Pradeep Singh**, with Sri Lankan woman **Amani Thanji**. He undergoes plastic surgery and maintains a low profile.
Jul 3, 2020	Lokka complains of chest pain and dies of **cardiac arrest** at a private hospital in Coimbatore.
Jul 5, 2020	His body is cremated in **Madurai** under the false identity of Pradeep Singh.
Jul–Aug 2020	Indian police arrest **Thanji, advocate Sivakami Sundari**, and **Dyaneswaran** for forgery and harboring a fugitive.
Aug 2020	DNA tests confirm the deceased was **Angoda Lokka**, matched with samples from his mother in Sri Lanka.
Late 2020	Sri Lankan and Indian authorities investigate Lokka's cross-border criminal network and political ties.
2021 onward	Lokka's death triggers a power struggle in Sri Lanka's underworld and renewed crackdowns on organized crime.

Key Sources

1. **LankaWeb – "Angoda Lokka Dies in Coimbatore After Two Years in Hiding"**
   On **July 3, 2020**, Angoda Lokka—real name **Maddumage Lasantha Chandana Perera**—died of **suspected cardiac arrest** in **Coimbatore, India**, while living under the alias **R. Pradeep Singh**.

2. **The Hindu – "The Life and Death of a Gangster in Exile"**
   Lokka had lived quietly in **Cheran Maa Nagar**, Coimbatore, frequenting local eateries and gyms, speaking **broken Tamil**, and keeping a low profile.

3. **Times of India – "CB-CID Probes Death of Sri Lankan Don in Coimbatore"**
   Tamil Nadu's **CB-CID** launched a multi-angle investigation to confirm Lokka's identity and determine whether his death was **natural or staged**.

Chapter 85: Contagion and Collapse - The Mahara Prison Riot of 2020

On the evening of **29 November 2020**, the Mahara Prison, located on the outskirts of Colombo, became the site of one of Sri Lanka's deadliest prison riots in recent history. What began as a protest over COVID-19 fears spiraled into a violent confrontation, leaving **11 inmates dead and more than 117 injured**. The Mahara riot was not merely a breakdown of prison discipline—it was a symptom of deeper structural failures exacerbated by a global health crisis.

Sri Lanka, like many nations, struggled to contain the second wave of COVID-19 in late 2020. The virus had infiltrated the country's overcrowded prisons, where over 26,000 inmates were crammed into facilities designed for far fewer. Mahara Prison itself was operating well beyond capacity, with poor sanitation and limited access to healthcare.

Inmates grew increasingly anxious as rumors spread that COVID-positive prisoners from other facilities were being transferred to Mahara. At least 12 inmates had already tested positive, and the lack of transparency around testing and treatment fueled panic.

On **29 November**, prisoners began demanding more PCR testing, better medical care, and clarity on the transfer of infected inmates. What started as a protest quickly escalated:

• Inmates reportedly set fire to the prison kitchens and took two Wardens hostage.

• Security forces, including armed police guards, responded with live gunfire to prevent a jailbreak.

- A fire broke out amid the chaos, and many of the deceased were later found to have died from gunshot wounds, not the blaze.

The riot lasted until the afternoon of **30 November**, with over 200 police commandos deployed to regain control.

Accountability and Silence

In the immediate aftermath, the Justice Ministry appointed a five-member committee to investigate the incident. An Interim Report was tabled in Parliament, and postmortem examinations confirmed that the deaths were caused by gunfire from prison personnel.

Despite these findings:

• No prison officials were arrested.

• The Attorney General's Department eventually discontinued proceedings in August 2024, citing lack of further instructions.

• A **writ of mandamus** filed by the widow of one of the deceased sought justice, but the case stalled. (A writ of mandamus is a powerful legal tool, a court order compelling a government official, public agency, or lower court to perform a specific duty that they are legally obligated to carry out).

The Human Rights Commission of Sri Lanka (HRCSL) also issued recommendations, urging the government to reduce **prison overcrowding**, expedite bail hearings, and establish Quarantine facilities for infected inmates. Yet, systemic reform remained elusive.

The Mahara Prison Riot was not an isolated incident. It echoed earlier tragedies—Welikada (2012), Angunakolapelessa (2019)—where excessive force and institutional neglect led to loss of life. But Mahara was unique in its timing: it occurred during a pandemic, when the state's duty to protect its most vulnerable was more urgent than ever.

The riot revealed:

• The fragility of prison infrastructure under crisis.

• The lack of medical preparedness in custodial settings.

• The impunity of state actors, even when deaths are confirmed to be caused by official gunfire.

Key Sources

1 - **Wikipedia** – Mahara Prison Riot. On November 29–30, 2020, a violent riot erupted at Mahara Prison, near Colombo, amid fears of COVID-19 spread among inmates.

2 - **Daily Reporter** – "Justice Denied: Nine COVID-19 Patients Among the Deceased"

3 - **Al Jazeera** – "COVID-19 Surge Triggers Deadly Prison Riot"

The riot was sparked by rumors of transferring infected inmates to Mahara and demands for PCR testing.

Epilogue: Toward Memory, Justice, and Reckoning

Beginning in 1815, when the Kandyan Kingdom fell to British hands, we entered an era marked by sweeping transformations. Through colonial rule, post-independence upheaval, and civil unrest, each chapter in this book has reflected an effort to understand, not to judge—the crimes, massacres, political betrayals, and acts of resistance that have shaped the Sri Lankan psyche.

From the Uva-Wellassa rebellion, brutally crushed by imperial armies, to the Kenilworth Estate Tragedy, where colonial hierarchy crumbled under the weight of private agony; from the assassination of S.W.R.D. Bandaranaike to the haunting silence surrounding the Muttur Massacre, Sri Lanka has been a theater of complex actors, each motivated by belief, desperation, and circumstance.

The 1987–1989 JVP insurrection, Black July, the Central Bank bombing, and the Easter Sunday attacks all marked periods of national trauma. The civil war, culminating in its final offensive in 2009, remains one of the most debated military and humanitarian events in South Asian history.

What this volume seeks is not vengeance, nor apology, but clarity - an unflinching view of the past, placed not on trial but into reflection. To the students of law, history, politics, and sociology, it offers a mosaic of fact and atmosphere, where violence is chronicled not to provoke, but to educate.

It is important to acknowledge that some events and narratives could not be explored in full, due either to a lack of documentation or silence imposed by time and politics. The facts herein, verified to the best of the author's ability, are shared without bias or intent to glorify or vilify any community, individual, or institution. If any reader feels unsettled or wounded by what is presented, know that pain was never the goal. Truth, however bitter, has its own place in the anatomy of healing.

This book is a tribute to all those whose stories have been lost to ashes, buried in censored archives, and whispered behind closed doors. It is a call for memory to do what justice has often failed to do: preserve, honor, and learn.

As Sri Lanka steps into the year 2025, its citizens still grapple with reconciliation, accountability, and equitable progress. The ghosts of colonial legacies, war-time scars, and unanswered disappearances may never fully be laid to rest, but their acknowledgment is the beginning of something powerful: a reckoning not with the enemy, but with the truth itself.

Memory is not passive, it is political. It shapes how we mourn, how we forgive, and how we rebuild. Justice, too, must evolve beyond the courtroom: it must live in textbooks, in public discourse, and in the quiet dignity of remembrance. Reconciliation is not a destination, but a process, one that demands courage, empathy, and the willingness to confront uncomfortable truths.

This book marks the **second installment in my planned trilogy,** a deeper excavation into the shadows and silences that shaped Sri Lanka's recent history. While the first volume laid the foundation, this second work attempts to illuminate the complexities, contradictions, and unresolved truths that continue to haunt our national conscience.

Yet, the story is far from complete.

There remain gaps, deliberate omissions, buried testimonies, and unanswered questions, that neither this volume nor its predecessor could fully resolve. It is my intention to confront these in the third and final installment of this series, which I hope to complete in due course. That sequel will not only revisit the narratives introduced here but also weave together the threads that have eluded clarity, offering a more cohesive and comprehensive reckoning.

History, after all, is not a closed chapter, it is a living archive. And as long as truth remains contested, the work of documenting it must continue.

Let this book be not only a record, but a reminder. Let it stir reflection in classrooms, in courtrooms, in homes, and in hearts. Let it challenge silence and inspire dialogue. And above all, let it ensure that the echoes of blood are not lost to time, but carried forward as a call to conscience.

Acknowledgements

This book would not have been possible without the generosity, insight, and support of many individuals—named and unnamed—who helped illuminate the shadowed corners of Sri Lanka's history.

To the families of victims and survivors who shared painful stories with courage and honesty: your voices gave this work its soul.

To researchers, librarians, archivists, and journalists who preserve historical records despite the risks and challenges—your commitment to truth is the backbone of this project.

To friends and fellow writers who offered thoughtful feedback and encouragement throughout my journey, and to those who challenged my perspective and pushed me to dig deeper—I thank you for sharpening my vision and widening my understanding.

To the people who kept memory alive when institutions failed to do so, who mourned not just privately but insistently and publicly—you embody the spirit of resilience that this book hopes to honor.

And finally, to the readers who carry this conversation forward: may these pages prompt reflection, dialogue, and above all, remembrance. citizens still grapple with reconciliation, accountability, and equitable progress. The ghosts of colonial legacies, war-time scars, and unanswered disappearances may never fully be laid to rest, but their acknowledgment is the beginning of something powerful: a reckoning not with the enemy, but with the truth itself.

Memory is not passive—it is political. It shapes how we mourn, how we forgive, and how we rebuild. Justice, too, must evolve beyond the courtroom: it must live in textbooks, in public discourse, and in the quiet dignity of remembrance. Reconciliation is not a destination, but a process—one that demands courage, empathy, and the willingness to confront uncomfortable truths. This book marks the second installment in my planned trilogy—a deeper excavation into the shadows and silences that shaped Sri Lanka's recent history. While the first volume laid the foundation, this second work attempts to illuminate the complexities, contradictions, and unresolved truths that continue to haunt our national conscience. Yet, the story is far from complete.

There remain gaps, deliberate omissions, buried testimonies, and unanswered questions—that neither this volume nor its predecessor could fully resolve. It is my intention to confront these in the third and final installment of this series, which I hope to complete in due course. That sequel will not only revisit the narratives introduced here but also weave together the threads that have eluded clarity, offering a more cohesive and comprehensive reckoning.

History, after all, is not a closed chapter—it is a living archive. And as long as truth remains contested, the work of documenting it must continue.

Let this book be not only a record, but a reminder. Let it stir reflection in classrooms, in courtrooms, in homes, and in hearts. Let it challenge silence, and inspire dialogue. And above all, let it ensure that the echoes of blood are not lost to time, but carried forward as a call to conscience.

Bibliography Page: References by Chapter

Part I: Colonial Crimes & Early Courtrooms (1815–1948)

Chapter/Event	Refedrences
Uva–Wellassa Rebellion (1817–1818)	Ceylon Blue Books, Kandyan Convention (1815), UK Colonial Dispatches, K.M. de Silva – *A History of Sri Lanka*
Madulla Massacre	British Army Reports, Colonial Intelligence Archives
Saradiel & Mamale Marikkar	Michael Roberts – *Caste Conflict*, Local folklore archives, Police trial transcripts
Attygalle Murder Case (1907)	Supreme Court Records, D.C. Wijewardena – *Early British Rule*
Sinhalese–Muslim Riots (1915)	Hansard Debates, S.J. Tambiah – *Leveling Crowds*, Colonial Legal Reports
Duff House Killing (1933)	Colombo Police Reports, Press clippings – *Ceylon Observer*
Kenilworth Tragedy	Estate Labor Inquiry Reports, Oral Histories
Pope Murder Case (1941)	Supreme Court trial archives, *Daily News* articles

Part II: Post-Independence Era (1949–2020)

Chapter/Event	References
Whitehouse Estate Murder (1949)	Estate Management Records, *Sunday Observer* coverage
Sathasivam Murder Trial (1951–53)	Criminal Court transcripts, Legal journal essays
Assassination of S.W.R.D. Bandaranaike	Commission Reports, News clippings (*The Island, Ravaya*)
Manamperi Case, Duraiappah Assassination	Truth commissions, Rajani Thiranagama – *Broken Palmyra*

1983 Pogrom & Jaffna Library	Groundviews.org archives, UNDP cultural heritage reports
1987–89 JVP Insurrection	Amnesty International reports, Rohan Gunaratna – *Sri Lanka: Feeding the Tamil Tigers*
Richard de Zoysa, Embilipitiya Boys	Human Rights Watch, UNHRC documentation
Kattankudy Mosque, Trinco Five, Muttur Massacre	LLRC Report, Al Jazeera & BBC investigations
Lasantha Wickrematunge	*Sunday Leader*, Free Media Movement files
Civil War Final Phase (2009)	Channel 4 – *Sri Lanka's Killing Fields*, UN war crime reports
Post-war violence, Kotakethana Murders, Political Assassinations	NGO briefings (CPA, International Crisis Group), Judicial records
Angoda Lokka, Makandure Madush	Interpol notices, Tamil-language press, Criminal Intelligence briefings

Additional Sources Across Chapters

- **Academic Journals**: *Contemporary South Asia, South Asia: Journal of South Asian Studies*
- **Human Rights Documentation**: Amnesty International, Sri Lanka Brief
- **Documentaries**: *No Fire Zone, Phantom of Coimbatore*
- **Books & Studies**: K.M. de Silva, Tambiah, Roberts, Thiranagama, Gunaratna, Senanayake, Sasanka Perera
- **Media Archives**: *BBC Sinhala, TamilNet, Daily News, Ravaya*

ABOUT THIS BOOK

Echoes of Blood: Sri Lanka's Legacy of Violence, Resistance, and Memory

Two Centuries of Killings, Disappearances, and Defiance

(1815-2020)

This volume is a sequel to my earlier publication, ***Contours of Conflict – The Making & Remaking of Sri Lanka,*** which explores the turbulent journey of democracy under siege and the nation's struggle for stability from 1948.

My work continues in my 3rd book of the Trilogy, with the forthcoming title, '**The Weight of Memory – Sri Lanka's Solved and Unsolved Crimes Since 1948'**, a deeper investigation into the shadows of justice and the echoes of unresolved truths that have shaped the country's post-independence history.

www.ingramcontent.com/pod-product-compliance
Lightning Source LLC
Chambersburg PA
CBHW052109020426
42335CB00021B/2687